GUILT

GUILT

+

by

CARYLL HOUSELANDER

GORDIAN PRESS
NEW YORK
1971

First Published 1952

Reprinted 1971

Library of Congress Catalog Card Number 76-131251

SBN 87752-053-4

CONTENTS

CONTENTS

Part Four: ILLUSTRATIONS

LIST OF PLATES

INTRODUCTION

THE most striking characteristic of the age in which we are living is psychological suffering. Even against the background of unparalleled physical and material suffering, this psychological suffering stands out as vividly as scarlet stands out on a background of drabs and greys. The mental hospitals and psychiatry clinics are full to capacity and a steady stream of sufferers is making the waiting lists longer and longer; in England "borderline cases" have been told, in some instances, that they may have to go on waiting for eight years. An audience with the Pope or the King could hardly be more difficult to get than an appointment with a psychiatrist.

There are, however, other places besides hospitals and clinics where one can at least be sure of examination and diagnosis from expert psychologists, though not always sure of the right treatment—the prisons and Borstals: but these too are filled to capacity with psychotics, neurotics, hysterics, schizoids and psychopathic personalities.

The contrast between life inside a hospital or prison today and life in the world is not so great as might be supposed, perhaps the greatest difference being that inside the institutions it is more regular and more disciplined, and that among all the emotionally and mentally disturbed people there are a few, sane or very nearly sane, trying to help the sufferers. Outside, there are just as many insane, psychotic and neurotic people, just as many borderline cases, just as many people who are their own torment; but there is no regularity, no order or discipline that they accept, and in most cases no one to help them.

There is one form of psychological suffering for which there is as yet no medical term and no admission to hospital or clinic—usually, but not always, the sufferers even keep out of prison. I have named this *ego-neurosis*. Ego-neurosis is a disease of the soul, a spiritual rather than a psychological ailment. It consists in a thrusting forward of the self; it may take the form of self-analysis, self-defence, self-obsession, self-aggrandizement, humiliation in being self, self-frustration or countless others, but it is grounded in self-love.

For the most part, ego-neurotics do not go to extremes; they are not listed among the abnormal. Their condition is a condition of spiritual weakness; it is largely because their souls and their minds are half-starved that they are ill in this way at all.

Usually they are people who suffer consciously merely from a vague and persistent unhappiness, an inexplicable sense of guilt about everything they do or don't do, a shrinking from effort, especially mental effort, a certain sense of frustration and a hidden stirring of shame because they feel inadequate before life—they suffer continually from embarrassment, very often from boredom (which is inability to respond to stimulus) and always from anxiety in some form or other. Their tragedy is less that they are most of the time unhappy, than that they have lost the capacity for ever being really happy at all. Of such people, the greatest of all the psychologists, C. G. Jung, wrote: "About a third of all cases are suffering from no clinically definable neurosis, but from the senselessness and emptiness of their lives."*

It is of ego-neurotics that this book has been written.

The depressing condition of mankind I have just described is not wholly depressing. Indeed, in the psychological suffering of modern man, I see the first great beam of hope for human beings. Pain is a merciful thing when it comes as a warning that there is something wrong with the body; it is intended to warn the sufferer of some invisible disease, so that it can be diagnosed and cured before it kills him; and in most cases, when one is wise enough to do something about it at once, at the very first stab of pain, the result will be restoration to health and the capacity to enjoy the life that has been saved.

Now mankind has for at least three hundred years been suffering from a deadly disease, materialism. A body must become ill if only some parts of it are used for the functions they are there for. If a man decided never to use his legs, they would atrophy and he would begin to feel the effects in other parts of his body

* C. G. Jung, *Modern Man in Search of a Soul*, Kegan Paul (London, 1936).

too, and if he did at last attempt even to walk across the room, he would break down. To refuse to use vital organs causes fatal disease.

For several hundreds of years, the majority of mankind in England and America have ceased to exercise the spiritual part of their nature.

Human nature is soul and body—men have treated it as if it were only body. They have not allowed their souls to function at all. In a vast number of cases they have not allowed even their minds to function, and besides having a disease of the soul, they have atrophy of the memory, understanding and the will.

Wars, exploitation of labour, men turned to machines, over-industrialization, regimentation, destitution, totalitarianism, are not the cause of man's psychological disorder, they are the result of it. All these things have happened and could only have happened because the majority of men ceased long ago to use these three powers of the soul, memory, understanding and will.

The psychological suffering of our generation means that the disease in man's soul is at last giving him pain; it proves that he really *has* a soul, for had it been possible for men to adjust themselves without ill effects to the wholly material world they have built for themselves, one might be excused for questioning whether a creature who *could* so adjust himself really possessed an immortal spirit. We might be forgiven for thinking that after all man is not made of soul and body, but of animal and machinery; that he does not need love, or beauty, or poetry, or art, or peace of mind; certainly he does not need to adore. All that he needs is material bread, sexual intercourse, oiling from time to time, and a tightening up of the screws which are so conspicuously loose.

But man has *not* been able to adjust himself; the pain of his soul's disease is being felt by nearly everyone, and in many cases it has become unbearable.

The insane, the psychotics, the neurotics are serving a tremendous purpose—they have revealed the disease in unmistakable terms, and they have forced the enquiry, so long needed, into the nature of man. We have realized that, just as surgeons could not operate before they knew the anatomy of the body, a doctor nowadays cannot treat a patient at all, unless he knows how the *whole* man is made and functions. Above all he must know what a man *is*.

The enquiry has begun, and gradually scientific research is pointing to mysteries beyond its own scope; the great ones among the doctors are beginning to make their researches on their knees.

All this is matter for thanksgiving. But the vast multitudes of ego-neurotics, whose suffering, though real and persistent, has not yet become unbearable, have a huge part to fulfil in this enquiry into the nature of man.

They should not accept the ache of self, like people who let their teeth ache until the nerves are exposed, because they are afraid of the dentist. But many do; they accept their own impotence and mediocrity, their distress and boredom, they resign themselves to it. This is very near despair.

But just as chronic invalids sometimes find it impossible to believe that they can ever be cured, ego-neurotics often find it impossible to realize that they can be happy, that they can have a zest for life, know the fulness of joy, and even add to the sum total of life-giving love in the world themselves. The ego-neurotic is usually lonely, he finds it difficult to explain his unhappiness; when put into words it sounds trivial, he finds it difficult to find a sympathetic listener, or one who could help even if he did listen. As for professional help, the experts have not time enough to give to all the insane; they have no time at all for the officially sane, however mad they may be.

The ego-neurotic has got to help himself; with God's help, he must cure himself.

He *can* do it. If he could only realize the delight that awaits him, the joy that he could know, the fulness of life that could be his, he would make the effort required to cure himself.

The single hope that has sustained me in writing this book is that some ego-neurotic may discover from it the possibilities of his own happiness, and so begin to make the effort that will bring him to its realization.

I do not want to force my own theories upon anyone, but to offer them to those who care to examine them as the only contribution my own ego-neurosis can make to this great enquiry into man's nature, in which all mental sufferers can take part.

I offer only what I have learned from my own wrestling with self-love, and I do so because I believe with Dostoievsky that "one is really responsible to all men, for all men, and for everything."

Feast of Our Lady of Sorrows, 1950.

In nature we have our being
In mercy we have our increasing
In grace we have our fulfilling.
JULIAN OF NORWICH

PART ONE

THE SENSE OF GUILT AND
THE REALITY

I

SOME PECULIARITIES OF THE
GUILT FEELING

*In our days an individual of exceptional powers can hardly hope to
have so great a career or so great a social influence as in former
times, if he devotes himself to art or to religious and moral reform.
There are, however, still four careers which are open to him; he
may become a great political leader like Lenin; he may acquire
vast industrial power, like Rockefeller; he may transform the world
by scientific discoveries, as is being done by the atomic physicists;
or, finally, if he has not the necessary capacities for any of these
careers, or if opportunity is lacking, his energy in default of any
other outlet may drive him into a life of crime. Criminals, in the
legal sense, seldom have much influence on the course of history,
and therefore a man of overweening ambition will choose some
other career if it is open to him.*

BERTRAND RUSSELL, *Authority and the Individual.**

THE OUTSTANDING CHARACTERISTIC of the guilt feeling is
its bewildering inconsistency. People who lead blameless lives are often overwhelmed by the sense of guilt,
while those who lead guilty lives may as easily be devoid of it.

Sometimes guilty people are even elated by the thought of the
evil they have done and its tragic consequences. Men have been
known to boast that the eyes of the world are upon them, within
minutes of their own execution for murder. But it is also not
without a certain relish that a particular type of pious person,
with a mania for self-perfection, proclaims herself the "Worst
Sinner in the World". Is there not some resemblance between
her mentality and that of the megalomaniac with the noose
around his neck?

Among people generally considered to be more normal there
are equally surprising peculiarities.

One would expect a reasonable person to feel more guilty after
repeating some particular sin some hundreds of times, until he

* Allen and Unwin (London, 1949).

has become enslaved and degraded by it, than after the first, isolated occasion. Of most people the opposite is true. The more often we do wrong, the less do we recognize ourselves as wrongdoers; the more we degrade our nature, the less do we suffer humiliation through our degradation. The more guilty we *are*, the less guilty we feel.

When we have so attached ourselves to some evil that it has become part of ourselves, we cease to admit that it is evil. Not only that: since, in this situation, we need to compensate our vanity as well as to delude ourselves, we are ingenious in finding ways by which our wrongdoing can flatter us.

A man who is an adept thief more often considers himself to be a clever fellow than a dishonest or mean one. Dickens' Artful Dodger did not consider picking pockets a mean crime but a brilliant accomplishment. He focused his mind not on the poverty of his morality but on the skill of his hand. He was artful —full of art!

In sins of sensuality particularly, repetition leads beyond mere callousness to a delusion of superiority. When conscience has been so thickened and blunted by habit that it has lost its fine edge altogether, and the feeling of release (both physical and psychological) which frequently accompanies such sin has swamped reason, the sinner believes himself, or more accurately *feels* himself, to be above the mass of men: for they are restrained—or, as he would say, inhibited or frustrated—by the law of God, by considerations of honour or pity, and in the last resource by the blind feeling of guilt. For all such things, he has or thinks he has a contempt; he believes that he is now different, superior to other men.

In the violent guilt conflict that in modern times is almost bound to occur in the lives of creative artists, when sensuality becomes debauchery and the compensation must be as extreme as the failure, people are able to believe not merely that they are supermen, but that they are supernatural, and dispensed from natural law. So it was with the poet Rimbaud. His most sympathetic biographer, Enid Starkie, writes of him: "Baudelaire always kept, in the midst of his worst aberrations, a sense of sin; Rimbaud, however, would not feel that for him debauch was vice: he was certain that he himself was above the reach of sin.

Later, looking back on the errors of this time, he said 'Moi!
Moi, qui me suis dit mage ou ange, dispensé de toute morale,
je suis rendu au sol.' "* This poor boy regarded his life of
cruelty and vice as a martyrdom, and is the hero of many
unstable members of our own intelligentsia—for whom he
would undoubtedly have had contempt, since they are able to
identify themselves with him as martyrs to vice, but not as poets
of genius.

One cannot fail to observe that the criminal lunatic, the
pseudo-pietist, and the sexual dilettante and debauchee are
brothers and sisters under the skin—each of them saying, with
perhaps a slight difference in accent, "Thank God, I am not as
other men."

People suffering from religious scruples present further remarkable discrepancies in guilt feeling.

The subject of scruples generally is a delicate one. They may
be a trial, allowed by God, purifying as the fierce bright fire of
Purgatory. Again, there are really sensitive souls, sensitive not to
themselves, but to the purity and beauty of God. To such a one
the tiniest shadow on the light of the soul, created to reflect and
radiate God, is grief hardly to be endured. To the vulgar eye he
will appear to be just another scrupulous person, but he is
beyond the comprehension of the vulgar and outside the scope
of this book. Outside it too is the sufferer from scruples who is
really pathological and requires the help of a doctor.

The type of scrupulous person who is interesting from our
point of view is one who is frequently tormented by some fantastic, trivial scruple, which is not a sin at all, but at the same
time blind to the fact that he habitually commits real sin of
another kind. For example, it is by no means rare to find people
obsessed by anxiety about involuntary suggestions of impurity,
but completely oblivious to their sins of habitual selfishness,
mental cruelty, betrayal of confidences, and omission of every
aspect of charity. Once again, our pietist leads straight back to
the criminal lunatic. One simply cannot fail to see his likeness to
certain maniacs, indifferent to the fact that they have just
clubbed someone to death, but embarrassed because they have
disarranged their own clothing in the process!

* Enid Starkie, *Arthur Rimbaud*. Hamish Hamilton (London, 1947).

In real neurosis, the guilt feeling, which is often hidden from the sufferer, is revealed by so many contradictory symptoms that the uninitiated can hardly fail to be either sceptical or baffled by them. This book is concerned with people classed as normal; but one can hardly observe the normal without the help of the abnormal, for in neurotic and even psychotic states we see the so-called normal, including ourselves, under the magnifying glass.

The neurotic symptoms that many specialists in psychology attribute to inhibited guilt feelings are like the name of Satan, legion. Only a few of them can be listed here. There are self-starvation and its opposite, excessive overeating. Shoplifting, petty crime. Pathological scrupulosity. An obsession about being fat, an obsession of fatigue, a compulsion to apologize continually, a compulsion to continual hand-washing. Puritanism, exhibitionism, personal dirtiness, excessive personal cleanliness. Masochism, aggression, sadism, self-pity. Crippling indecision, delusions of persecution. A mania for being flattered, which is often found in company with constant disparagement of others. A mania for being loved, often present in someone without any capacity for loving. A mania for eroticism, a mania for prurient talk, often found together with sexual impotence. Confused eyesight, deafness, failure of the sense of smell. A mania for wishing to be invisible; sustained attempts to be *inconspicuous* by eccentric dress and behaviour! A mania for walking or cycling to the point of exhaustion. Hypochondria, melancholy, dypsomania, amnesia, religious manias, and a host of other disorders, ranging from blushing to nervous paralysis.

But there are, as well, states symptomatic of buried feelings of guilt to be found among the members of almost any family accepted as normal. These could be described as "nuisance states".

Among them is love of making scenes—which may take the form of bursts of temper, quarrelsomeness, fits of sobbing and moaning, or almost insufferable demands to be loved.

Again, there is a very common nuisance state which I call the "pre-pleasure gloom". Certain people invariably anticipate pleasure by intense gloom, almost like a psychological "hang-over", coming before the event instead of after. It seems that it is necessary for their pleasure that they shall first punish themselves for enjoying it—and, of course, this includes punishing others too. For days before a celebration, or even a family wedding, they cast out an atmosphere of gloom. I have known the mother of a large family who could not enjoy the Christmas celebrations unless she spent Christmas Eve and the morning of Christmas Day in the cemetery. Not because she remembered her own dead, or that she was impelled to pray for their souls— any prayers she *did* utter on those occasions were objurgatory prayers against her living relatives. I believe her impulse for going to the cemetery was that there she could indulge her need to feel gloomy, and, moreover, could to some extent make her family feel guilty for their easy attitude to the coming pleasures. When these pleasures actually came, she appeared to be able to abandon herself to them more completely than her children, or even her grandchildren, provided that she had already punished herself for the fun!

This attitude, directed to pleasure rather than to evil, is among the commonest idiosyncrasies of the guilt feeling. It has eaten into large sections of British society like corrosive acid.

We are infected by puritanism, just as many French Catholics were at one time infected by Jansenism. Puritanism is the prudish, but rebellious, younger sister of Protestantism, and these sad sisters are both suspicious of pleasure and of beauty. Between them, they have given our critics every excuse to dub us hypocrites, for to those who have never lived in a Protestant environment, and cannot imagine our peculiar national guilt conflicts, there seems no other explanation of the phenomenon of people who are more shocked by pleasure than by sin!

When anger enters into the guilt feeling, it is nearly always complicated by this puritanical attitude to pleasure, and it takes terrible, sometimes diabolical forms. One of these is a variety of projection, that is of projecting the evil in oneself on to some other person. There are people who will not admit the existence of evil in themselves; they will not, and ultimately perhaps cannot, allow the dark side of their nature to invade their consciousness. They refuse to know it. They have formed a superhuman ideal of themselves and will not countenance the possibility of frailty and sensuality within them, even as a potentiality. But let them maintain this class division within their own breast as rigidly as they may, the fact remains that they, like the rest of us, are children of a fallen race: concupiscence has become part of their nature, in them as in everyone lurks the dark heritage of all the evil that has come into the world through original sin: and not only the majestic sombre shadows of that mysterious evil, but its more popular aspects—its bawdiness, its insobriety, its vulgarity. All this they project on to other people. So when they go out from the shelter of their homes they meet, at every turn, the wanton whom they have cast out of their own hearts. From the brazen faces of irresponsible little girls their own frivolity mocks them. They hate all that is young and provocative, with a hatred which is immeasurably more evil than the frailty which provokes it. But this is because it is *not* really that frailty that raises such a demon, it is the festering, repudiated evil *self*, walking out all unaware in an Easter bonnet!

There is hardly an evil force more terrible than projected self-hatred. It is not for nothing we are told to *love* our neighbour *as ourself*, we must tremble lest refusing to come to terms with *all* that is self, we *hate* our neighbour as ourself.

Self-pity often accompanies guilt projection—the pious person, poisoned by hate, is easily able to believe that it is she who is the victim of hatred. Mild people with persecution manias are usually great haters; this, however, is a secret, even from themselves. A classic story of projection and self-pity is told of Hitler who, when visiting a village where one of his cruellest purges had been carried out, wept bitterly, saying, "How wicked these people must be, to have made me do this!"

There is such a thing as an artificial guilt feeling, a synthetic conscience which comes from outside and is imposed by other people. This is the explanation of many taboos among primitive people, tribes who, motivated by a natural desire for survival, imposed prohibitions and laws designed to achieve that end, to which they gave the solemnity of religious rites.

In Victorian society, we discover taboos and superstitions which, though they were given the gentlest new names and camouflaged in the soft drabs and greys of respectability, had much in common with those of the primitive savages. But it was not only to preserve life itself, or the life of the race, that these false consciences were imposed, but to preserve the tyranny of petty power and the servile homage paid to money and those who possessed it, no matter whether they had come by it honourably, or by selling slaves or sweating child labour.

Patriarchs and matriarchs, as parents too often were, had a positive genius for imposing a sense of guilt on the more devitalized of their children, who were educated successfully to feel that the most harmless action, sometimes any positive action at all, was guilty.

On the other hand, the more robust members of the family— in those days, unlike ours, usually the sons—were often driven by the same thing to outbreaks of debauchery, as the only relief for the nervous tension caused by the sacrosanct atmosphere of the home, as well as a discharge for their sense of personal guilt, for which they could not find any reason.

In those Victorian days when the contrast between poverty and wealth was appalling, the rich were actually able to make their poor dependants ashamed of having anything that was joyful or frivolous for their consolation. A governess of the period, for example, would not have dared to face her God, let alone her employer, in a "nonsense" hat; while the employer, who did actually exploit dependence as cruelly as that, was able to regard her own greater (and superfluous) possessions—her estates, her antimacassars and furbelows—as a sign of God's particular favour.

It would, however, be an injustice to compare the Victorians unfavourably with ourselves, in the matter of creating synthetic consciences, or to presume that this is done less cruelly nowadays, because the "working class" people are now perhaps more gaily dressed than the rapidly dying out "leisured class".

Selfishness and fear are just as skilled in producing false consciences as ever they were; today, it is not for having a hat that a young woman is made to feel guilty, but for having a family. Here in England, which is rapidly becoming predominantly a land of old people, there are millions of young men and women who have been deliberately conditioned to feel that the wholesale murder of their unborn children is a right and proper thing, whilst giving children life is a sin against society.

Compare this with the custom (imposed, no doubt, by arguments similar to those used to introduce the teaching of contraception into the government clinics) in certain primitive tribes, which compelled the aged to climb a high tree, and swing from the topmost branch, so that if they lacked the strength to cling thus literally to life they should die. In both cases, murder of the defenceless is the basic idea, and in both cases it is accepted as the right thing to do.

Individuals, as well as groups, are able to impose guilt feelings on one another, and the more deeply the emotions are involved, the more crippling the sense of guilt is likely to be.

Who does not know the young—and old—man who has a morbid attitude towards women, the result of the stranglehold of a positively suffocating maternal love during his adolescence, which has instilled guilt like a cumulative poison into every potential relationship with any other woman?

In a lighter vein (though, if this has anything to do with the present almost universal failure to read a book that requires concentration, it is not after all so light a matter) is the odd little quirk so many people have about reading in the daytime, especially the morning—they hardly feel it can ever be right to read excepting when the brain is already tired, or else in order to tire it and so to induce sleep! How many mothers and governesses there must have been who believed that the devil found even more work for minds that were not idle than for hands that were!

It is, however, group or herd false consciences that lead to the worst cruelties. Individual cruelty pales into insignificance beside that of the many-headed monster, for it is imperative for the monster's preservation that not one of its heads must think.

No one must come into a herd, who challenges its conventions —for these keep it not only in existence, but in complacency. These conventions are not built in a single generation, they are always upheld by long traditions which give a certain romance to their stupidity, they are handed down by generations of wishful not-thinking. The first one that thinks is a threat to the security of the group. This is why schoolboys, who profess contempt for cowardice, are able to bully and torture any single small boy among them who does not take the impression of the group, like soft wax; and this the tormentors do, not only with undisturbed consciences, but with elation in their sense of solidarity and power, and their touching loyalty to the spirit and traditions of the old school.

Not unlike the worst that schoolboys are capable of is the extraordinary conscience which enables Christians to think it right to encourage hatred of Jews and oppression of coloured people, and to shudder at marriages between those whose skin is of different colours, as though such marriages were sinful! What intricacies of fear and projection and suggestion, of convention and tradition, have gone to the making of such consciences as these!

Whenever a murder is committed and the police are still looking for the murderer, a number of people who are perfectly innocent of the crime give themselves up for it. Under a similar compulsion school-children have been known to "own up" to misdeeds of which they know nothing—the atmosphere of guilt was created by the solemnity of the teacher, and suggestion combined with the inner compulsion to relate the feeling of guilt to something definite. On the other hand, it is often because the real murderer, though perfectly aware of what he has done, feels no guilt, and the real offender at school likewise feels none, that they are able to evade suspicion.

A curious example of guilt feeling, which is at once imposed and repressed, is that suggested by the attitude of the average Englishman to Roman Catholicism. He prides himself, this Englishman, on being broad-minded, a respecter of every man's conscience or lack of conscience, tolerant of everyone's belief or unbelief. If one of his friends chose to become a Quaker, a Plymouth Brother, a Baptist, an Anglo-Catholic, or even a Mormon, he would consider it no business of his. But let one become a Roman Catholic!—all toleration is thrown away; he will not hesitate, when remonstrance fails, to resort to aggressiveness, even sometimes to insults. His friend, he tells him, has taken leave of his senses, he has proved himself a coward unable to face the burden of thinking for himself, an escapist from life, a traitor to his country. Moreover, he suspects him henceforth not only of trying to convert himself, but even of trying to get him into the Church by trickery. He is always on the defensive.

Sometimes he admits that the church services have a certain beauty but he fears their attraction, which he feels is another lure to something undefined, but sinister and threatening. In fact, he reacts much as a man who is painfully aware of a hereditary tendency to drunkenness: he dreads it because he knows that it is in his blood, yet for that very reason he can hardly resist it. So it is with the Englishman's fear of Catholicism. Whether he is good or bad, Catholicism is in his blood. Few if any of us are not descended from apostates. Few if any English families were not once Catholic: and Catholicism, even in the blood, is stronger and more ineradicable than drink. Our forefathers, if they were to endure going on living with themselves and with their children, had to justify their infidelity. Therefore they built up a sinister picture of Catholicism, which has been handed down the years, and has set up a conflict between the irresistible attraction and the bogey lurking just below the surface of memory.

There are many curious delusions brought about by the sense of guilt. To give only one of them as an example, it is a popular delusion that time lessens and ultimately wipes out sin, merely because the *sense* of guilt grows duller with the passing of time— it is like a chronic ache, such as rheumatism, which we can undoubtedly get used to, and actually feel less when we have borne it longer. Moreover, chronic aches and a chronic sense of guilt both respond to innumerable drugs.

Perhaps the most curious of all the manifestations of the guilt feeling is to be found in the saints. While criminals are often free from it, the saints never are, they are more aware of the sense of guilt than any other people. They too, like the over-scrupulous pietist, frequently declare themselves to be the greatest of all sinners, but there is this enormous difference between them— the pietist says this in an attempt to find a formula that will relieve her of suffering, but the saint says it as an invitation to the suffering of the whole world. St Teresa of Avila, with her tremendous "To suffer or die," spoke for all the saints.

Yet another curious discrepancy: while the guilt feeling disintegrates all others, even those who manage to escape the actual pain of it, it integrates the saints. In them it is the blackness of the alchemical gold.

II

THE REALITY OF GUILT

I do not see that we can possess the light of intelligence without the pupil of the holiest faith which is inside the eye, and if this light is darkened or clouded by self-love the eye has no light, and therefore cannot see, so not seeing cannot know the truth.

ST CATHERINE OF SIENA*

AFTER even so brief a glance at only a few of the inconsistencies of the feeling of guilt, we can hardly wonder that there is a popular inclination to think that guilt itself is not a reality at all, but something purely subjective, an emotional malaise, which can be cured by a psychotherapist, or even in milder cases by reading superficial articles on psychology in newspapers and magazines, or having tea and a chat with a friend "who knows something about psychology".

Widespread faith in psychology encourages this view. I say *faith*, because it is a fact that many people accept psychotherapy not as a form of treatment for functional neurosis, which is all that it claims to be, but as a faith. This is not surprising, because psychotherapy, *as it is imagined to be* by the multitude, is an escape from facing the reality of guilt and the personal responsibility which it involves. Escape is a keyword in the study of guilt. If the feeling of guilt is no more than a psychological disorder, not only can we hope to be rid of all individual responsibility for sin, but even of the guilt *feeling*.

It does seem at first sight that a feeling so divorced from reason and common sense cannot have its origin in reality. If this feeling is no indication of the true state of our conscience, no guide to what is wrong and what is right; if we can be made uneasy equally by what is bad, indifferent or positively good; if the feeling can manifest itself in so many different ways, fantastic, contradictory, and apparently as little within our control

* Piero Misciattelli, *The Mystics of Siena*. W. Heffer and Son (Cambridge, 1929).

as a rise of temperature; if moreover it can be imposed upon us from outside—what possible coherence can it have for us at all?

Yet this unreality surrounding the *feeling* of guilt points straight to the *reality* of guilt.

There must be a reason why proneness to the feeling of guilt is almost universal; why, even when there has been no outside influence to induce it, it exists, often in people of unquestionable purity of heart, varying from a vague floating anxiety to a slow cumulative poisoning of the whole personality. There must be a reason why those who do not feel guilty at all are usually the most corrupt, and why the feeling of guilt can be induced and imposed by a countless variety of means, and meets with so little resistance. Can we really avoid the conclusion that there is something within us all which responds immediately to the suggestion of guilt?

Clearly human nature is fertile soil for this suggestion. The sowing of good seed in human nature is always precarious. It may take root, it may not. It may come to flower, it may wither away. But the sowing of the bad seed of synthetic guilt is never precarious: that always thrives in our fetid soil. It always bears its poisonous flower, taking a thousand grotesque shapes and colours, like evil, luminous fungi, in dark undergrowths, swamps and cellars.

It is difficult to avoid the conclusion that guilt is a reality, that we *feel* guilty because we *are* guilty, *but that the feeling has been misplaced, dislocated from its true cause*, and is seeking some cause to which to attach itself.

We resemble those people who are suffering from cancer, but who, because cancer is something which they will not face, seek desperately for some other explanation of their symptoms.

By all means let us have any illness, any peculiarity, to explain our uneasiness, provided it lets us escape the real explanation— guilt in the roots of our being, involving us in the responsibility and in the suffering of the whole world, compelling us to lifelong conflict within ourselves. We prefer a thousand times to think of ourselves as neurotics, even as psychotics, rather than as responsible human beings, carrying the burden of sin, and threatened by the torrent of darkness that we are trying to dam up in the depths of our being.

We will not, and, spiritually devitalized as we are today, cannot, face our own guilt, that terrible force of agelong evil and suffering which is the inheritance of every descendant of Adam, of every man who comes into the world. Man was created for joy, but the first man sinned, and as a result of his sin suffering came into the world.

The immediate result of the first sin was psychological suffering, that kind of suffering which can be experienced only by human beings, who have minds and souls as well as bodies.

In the penetrating light of God, self-knowledge became unbearable to Adam. Bitter, inescapable conflict had entered his nature and divided him against himself. God was the source of his joy, but now he was constrained to hide from God. Now, instead of keeping its unhindered capacity to delight in good, his whole nature lurched downwards and dragged him towards evil.

The effects of his sin had in some mysterious way entered into nature. He was no longer lord over the animals, they were no longer his gentle comrades, but a danger to him. Even the earth and the skies had become incalculable and menacing; from now on he could not have even the simplest good thing, such as bread, without effort and self-conquest. In order to eat and to feed his wife and children, he would have to wrestle unceasingly with the elements, with storm and frost, driving winds and withering heat, with the weeds and the thorns and the thistles choking the seed he had sown.

His passions, which before he sinned had been at his command, a source not only of delight but of sanctity, had become like demons possessing him, ready at any moment to swamp and shatter him, to destroy him and with him the woman he loved. He must wrestle with them, even more fiercely, even more unceasingly, than with all the rest of creation. He must experience hunger and thirst, cold and heat, fatigue, pain, sickness and death. Everything had been violated by his sin—his soul, his mind, his capacity to love, his work, his environment, his body. Everything that applies to Adam applies to us, who are his children.

Our human nature, inherited from him, is fallen human nature, therefore suffering human nature.

Psychological suffering is our portion. Self-knowledge is

unbearable to us, unless we have the rare courage that is willing to be purified by fire. We are in conflict with ourselves. We long insistently for happiness, yet our inclinations drag us, remorselessly and always, towards the things which ultimately destroy even the capacity for happiness. We cannot get, let alone keep, the simplest good thing without waging war on self, without irksome self-discipline and self-denial. Like Adam we must wrestle continually with the elements, our vast cities do not save us from them, and the forces which scientific discovery could have harnessed for man's healing and good threaten his very existence.

Our passions are always ready to destroy us, and with us those whom we love.

Work, intended to be a delight, has become an almost intolerable burden.

> Generations have trod, have trod, have trod;
> And all is seared with trade; bleared, smeared with toil;
> And wears man's smudge and shares man's smell:
>   the soil
> Is bare now, nor can foot feel, being shod.

Man did not stop sinning after Adam. On the contrary, each one of us, besides having inherited original sin and the suffering that it has caused, has added to the world's suffering by his own sins.

We have therefore a double obligation as human beings. As children of Adam we share with all other human creatures the guilt of our whole race, and the obligation to shoulder our share of the burden consequent upon it, and as individual sinners we have an obligation to wrestle unceasingly with ourselves.

The human race is bound together by a solidarity of guilt; personal strife and personal sorrow are a debt which we owe to one another.

We have a double obligation which at first sight seems paradoxical, both to accept suffering and to wrestle with it. We are obliged to do all that we individually can to alleviate the pain and sickness of mind and body that afflict mankind, to wage war on misery, want and injustice, to use every natural means given to us to do this, as well as to strike straight at the evil that is the root cause of it all, with supernatural weapons of prayer and sacrifice. But at the same time we are obliged as human creatures to accept the common lot, the continual assaults of temptation, the continual necessity for effort, the sweat and toil of work, the frustrations and failures, the hardships and difficulties and contradictions of daily life, its sickness and insecurity, its fatigues and pains, its sorrows and bereavements, and our own death. To regard ourselves as exceptions, somehow exempt from the common lot of fallen men, is to attempt to separate ourselves from humanity.

There is another result of Adam's sin—I shall only refer to it here, but it will be discussed more fully a little later—which changes the whole face of suffering, and lifts our labours on to a different plane, a transfiguration of sorrow; and yet from this too modern man shrinks.

Christ chose to use suffering and death as the means of our redemption. It was Christ who paid the debt that the human race owed to God, for no one else could have paid it; it had to be one who *is* God and *is* Man; he made it possible for each man individually to work out his own salvation.

Christ could have redeemed the world by a single tear or a single breath, but he chose to redeem it in the way that showed the utmost possible love, through taking all the suffering of guilt on himself, wedding himself to our sorrow, and offering the sacrifice of his own death on the cross. "Greater love than this no man has, that he lays down his life for his friends."

We as Christians live with Christ's life. He lives our life, we are offered the glory of living his. But on earth it is impossible to respond to this offer, which involves loving with his love, without accepting what he accepted as man, that is, not only a fragment of the world's guilt, but all of it, all the suffering caused by sin, the world-sorrow. The suffering of the whole world is the concern of each one of us.

It is from the responsibility of guilt that modern man turns away, from the constant effort of self-conquest, from the acceptance of the world's suffering as his own business which he cannot shelve, and most of all from the mysterious destiny of his Christhood, with its imperious challenge to surrender himself body and soul to Christ's uncompromising, illimitable love.

III

RELIGIONS OF ESCAPE

ESCAPE, I have said, is a keyword in the study of guilt. Today Freudianism is the popular religion of escape, but it is not one which has broken on mankind with the sudden lightning of a new revelation. It is merely the latest logical step in a series of escape religions, which have been evolving since the Reformation.

The most striking contribution to escape given by Protestantism is the escape from self-knowledge. From the beginning and all through its changing phases it has failed to guard men from self-delusion. In the Church there are three great safeguards against self-delusion: an infallible moral teaching, the sacrament of Penance, and the doctrine of Purgatory. The teaching leaves man under no mistake as to what actions are sinful. The sacrament of Penance forces us to examine our own conscience in the light of the authoritative moral teaching, so that we can be under no mistake as to our own sinfulness; further we must put our sins into spoken words and admit them to another sinner, we must abase ourselves before God and offer personal penance, self-denial, some touch at least of asceticism. The doctrine of Purgatory insists on the reality of sin as holding men from the realized presence of God in Heaven till every smallest stain and shadow of it is gone from the soul.

And all three the Reformers let go: and with them the means by which men would know what sin is, would know their own sinfulness, would be kept in continuous awareness of sin's enormity and the means of its healing.

Never, at any time in its fluctuating history, has Protestantism been the religion that sinners need. When it reached its peak in Victorian England, it had become, in its mainstream anyhow, a religion of the virtuous and respectable, or rather of those who really believed in their own virtue because they were able to sin so respectably!

It was the respectability of the country houses, smooth green lawns, garden fêtes, croquet, soothing and soporific hymns and equally soothing and soporific port, depending not a little on ample material resources, and giving, to those who enjoyed them, a quite special twist to the psalm which declares that "The Lord is my Shepherd, I shall not want."

Men went to church because they felt themselves to be good enough to go, not because they knew themselves to be bad enough to have to go.

There was a curious idea that goodness and prosperity were identical. A favourite book of the period, *The Fairchild Family*, which was put into the hands of adolescents to "improve" them, advances this idea without a shred of humour: Mrs Fairchild, who constantly preaches sermons to her children, makes no bones about telling them that their family's ample means is a sign of God's preference for them!

Undoubtedly it is easier for the rich to *feel* good than it is for the poor, not because wealth shields them from temptation and sin, but because it makes it less easy for them to recognize temptation and sin for what they are. It is more difficult for the revered master of the house, who has to be helped to bed by his tactful valet, to feel degraded, than it is for the homeless old man in the street who has to be helped to a bench in the cells by a policeman. The poor commit as many sins of pride as the rich, but pride is a painful sin to the poor, a pleasurable one to the rich; the pride that is roused by a snub hurts, the pride that is inflated by flattery soothes. All too often the dependents of wealthy people share the guilt of their complacency through flattery; so too do the social climbers and hangers-on. Wherever there are people who are inflated like frogs in wet weather by their position and prestige there are certain to be servile people, who like to be patronized and who are partakers in the guilt of their patrons.

Again, it is easier to imagine oneself possessed of the charity that covers a multitude of sins if one can give easily of material things, than if one has in fact nothing but oneself to give. So far as benevolence in his own home and his own village went, the Victorian was usually above reproach, but he did not understand the need to give *spiritual* alms—prayer, self-denial, reparation.

His conscience, lulled to complacency from which there was nothing to rouse it, was not often troubled by the state of the world beyond the village. That is why his religion in its hey-day did better in the country than in the town, and tended to become more parochial than universal.

In the big cities guilt is always visible. Today it is visible in the ruins. In Victorian days it was visible in conditions that brought our disasters about, and which exist still, but are more carefully hidden. Material destitution, moral dereliction, drunk-enness, misery and vice were seen openly in the streets. The most spiritually blind person cannot come face to face with the evidence of guilt day after day, without his complacency being ruffled by some stirring of doubt about his own immunity from responsibility.

The blindness following the loss of the sense of sin in the good Victorian did not consist in not seeing the dreadful contrast between wealth and poverty which existed, but of taking it for granted that there was nothing that the individual could do about it. Particularly the poor individual.

The rich man did not know that he was not only in need of contrition himself but that he owed it to all other men; the poor man did not know that it was within *his* power to bestow alms upon the rich man who passed him by in the street.

Even the dead went without spiritual alms. The Evangelical made a cult of his own dead relations, but no matter how arro-gant, selfish and greedy they might have been on earth, they were presumed to have gone straight to Heaven, jet-propelled, when they died. I can remember with what secret, fascinated horror I once gazed when I was a child on the graven image of a friend's ancestor, a massive old lady stretched out on top of her vast family tomb, who, I was informed, had died of apoplexy brought on at table by overeating; but nothing daunted, she had reached the bosom of Abraham before the chicken bone she was gnawing could be removed from her mouth!

The good Protestant was unable to imagine the torment to a soul, conscious of sin, and rushed, so to speak, into the presence of God, without the sweet and terrible mercy of purifying fire. She was also unable to believe that the members of her own family could need spiritual cauterization, or the mercy of the prayers that fall into the fires of Purgatory like drops of cold water.

Consciousness of sin and of the common responsibility for guilt unites men, spiritual alms are the hand of love reaching from end to end of the world, and beyond the world to those who have died. Awareness of the reality of the common responsibility for guilt leads to communion between all living men, and between the living and the dead.

On the contrary, every escape mechanism, every denial of guilt, and particularly every conviction of personal righteousness, leads to exclusions, to a narrowing down of compassion, to spiritual cliques, and parochialism.

In that serene atmosphere of security, of beautiful manners, of church bells ringing across green meadows, of grey spires pointing to skies of delicate blue, of quiet graveyards, reassuring the living from every mossy headstone that all their dead were "Safe in the arms of Jesus", religion blossomed in the peace that this world gives, and from it, a little flowering offshoot, there blossomed another escape, namely the sentimentalized, sugary conception of the human character of Christ. The unreal Christ of the lace-bordered texts, waved hair and beard, white robes and white sheep. A *whole* conception of Christ could hardly have grown out of the polite and gentle piety that prevailed, and freedom to interpret the Scriptures which every individual was allowed resulted in freedom to ignore the less congenial passages, such as the whipping of the traders in the Temple, and Christ's teaching on the subject of Hell. A writer of the time, Samuel Butler, described a typical congregation as one "that would be equally horrified at hearing the Christian Religion doubted, and at seeing it practised".

I have been describing what I have called the mainstream flowing out of the Reformation. What of those who could not stay in it, the unmistakably sinful who could not deceive either themselves or their neighbours about their state; and the souls of intenser spirituality? Take the black sheep first. One result of the loss of the sense of sin was the division of the flock, separating the black sheep from the white, while forgetting the divine Shepherd's declared preference for the black. To this day we hear people say "I am not good enough to go to church". They are the spiritual descendents of those Protestants who were simply not able to *feel* good. There were many such people, who gave up going to church or any other public worship. There were others who not only did not feel good, but felt positively bad; they were conscious of some definite grave sin, and felt that to take the Communion in these circumstances would be very wrong. They knew of no way to know they were absolved from the sin, so they too simply drifted away from their one conscious contact with God. There were some among the latter who entertained the curious idea that a long lapse of time automatically absolved sin. But usually before long enough time had passed, their faith had faded into fainter colours than their sin had done, and they never resumed the practice of their religion. What then became of them? Either they became completely de-spiritualized and materialistic, or they resorted to one of the many escape mechanisms outside of religion, which will be described in the chapter on Mechanisms of Escape, or, and this most frequently, they drifted into the great colourless mediocracy, who profess what is called "my own religion".

There have been countless new religions started, as by John Wesley, with the most magnificent spiritual ideals, but for want of the three elements in Catholic life already described, they have tended to revert to the mainstream atmosphere. And beside these, what of the spiritually sensitive? One of the results of the Protestant religion, from its beginning until now, has been a spate of reactions, putting *all* the stress on man's guilt and none on God's love. It is characteristic of all these sects that the often overwhelming sense of guilt is dislocated, removed from its real cause, sin, to some other cause altogether.

For example, puritanical sects attach more guilt to pleasure than to sin, and lay a great burden of guilt on to innocent recreations, such as a game of cards on a Sunday. Some such sects project their feeling of guilt on to everything that is either gay or beautiful, especially that quality which has the lovely little lilting name "levity" and teases pomposity and solemnity. Everything lighthearted comes under the censure, and even everything entertaining: dancing, wearing pretty clothes or trinkets, curling the hair, reading fiction, going to the theatre, and hearty laughter!

The worship of God itself must be stripped of every outward beauty, even the offering of flowers in church for his glory who made the flowers.

Again the two elements that are always found in attempts to escape from the real cause of guilt appear—separatism or exclusiveness, and a false conception of God: this time a travesty of God yet more deplorable than the picture of the sentimental human Christ, a dour censorious God, condemning his children for delighting in the loveliness of his own gifts to them!

Countless men and women have abandoned religion altogether because this conception of God overshadowed their childhood and adolescence.

One of the most tragic reactions to the deficient sense of personal sinfulness that have flowed out of the Reformation is the Salvation Army. *Tragic* because it is a body inspired by such great love, in which not only the guilt of personal sin is profoundly felt but responsibility for the world's suffering too, but once again the answer is lost, and just as the old type of Protestant depended on *feeling good* to be saved, the Salvationist depends upon *feeling bad* to be saved; and feeling good or bad, once spiritual adolescence passes, can usually be induced only by orgies of emotional stimulation, hymn-singing, exhortation, clapping hands, beating drums and so on, all too often resulting in emotional excitement of the kind that is followed by spiritual hangovers, moral lapses, and nervous exhaustion.

Significantly towards the turn of the century Christian Science appeared. Without any reflection on the sincerity of its inventor, it is easy to see that this would have given considerable satisfaction to Satan. He had succeeded for at least three centuries in making the majority of men abuse almost every gift that God had given to them. They had used science more often to destroy the souls and bodies of men than to benefit them. They had made work, not a thing of joy and redemption as it could have been made, but a treadmill that had broken the spirit of multitudes. They had almost all lost sight of the true God and had either distorted conceptions of him or none at all. The scene was set for the centuries of sin and guilt to break out in visible suffering all over the world, like a great rash of evil.

There was one thing, however, that could frustrate Satan,

undo his plan and break up his work of centuries, and that was if, instead of being completely demoralized and dragged down into despair by the suffering that was about to break out, man should suddenly go into reverse, and use it for good.

How excellent then, from his point of view, that just now a new religion of escape should seduce hundreds of thousands of people to the astonishing belief that there is *no such thing as suffering*! No evil, no body, no sickness or pain, or hunger or thirst—and even no death!

It has always been to Satan's advantage that people should not believe in himself, and what could better serve this end, besides causing a wholesale waste of suffering as a means of redemption, than making them believe that there is no such thing as suffering?

It is a bewildering fact that there were vast numbers of people who became convinced that they had no body; but there were, and there still are. It is more bewildering still, that many of them went on believing that there is no evil, no body, pain or death, when wars and man's illimitable cruelty forced them to see people wounded and dying in their streets, and brought irrefutable reports of multitudinous misery and starvation and mass murders to them. But most astonishing is the fact that these people are most convinced of all that they have no bodies, when their own bodies are racked with pain! The only possible explanation is that Christian Science offers human beings something which they want so intensely that they are prepared to violate their reason in order to have it. The faith of the Christian Scientist is the limit of wishful thinking, and Christian Science the most transparent religion of escape. Virtually it teaches: "If there is no guilt, no one has any responsibility to his fellows for suffering. If there is no suffering, I cannot suffer; if there is no death, I shall not die." Here indeed is a complete expression of fear of responsibility, fear of suffering, fear of death!

In common with every escape religion and with every escape mechanism, Christian Science tends to isolate its members from the world of men and women; the invisible rivers of compassion which flow between most human creatures do not flow from Christian Scientists. Even for members of their own church they have no ordinary sympathy and compassion. What sympathy can they feel or give for the pain that they deny exists? And what compassion to the bereaved, if they deny the existence of death? So far as they can, they cut themselves off from the solidarity of sorrow which comforts and unites other men.

Mary Baker Eddy claimed to have "discovered" Christian Science in the year 1864. At that time Sigmund Freud was eight years old—oddly enough, it fell to his lot to start a faith that would teach that man had a body and no soul, exactly the opposite to Christian Science, in which man has a soul but no body.

The really evil thing about Freudianism is the abuses of it which have made a faith of it and distorted Freud's theories. It is true that Freud was a materialist, and his theories material; this is his limitation. But he believed that he was only dealing with material things, and with morbid cases. To apply his theories to the spiritual is ridiculous. Freud himself was a fearless seeker for truth, and one who often stood alone. Undoubtedly his mistakes—especially the profound pessimism that marks his theories—have done an immense amount of harm; but he opened the gate to more human sympathy and hope than any doctor before him. After all, we should be grateful to the hen that lays the eggs, even if it is a rather sad, limited little hen, and some of the eggs are bad.

Freudianism is a religion which has grown from the heart of a twisted humanity. It would be as unfair to attribute all the dogmas that are proclaimed as "Freudian" to Sigmund Freud himself, as it would be to attribute to Cranmer the ingenious technique of escape that has grown up in the Church of England.

The Freudian faithful, conditioned as they are by generations of more and more vague and elastic Protestantism, do not ask to know, let alone to understand, a great deal concerning their belief; neither would many of them be prepared to face the task of learning their master's vocabulary and reading his works. They are not disturbed, either, by the fact that psychiatrists usually disagree with one another. After all, the reformed religions have done the same: so that the ordinary layman can believe or disbelieve almost what he will, without necessarily being quite sure what it is: or, which matters more, without being committed by it to any definite line of conduct in the future.

The average "Freudian" has no very clear knowledge of what Freud taught about the "oedipus complex" or "infantile sexuality"; and though he is familiar enough with "the Ego", the "Id" might as well be a harvest bug for all he knows. He is content to accept as dogma that any persistent feeling of guilt is morbid; and should it become acute, it should be extracted by a psychiatrist, almost as easily as an aching tooth can be extracted by a dentist.

Why is it that it is Freudian psychoanalysis, and not the enormously suggestive philosophy of Jung, that has captured the popular imagination? In the philosophy of Jung there is all the beauty and terror and dream of mankind—its myths, its fairy stories, its magicians and its heroes. All its symbols too, water and light and earth—spiritual rebirth, resurrection, and ever-returning childhood.

In the land into which Jung invites the troubled soul, we walk in dark primeval forests beside the waters of the living stream of life, sometimes with its loveliness sparkling in our eyes, sometimes blindly through great chasms of darkness. Here we meet those figures of our childhood and our dreams, who deliver us from the drab material world—Merlin and Aphrodite, the witches and the gnomes, the immortal little child and the divine Shepherd playing eternal music on his reed. To this land there are no boundaries.

No boundaries: there we have part of the answer: modern man is eager for boundaries. He *prefers* to shrink to the limitations and spiritual frustrations of life offered by Freud, for they offer him an escape from the responsibility of being guilty; in fact, they even offer him an escape from the responsibility of being human, for a soulless man is not a human being. Psychoanalysis, the technique of Freudianism, claims to help men to know themselves, but the most frequent result is just the opposite; it is too often a case of the blind leading the blind, and results in a man ceasing to know even what a man is.

From ceasing to know what he is *like*, man has ceased to know what he *is*.

We have seen that in his attempts to escape from self-knowledge, man loses his knowledge of God: like Adam he tries to hide from God, because in the penetrating light of God he sees himself as he is. But he cannot really escape from the light of God; he can only hide his eyes and blind himself to it.

For three hundred years men have been blinding themselves to God, and with each attempt to escape from guilt their conception of God has become more negative or more distorted. The result is, as we have seen, that today the majority of people have either no conception of God at all, or one that is vague and negative, or even one that is repellent: and this is the tragedy of modern man, because, while he is aware that he is a psychological failure and seeks desperately for a remedy, he turns away from the only remedy that can save him—namely, the response of his whole being to God.

He tries to accept a wholly material explanation of himself, because his misconceptions of God lead him to an instinctive fear that any surrender of his mind to him would interfere disastrously with his life. He feels that contact with God, even if not positively disastrous, would be depressing.

He cannot persuade himself in his heart of hearts that it is certain that there is no God. But the subject is so embarrassing that it has become accepted as "bad taste" even to refer to God in conversation, and in so far as he can he avoids him in thought.

His vague uneasiness about God, which can never be finally put to sleep, is overshadowed by the distorted ideas of him so indelibly impressed on nearly everyone by the escapist religions —the sentimental, sweet God who would surely not have created the tiger, and the dour, vengeful God who would surely not have created the sparrows.

His own guilt feeling aggravates the difficulty, for even if his life is blameless by his own standards, the feeling of guilt will waken in him, as it does in everyone; and because it is a feeling of anxiety and fear and uneasiness generally, it will increase the sense of being somehow in danger from, and being watched by, a vengeful and all-powerful Being. Thus through the unhappiness and confusion of his own blind and unexamined feelings, he at once fosters and represses a tragic misconception of God.

Since the majority of people have hardly used their spiritual functions at all, the idea of self-discipline or the least degree of austerity is irksome; in the matter of temptation, even when it is known to be temptation, they have for so long taken the line of least resistance that any other line seems unthinkable.

While he wants to live fully and to be a complete human being, man does not know that God *is* the Source of Life, and that the fulness of his own human life depends wholly on his response to God. He does not know that in the uncreated Light of God, the drabness of his personality would be changed to rich and brilliant colour, as everything is coloured when the light of the sun shines on it. Rather than risk the cost of surrender to God, he forgoes everything outside the little shell of his materialism—not only the mysteries of the world of the spirit, but the wholeness and beauty of the sacramental life of soul and body living in harmony with God and with all creation.

He is unable to desire God; he cannot conceive of Heaven being the knowing of God; or desire Heaven, in eternity or now in his own heart, because its attraction does not compensate at all for the trouble and possible pain and sacrifice involved in having it, or for the awful risks and possibilities of the unknown.

He has become like the pitiful old woman in Samuel Butler's *Way of all Flesh*, who, when she is dying, implores the visiting parson in vain for some hope or comfort in the face of eternity, and then shocks him by saying, "I can do without the Heaven, Sir, but I cannot do with the Hell."

IV

MECHANISMS OF ESCAPE

It is certainly better to know that your worst adversary is right in your own heart. C. G. Jung, "The Fight with the Shadow"*

M ODERN MAN, having succeeded in blinding himself to the reality of guilt, and lost or numbed his sense of sin, is intent upon ridding himself of the misplaced *feeling* of guilt. This is as hopeless an attempt as it would be to cure a malignant growth by treating the symptoms—for example, by drugging a headache associated with it, or sitting in a draught to cool the fever. Nevertheless the ways of escape, like the manifestations of the guilt feeling, are legion and ingenious, and sometimes they are, for a time, successful.

Every one of them reveals an attempt to escape from one, or all, of three things. They are:

> self-knowledge
> suffering
> responsibility.

In the few examples of the inconsistency of the guilt feeling listed already in the first chapter, the mechanism of escape from these three things is self-evident, but there is much to be learnt from a more careful consideration of some of them, and of others which we meet every day in ourselves and in other people.

A common attempt to escape *self-knowledge* is the practice of continually confessing moral lapses to friends. These confessions are always punctuated by exaggerated expressions of self-disgust, and go together with a complete absence of any determination to take practical steps to break off the habits in question.

* From *The Listener*, 7th Nov., 1946.

Just below the surface of deliberate thought, the person indulging in these confessions reasons thus: "I am not just an ordinary sensualist; if I were, I should not suffer like this for my peccadilloes. Only a sensitive person like myself could suffer such distress for these things." Thus he restores his self-esteem by creating an imaginary, sensitive self who, once more, is "not as other men," and at the same time he is paving the way for future lapses.

There are other ways, too, in which confession, outside sacramental confession, temporarily relieves the sense of guilt, builds up complacency and paves the way to further sin. The debauches of confessing in company practised by the Oxford Group go far to explain the marked complacency that is characteristic of its members.

People who are trying to escape from humiliating self-knowledge frequently do so by putting on psychological fancy dress.

Fancy dress helps people to imagine themselves to be like the type of person they have dressed up as; sometimes even to think that they are that person. It is the greatest help to the morbidly self-conscious, especially if it is a costume that hides the face. I have seen a little man, who in ordinary life had the disposition and appearance of a canary, completely transformed by a suit of armour at a dance, and temporarily changed from his twittering little self to a reckless gallant, so forward and daring that in a few hours he complicated his life for months.

The psychological fancy dress worn by the guilty must do more than the ordinary fancy dress; it must not only give the wearer confidence and hide what shames him from others; it must also hide it from himself. It must not only justify his conduct, it must glorify it. Guilty man is not content merely to excuse himself; he needs to boast; he craves the support and reassurance of his fellow men; he wants their flattery and applause, and he wants it exactly in proportion to his misgiving about himself.

Many a boy, at the most impressionable age, has become a thief because he was able to hide the contemptible meanness of the thief's life under the fancy dress of a romantic figure in crime. A hold-up man will see himself as a Dick Turpin in scarlet and gold, redeemed in his own eyes by an imagined discriminating chivalry. For those who are wanting in imagination, the cinema supplies models of crooks and gangsters who, though they ultimately come to grief, to satisfy the vague morality of film censors, win the public sympathy by their charm, their loyalty to their own kind, and their qualities of romance and pathos. The lowest kind of crook, in the film world, is often the man who keeps the deepest love and loyalty of women.

I once enjoyed the passing friendship of a burglar, who constituted himself my escort through some streets surrounding a place where I was working. He declared that those streets were dangerous; I had only his word for it. He was very large, very tough, an amateur boxer and an ardent churchgoer, with strong leanings towards the Roman Catholic Church which were frustrated by what he considered her unreasonable insistence upon restitution as a condition for absolution. He had a little son, a fragile child whose straight thin body and mop of yellow hair made him resemble a dandelion, whom he meant to bring up in his own way of life.

This man justified himself by the stock excuse of burglers generally, that the burglar's trade is as honest as that of the banker or the stockbroker. He glorified himself by saying that it needed far more courage. In fact, his fictitious self was a hero. He used his black mask not only to conceal his identity at work, but to hide from himself under cover of the romantically brave man. He had to hide from himself that other man, whose victims were very often defenceless old ladies, lying in the shallow night sleep of the very old, as helpless and pitiful as sleeping children. But those old ladies would never enjoy that quiet sleep again after his visit. Together with many others who had only read about him in the newspaper, they would lie, night after night, their eyes wide open, listening, listening, listening—for someone breathing, close to them in the darkness.

The immoral woman will often see herself, not as degraded, but as superior to other people. If she can attain a real state of amorality by completely destroying both her conscience and her fastidiousness, she will regard herself as not only not impure, but as uniquely pure and innocent, an emancipated human being, free of all the dirty little restrictions and inhibitions which contaminate the mind of the prude.

The adulteress and the ageing wanton each thinks of herself as an "enchantress"; and if she happens to move in society, she hides from herself both the sordidness of her present life and the tragedy of her coming old age by putting on a psychological fancy dress of one of the famous adulteresses or courtesans who are remembered as they were at the height of their beauty or charm, and whose sins are glorified by the vulgarity of their many envious admirers. Favourites among them are Jeanne du Barry, Ninon de l'Enclos, and Lady Hamilton.

Unctuous piety is a not uncommon fancy dress put on by degraded characters—often by those who are very diverse in every other way. Charles Peace, the most obscene of murderers, wrote letters of pious exhortation from the condemned cell, and the father of Elizabeth Barrett Browning pressed his odious emotional demands on his daughter in the rôle of a deeply religious and prayerful man.

In the type of scrupulous person capable of torturing herself about imagined sins while remaining blind to her real sinfulness, the desire to evade self-knowledge becomes mixed quite obviously with the desire to get relief from *suffering*. This is not the same thing as the desire to *avoid* suffering, which is more closely locked up in the attempt to avoid responsibility—the common burden of suffering resulting from the universal guilt of original sin, and the never-ceasing burden of self-conquest.

The type of person I have in mind is already suffering, and her repeated confessions and searchings of her conscience to find, not what *is* there, but what is *not*, are aimed at both keeping her illusions concerning her own spirituality, and trying to discharge the suffering of the guilt feeling by giving it a name, attributing it to some trifling imperfection which she can thus externalize. The same process is often seen in psychotics who attach their guilt feeling to something external, such as food, and seek relief by rejecting it.

The scrupulous pietist has built up an imaginary self in her own mind—a self quite incapable of crude and ordinary sin. Her ideal of perfection is based not upon God but upon a sinless

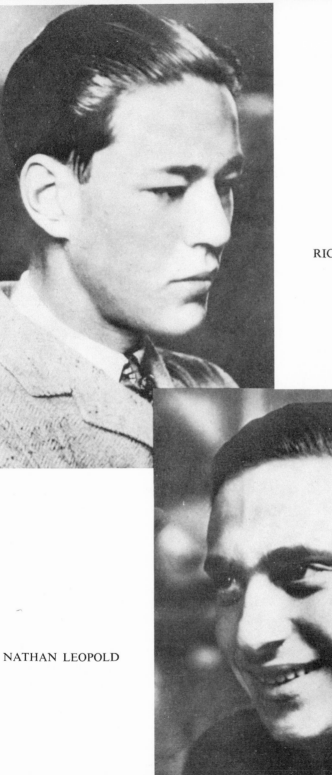

RICHARD LOEB

NATHAN LEOPOLD

self, a really "impossible she", who blinds her to all other people. But in spite of this she feels a continual, aching sense of guilt. Her examinations of conscience do not reach out from the "impossible she" to other people; indeed it does not occur to her that her distress, sometimes amounting to physical symptoms of anxiety, can be caused by anything less (in her own mind), or anything else, than a stain on the white robe of her own perfection. Naturally, then, her need for a sin to confess, which she expects each time to prick the blister and discharge the suffering of *feeling* guilty, tends to a search for sins against self, such as impurity; and in her case, of course, this could not be more than rather nebulous, vague thoughts or "suggestions". It is not surprising that almost immediately after the confession the uneasiness returns, and she then questions the confession itself, and returns as often as the confessor will allow, to confess the last confession.

It is always the sins against self which obsess this type of scrupulous mind—never the sins against God or against other people. Who has ever known a person of this kind who was tormented by her want of love, by her lack of justice, by such things as grinding her servants into giving the maximum work for the minimum wage, or letting others in her family take on all the drudgery of the home while she resorts to prayer? Or by condemning others for the sins to which she is not tempted, or giving a false and repellent idea of religion to children by her manner and speech? Again, does anyone afflicted in this way ever realize or grieve over the insult to God implicit in the anxiety which doubts his forgiveness, his mercy, his knowledge of her soul, and which closes her heart against his love? She is really unaware of her sins against God and against other people, for the simple reason that God and other people are not real to her. God, in himself, God as absolute Being, as Goodness, as Fatherhood, is unknown to her. Other people are unknown and unreal to her. She is too much aware of herself to realize anyone else.

It is in this that our pietist resembles the criminal and the lunatic. The characteristic which these three have in common is unawareness of anyone but themselves.

Egoism consists precisely in unawareness of other people. It is

G   D

one of the results of guilt, for it is the result of the unawareness
of God that has been brought about in many by their attempt to
escape from guilt. Only the beauty of God is sufficiently compelling to hold man's attention and to draw it off from himself.
When he turns away from God and becomes unaware of his
presence, his whole interest turns in and centres on himself and
becomes self-love. If he is obsessed by feelings of guilt, self-pity
will increase his self-love; if he has managed to delude himself
and to numb his sense of guilt and sin, he will become inordinately conceited and easily offended by the least affront to his
imagined splendour, brilliance, uniqueness or charm. He will
realize the existence of others only in so far as they affect himself, by gratifying his sensuality, flattering his rarity, ministering
to his needs, protecting him from life, and so on. He will see no
importance whatever in their lives apart from himself. He will
always be defending his loved self and will go to any lengths to
gratify a wish or to avoid a suffering.

The deliberate murderer who is sane values another human
life very much less than his own gratification. To the person who
has really touched the satanic perfection of self-love, even a
small personal gratification is more important than someone
else's life.

There is an instance related by the pioneer criminologist
Lombroso, of a child of eleven, a pretty little Italian girl, who
gave evidence against herself in court without a trace of embarrassment or shame, as if she were reciting a poem. She had
murdered a four-year-old child by pushing her out of a high
window. She first stole the child's ear-rings because she wanted to
sell them to buy sweets; then she murdered the child in case she
told of the theft, which would have led to a beating for herself.
This child murderess made no attempt to conceal or deny the
murder, and felt no shame or sorrow for it; she simply could not
see that the baby's life and the parents' grief mattered more than
her own deprivation of a few sweets or avoidance of a beating.

The notorious Smith, who murdered three wives by drowning
them in a bath, was extremely parsimonious; when the day
fixed in his own mind for the murder was approaching, he began
to bring home small gifts for the intended victim, in order to
make himself dislike her. He always came to dislike anyone who

cost him money, and he wished to feel sufficient dislike to destroy any feeble pang of pity or remorse which might make it less easy for him to commit the crime he intended.

We have seen that owing to the loss of the sense of sin and the loss of the knowledge of God, many people have an "unresolved" guilt feeling—that is, a feeling of guilt, sometimes amounting to an obsession, for which they cannot account in any reasonable way.

Sometimes this turns to anxiety and to curious obsessions, and the sufferer will often take fantastic ways to try to discharge the suffering. He will even seem to court a different suffering involving disaster to himself, to break the unbearable tension. He will want to be punished and will sometimes commit crimes in order to be punished; or he will give himself up for crimes committed by someone else.

In the opinions put forward by psychiatrists as evidence in the trial of the two boy murderers, Leopold and Loeb, one of them —Loeb—committed the crime as an indirect suicide. He said during the examination by psychiatrists while awaiting his trial, that he had often felt that he ought to commit suicide; and witnesses told of his having said this long before he was on trial for his life; he expected to be executed, and went joyfully to serve a life sentence. When he was a young child the daydream most pleasing to him was that he was in jail, undergoing punishment. Whether the psychiatrists were right or wrong about Loeb, there can be no doubt that people give themselves up for murder of which they are innocent.

In the case of Constance Kent, a girl about fifteen years old who murdered her little step-brother, but whose guilt was not discovered until, many years later, she confessed it herself, a young man who had nothing whatever to do with the crime gave himself up to the police as the murderer.

The most popularly accepted explanation of these false confessions is the power which suggestion exerts over certain weak-minded people by means of gruesome and detailed newspaper reports. There is, however, one outstanding example to show that neither this nor the "unresolved" guilt feeling is always the true explanation, and to raise many questions concerning how the mind works.

This is the example of Hans Strausberg, who confessed to two of the most terrible murders actually committed by Peter Kürten, "the monster of Düsseldorf".

While the townsfolk of Düsseldorf were in a state of fear and horror bordering on hysteria because of the presence among them of an undiscovered murderer whose crimes were multiplying, Hans Strausberg—an epileptic, who was twenty-one years old but unable to read or write, who was of subnormal intelligence and could hardly express himself coherently because he had a cleft palate and a hare-lip—lassoed and attempted to strangle two young women, but on both occasions the young women escaped.

Strausberg was arrested and accused not only of the two attempted murders he had really been guilty of, but also of the actual murder of a child and a man committed by Peter Kürten. He confessed to all four crimes, and gave detailed accounts of how he committed the two murders as well as the two attempts. It was only with great difficulty that he was able to make his speech understood, but he did so, and his descriptions of the murders were amazingly true to the real facts later confessed fully by Peter Kürten.

Hans Strausberg, being completely illiterate and a cretin, was incapable of reading newspapers, and as he had in fact attempted two murders, he hardly needed to seek for something to which to attach his feeling of guilt. Further, evidence which came to light during his trial and the examinations of the psychiatrists showed that he was among those who are without any sense of sin and whose conscience does not disturb them at all. He was found to be not responsible for his actions, and committed for life to a mental asylum.

The Russian writer Dostoievsky, himself obsessed by guilt, wrote novels springing from his intimate knowledge of men, acquired in the prisons of Siberia. He understood them as few writers have ever done, because the story of their agony was graven deep on his own heart and mind. In *Crime and Punishment*, the story of a poor student, the hero, Raskolnikow, who commits a murder to try to break down his feelings of humiliation, does everything he can after the murder to bring suspicion on himself, and finally confesses; after this he experiences what is apparently the first feeling of relief and joy in his life, because he is given a life sentence in Siberia!

Seeking *to be* punished is not the same thing as *self*-punishment, which seems to be a complicated drive, in which an attempt to avoid *responsibility*, and a fear of punishment to come, are mixed with an instinct, though a twisted one, for expiation.

An old circus clown who had travelled most of the world in a menagerie show told me of a lion tamer, his companion for many years, whose act, planned by himself, was putting his head into the lion's mouth every night: he did this to expiate a crime which he had committed and which was never discovered.

In seeking to avoid responsibility, one of the commonest escape mechanisms is self-punishment. We have already glimpsed this in the addicts to pre-party gloom, but it takes countless forms. The person who punishes herself cannot enjoy pleasure or happiness because she is haunted by a *conscious* sense of guilt. She certainly does not want to give up the good things she has, but she lives in dread of some catastrophe befalling her by way of punishment—punishment for what? She will tell you that she is afraid of being punished for being happy —or rich—or in good health. In reality she feels, and rightly, that to have managed to avoid doing anything at all by way of shouldering the common responsibility for guilt puts her in a precarious position. In the last resort what she fears is death. She may get through without a single personal sacrifice in this life, but what of the next—if there is one? What waits in the unknown worlds beyond this?

A frequent form of self-punishment is hypochondria, though it is complicated by other buried motives. Hypochondria is a means of obtaining a number of things that the neruotic feels a bitter need of, and it also satisfies the craving to be punished. For so long as the patience of the doctors lasts, it does much to give the poor sufferer the feeling of being protected from death. With the dread possibilities of the unknown facing her, she calls the doctor to her side at the first symptom of illness. She can even induce symptoms to bring him. She receives either his treatment—and protection—or his assurance that there is nothing wrong with her. If it is the latter, the relief will be short-lived, as the doctor will go away. She prefers him to be in continual attendance, and fears nothing so much as good health.

Of all the attempts to escape personal responsibility for the suffering of the world and for individual guilt, none is so dangerous as the loss of their own individuality which countless people seek by identifying themselves with a group. One of the most persistent miseries that sin has imposed upon men is a sense of personal insufficiency. This has become more than ever acute in our own days, because of the huge tidal waves of fear that are sweeping through the world, filling the individual with dread because of his helplessness in the face of gathering disaster.

His plight is more terrible because in his flight from guilt he has lost sight of, or perhaps never seen, how to save himself, and with himself his fellow men, from what he dreads. Because he is afraid to look into his own soul, lit up by the searching beam of the Uncreated Light, he does not realize that the enemy is *within himself*. Only in himself can he come to grips with the evil which threatens to destroy humanity. He is afraid to look inwards, and so he is aware of little but that which is outside of himself. He is aware that the threatening tide of evil is always gathering strength, but not that its relentless and seemingly uncontrollable force is streaming out of his own heart.

Moreover, that which he refuses to recognize in himself, he projects on to others, whom he makes his scapegoats. Everyone who fails to realize and to come face to face with the enemy in himself will always seek and always find an enemy outside of himself.

Most people try to banish the dark side of their nature and of their individual psyche, to force it out of their consciousness into the unconscious. We have already seen how diverse are the ways they use, ranging from scrupulosity to crime.

Jung calls this dark side, which is part of every one of us, "the Shadow". It is the evil in man and his proneness to evil, the persistent downward lurch in every one of us, the potential as well as the actual sin which is in us all. "Primitiveness, violence, cruelty, in short all the powers of darkness." "The Shadow" is the result of original sin.

If we succeed in banishing our evil side and become unaware of it, the primitive cruelty and wickedness in our hearts waxes stronger and stronger out of sight. The beast is preparing for battle in secret. It is crouching just below the thin surface of consciousness, with talons out, ready to break through and destroy.

The danger is great when we are *not* in conscious conflict with ourselves. We must bring the evil out into the light of consciousness, in order that we may meet it on the battlefield of our own souls.

We are safe only when we are consciously at war within ourselves.

This is one meaning that we may discover in those paradoxical words of the Prince of Peace, "I bring not peace but a sword."

But the danger is not to the individual alone. When a great many individuals are secretly possessed by forces which they do not understand, they are drawn together and united in a curious way by the forces they disavow.

There is a mysterious magnetism which unites them, and if they are organized into a group which identifies itself with an ideal that replaces the individual's sense of responsibility and his sense of his own littleness, by an inflated idea of the mission and power of the group, he becomes more and more unaware of the evil in himself.

When this happens, that evil is multiplied; it is no longer one man's "shadow", but the shadow of millions, all uncontested, all gathering force, ready to be released as soon as a leader is found who is himself so possessed by evil that he is the symbol and personification of the masses.

As the devil driven out of the maniac was liberated in the Gadarene swine and sent them rushing to their destruction, the devil that has been liberated from the leader's soul seizes upon and liberates "the Shadow" in the souls of the regimented multitude and drives them to their own ultimate destruction.

We have seen this illustrated in the tragedy of Germany. German youth, smarting under the humiliation following the war of 1914—demoralized and depressed—was a ready prey to the Nazi ideology. Lost in the new exhilaration, identified to the point of insanity with the rightness of the Cause and the idolatry of the Fuehrer, not one of those young men and women was aware of the evil *within themselves*.

As the blonde Hans, with the blue eyes and face of an angel and the slight smell of carbolic soap, swung along the streets in his S.S. uniform, exulting in the sacrifice of his personality to the Cause, the forgotten evil in his own soul, uncontested, waxed stronger and more furious. Straining at the chains that were already breaking, crouching in the darkness, the beast was ready to spring.

But the beast was not alone. The multitudinous evil in the millions was secretly united in an immeasurable force of destruction, waiting for the signal to break out into the open and plunge the world into a sea of blood.

The signal came from Hitler, because he was the most inferior and most irresponsible of them all. He was not the leader or the oppressor of the German people, but the expression of everything that was worst in them, which they were repressing in themselves. This is Jung's description of Hitler and his relationship to his people: "With the rest of the world they did not understand what Hitler's significance was: namely, that he was a symbol for every individual: he was the most prodigious personification of all human inferiorities. He was a highly incapable, unadapted, irresponsible, psychopathic individual, full of empty childish fantasies, but cursed with the keen intuition of a rat or guttersnipe. He represented the shadow, the inferior part of everybody's personality, in an overwhelming degree,—and this is another reason why they fell for him."*

It was that intuition of the "rat or guttersnipe" that warned Hitler that the wild beasts leashed in the darkness were already too thirsty for blood to be held back until the moment for the devastation of Europe, and impelled him to let them loose upon the Jews in Germany.

What happened to the Germans yesterday may happen to us tomorrow. We are creating conditions such as the Germans made for themselves.

First of all and most dangerous of all, we too repudiate "the Shadow"; we refuse to see that in each one of us, just below the brittle surface of consciousness, there is a "Beast of Belsen".

* C. G. Jung, "The Fight with the Shadow".

We prefer to think that those who committed outrages of cruelty on human beings in Belsen, Auschwitz, Lublin, Mauthausen and Ravensbrück were abnormal people, monsters suffering from some congenital psychopathic enormity; but this is not so. The most revealing finding at the trials of the "war criminals" was that they were, with very few exceptions, sane, normal people, people like you and me.

They did what we are doing; instead of fighting the evil in themselves and so preventing the collective force of evil from gathering, they escaped into the complacency and the false security of identification with a group—not that rightful tendency to associate with others, grounded in man's nature as a social being, whereby the individual personality is enriched, but a fleeing from the burden of being oneself.

Right through every stratum of society this tendency prevails here. Men and women hand themselves over willingly to be crowded together and controlled by forces outside themselves in industry; they lose sight of their helplessness before the rising tide of want and poverty. They even allow their pleasure to be organized for them, and herd together in huge groups to spend their holidays in camps, where every hour of the day is arranged for them.

Religious people form themselves into groups in which, through over-activity that is often "much ado about nothing", and the feeling that they belong to a great and vital force of righteousness with a mission to lead and dominate others, they lose the feeling of personal guilt and of insufficiency.

Thus by losing his individuality, in order to rid himself of his first responsibility—namely, to fight the evil in himself—man adds a sinister aspect to personal guilt, not only for the individual concerned, but for mankind as a whole.

Psychologists relate neurosis of many kinds to "unresolved feelings of guilt".

Although this is a book about normal people, we cannot ignore those who are considered abnormal, because not only, as I have already said, do we see in them the normal under a magnifying glass, but there are psychotic people and even insane people who seem to be chosen to suffer some typical universal suffering of our age, in an intensified form; and there may well be saints among them, to whom we owe an incalculable debt, and at the very worst they are warnings to us and scapegoats for us all.

All these neurotic obsessions can be traced to a compulsion to try to be rid of the suffering of an unbearable tension or unhappiness, but, as I shall explain in the chapter called "The Homing Toad", I believe that they have also another and more far-reaching significance.

Some of these obsessions are: constantly washing the hands: a mania for counting—counting the words spoken, the steps taken in walking, the lines on the paving stones, the stairs, and indeed everything that can be counted: repeated gestures, and sometimes the queerest antics, such as touching every lamp-post in the street. Anxiety, attributed to the same cause, leads people to open and re-seal their letters over and over again lest they be in the wrong envelopes; to write the same sentence literally hundreds of times; to go back over and over again to see if they have turned off the light; to become the victims of unreasonable fears, and so on.

Dr Russell Brain describes many of the guilt complexes of writers in an article published in the *British Medical Journal*, called "Authors and Psychopathics". Samuel Johnson, he tells us, whirled, twisted and performed extraordinary antics with his hands and feet, especially when crossing the threshold of a door, and he had the habit of whistling and blowing and counting his steps, touching posts in the street, and—perhaps most disconcerting of all for his friends—of stretching out his arm with a full cup of tea in his hand, in every direction.

It is not only unresolved guilt to which the individual cannot attribute the cause, that may result in abnormality. Guilt for which the cause is all too well realized by the sufferer may also result in neurosis and morbidity, because he is unable or unwilling to cope with the situation.

The poet John Donne is an example of this. A Catholic apostate whose veins ran crimson with martyrs' blood, he became Protestant Dean of St Paul's Cathedral, and then grew obsessed—literally obsessed—by thoughts of death and the decomposition of the body. The statue of him in St Paul's Cathedral is a monument to his guilt.

In the article quoted above, Dr Brain tells how this statue was made; having consented to have a monument made of himself for his Cathedral, Donne had an urn made to fit his body, and wrapped in his winding-sheet he stood on it, posing as his own corpse. Thus it was he caused an artist to draw him for the monument. The drawing, when completed, he had placed by his bedside and gazed on it until the hour of his death.

Donne expressed all too cruelly his own anguish, and with it the anguish of all guilty men who do not know, or will not take, the remedy for guilt, in one sentence: "Any man's death diminishes me, because I am involved in mankind; and therefore never seek to know for whom the bell tolls; it tolls for thee."

V

THE HOMING TOAD

For those who offend me are also very close to me, though against their will.

Revelation to St Teresa of Avila

TO TELL the story of human guilt would be to tell the story of mankind through all the ages of creation until now, but all through that history from the very beginning until now man's reactions to guilt and his attempts to escape have been consistent, and have followed the pattern that they follow today.

Many people do not believe the story of Adam and Eve and the first sin, but it seems to me difficult to disbelieve a story in which human beings are so true to the psychological pattern that is recognizable in every kind of person today.

The immediate instinct following their awareness of their guilt was to hide themselves from themselves, to put on fancy dress: and then, even when they had done this, they must hide from God.

They were afraid of the light of God because they were naked, because they could not help seeing themselves in that penetrating light as they really were, as they had become now; and therefore the Presence of God, which until now was the source of their joy, was painful to them.

The curious thing is that they were not afraid of God because they had disobeyed him, but because they knew that something had gone wrong with their human nature as a result, and they could no longer endure self-knowledge in God's presence. They tried to hide from themselves and from one another. They found the truth about themselves confusing enough in their own company; in the presence of God they found it intolerable. Adam did not answer the voice of God calling to him in the cool of the day by saying, "I was afraid because I had disobeyed you," but "I heard thy voice in the garden, and I was afraid because I was naked and I hid myself."

But even so short a time ago as the dawn of that day in Eden, walking in the loveliness of the light of God, Adam and Eve had been naked, and they were not troubled by the fact. "And they were both naked, the man and his wife, and were not ashamed."

Human nature is made in God's image; only when it has been made in a sense unnatural by sin, so that concupiscence has infected it with its subtle poison, does it become that of which man is ashamed before God.

This applies to everything in human nature, not only, as countless people imagine, to sex; but undoubtedly there was a profound psychological effect upon the natural love of man and woman too, and the emotions woven into this love became split. The order of God's law no longer held man in the perfect balance and the unity within himself which made his expression of love a simple, complete act of pure joy, controlled by his own will. Human nature was disintegrated by the first sin, and instead of being, as Satan had promised, more like God, it was less like God, for in its every expression it had lost its wholeness. Inevitably this expression, life-giving love—which is the most Godlike of all—was complicated most of all.

The first sin was, above all else, a fearful abuse of the gift God gave to man by which alone he was able to love—namely free will. The result of the sin was that he was no longer able to use his will freely; he became the slave of his impulses and appetites and the use of his will must henceforth involve a struggle with them and with himself.

Probably, like a sign of what had happened inwardly, which would take many generations for man to understand, came the first matrimonial quarrel, the first disagreement and antagonism between man and wife who were made to be one flesh. For it is difficult to suppose that at least a little coldness did not result from Adam's prompt shifting of responsibility on to Eve! "The woman whom thou gavest to be with me, she gave me of the tree and I did eat."

To this day sexual love is split in its expression. It is complicated by conflicting elements of love and hate, sadism and masochism. There is a kind of schizophrenia of sex, which many people now accept as being "natural"; but, as we shall see, sex requires the unifying principle of redemption to restore it to

man's true nature, and to make it once more the supreme
expression of human love.*

Cain followed the same pattern as Adam. Because he had
murdered his brother he could not endure to remain in the
presence of God; but neither could he face the hardship of being
a vagabond on the earth that would yield nothing to him, and
the fear of being murdered in his turn by other men. The
wonderful touch of mercy following his sin is nearly always
ignored by those who tell Cain's story today, and we are told he
was "branded" as if it were to add to his shame by pointing him
out as a murderer. In truth God put a mark on him to protect
him.

"And Cain said unto the Lord, My punishment is greater than
I can bear. Behold thou hast driven me out this day from the
face of the earth; and from thy face shall I be hid; and I shall be
a fugitive and a vagabond in the earth; and it shall come to pass
that everyone that findeth me shall slay me.

"And the Lord said unto him, Therefore whosoever slayeth
Cain, vengeance shall be taken on him sevenfold. And the Lord
set a mark upon Cain, lest any finding him should kill him.

"And Cain went out from the presence of the Lord ..." (Gen.
4.13-16).

There is not only a pattern running consistently all through
man's reaction to his guilt, but there is also an equally consistent
pattern in God's reaction to it, which begins with Adam and
persists all through time to this day. It is an attitude of the
tenderest fatherhood, and the first men in spite of their guilt still
knew God well enough to know this. Note that it was not of
God's vengeance that Cain was afraid; he rather turned to him
for mercy, as if he felt confident that he would ease the punishment that he could not bear: what he really feared was what his
fellow men would do to him: "... and it shall come to pass that
everyone that findeth me shall slay me"—and God at once
brands Cain, not to scar him as a murderer, but to set the seal
of his own extraordinary protecting love on him. No one, seeing
that mark, could kill Cain unless *they* liked to risk the vengeance
of God.

Before that, what a significant little detail reveals God's

* See Chapter XVIII, "The Measure of Joy".

tenderness to Adam and Eve. He did not leave them naked or cowering away from him in their fancy dress of fig leaves, but he clothed them himself: "Unto Adam also and to his wife did the Lord God make coats of skins, and clothed them" (Gen. 3.21).

The story of man's wickedness and God's mercy goes on like this. When men had become wicked, "thinking only evil thoughts", and the flood came, the Ark was given to Noah and his family and the animals; and when the flood subsided, God filled the sky with the lovely sign of the rainbow—who but God would give a rainbow with his forgiveness! Again and again, the Israelites, who were to give us Christ, were forgiven and given lovely tokens of forgiveness when they had sinned. Even those punishments which God's love must give are inflicted on man by his own hand, he brings them on himself; only love and mercy come straight from God's hand.

Death, the most terrible punishment for sin, was brought into the world by man, and the first man to die died by a man's hand. The first death was murder.

Mercy upon mercy answers sin upon sin, and Christ is the complete mercy, which cannot be surpassed. We shall see a little further on how completely and how exactly Christ is the answer to Adam.

As to Satan, who is the ultimate cause of all guilt, and who first induced a woman to sin, God answers him with a woman: "And I will put enmity between thee and the woman" (Gen. 3.15). This woman is the Mother of Christ, who already stands before God, with the head of the serpent crushed under her foot.

There is one remarkable characteristic of human nature which seems to me to bear some relationship to the brand of Cain, the mark of mercy which shows that man, evil though he is, is protected by God.

In the heart of every fallen man there dwells a homing toad.

Toads are not very popular animals, except perhaps with witches; on the whole men think of them as repulsively ugly, squat, square, horny, coarse and altogether, in spite of the fact that they have beautiful eyes, unattractive. Superstitious people, presumably because of the poor toad's connection with witchcraft, think he is unlucky and spit on the ground when they see him. But there is one kind of toad (incidentally, he is the commonest kind, the large brown fellow we find under big stones in the garden) who is a most moving animal, as beautiful as he is grotesque, and for me at all events a symbol of mankind: the homing toad.

This toad has an undefeatable drive in him to go back to his home: he can be taken as far away from it as anyone is cruel enough to take him, and he always gets back. Some have taken a homing toad fifty miles from his home, and after marking him in order to be sure of his identity, have let him go, and after weeks he has turned up at home, dusty from many hot dry roads, thin, nearly dead from exhaustion, but back again in his own home, where mercifully he recovers, fills out, becomes a plump happy toad again and falls into a beautiful beatific sleep under his old home stone.

Now man, however evil he becomes, however twisted and grotesque—however far away guilt takes him from God, from his home, the environment in which he can regain the true shape of his manhood—always reveals the struggle, innate in him, to get back. He really wants to be in the Light of God, in his proper home, and even in the twists and contortions that he goes through in his abnormalities, even in his insanities, it is obvious that he is striving, without his knowledge, even without his will, to get back.

In every manifestation of his mind working in ignorance—but sincerely—man shows his desire for God's light. In all his psychological mistakes and oddities he shows a wish to be what God wants him to be, though he is often showing it unconsciously and by making his pseudo-self into a caricature of his real, God-made self.

There are certain things man was created to be, certain conditions for being restored to the original pattern which have come about through his redemption and his oneness with Christ; under all his confusion and folly, something in him strains and agonizes towards those things and tries to fulfil those conditions.

There is evil beyond all words in every man, but against that evil there is persistent good, which makes him like his symbol in the homing toad, lovable even when he is grotesque. It is as well to list some of these signs of the homing toad briefly here; they will be discussed more fully as we go on, and probably the reader will see others that I have not perceived; but the more they are kept in mind in discussing some of the miseries of human nature, the more hopeful one is able to feel for mankind.

First of all, the instinct to hide, with which we can include psychological fancy dress and many forms of self-delusion. It is observable that people assume a disguise which gives good points to the character they assume, though sometimes if those who are to be impressed by the character belong to a set that is degenerate or dishonest, they may wish to seem worse than they are in the general make-up. But the thief will have on the hero's fancy dress, the immoral woman will clothe herself in the fiction that immoral women are great-hearted, the degenerate will easily put on the self-delusion that he is anti-social because he is supersensitive, or more afflicted by social injustice than other men. It is the commonest thing in the world for the man who is jaundiced by envy to suppose that he is a social reformer, or the intellectual who has become déclassé and is a misfit in every class to find a virtue in his own class-hatred. The scrupulous woman in her fancy dress of angelic perfection cannot bear to know the hard kernel of her own heart that is so far from the likeness of eternal Love.

All of them are crying out in a most incongruous, involuntary chorus—but a chorus all the same—"Thank God we are not as other men."

Deep in the heart of man there is a longing to be as God created him: to be a man made in the pattern of Christ. St Paul speaks of "putting on Christ". That is man's real need, to "put on Christ" like a garment, covering himself not with a disguise, a falsehood, but with the humanity of Christ, for which he was made.

Guilty man cannot face himself as he is. In spite of the fact that this is an age in which introspection has become almost a science, it is also an age in which few men dare to face themselves and to see themselves as they are. Consequently nearly everyone has made a fictitious self, and in contemplating this, he is able to forget "what manner of man he is".

G   E

This desire to escape from self-knowledge is, like the desire to escape from suffering, a symptom of self-love, and it is interesting to observe that twisted as he is, man *cannot* love himself as he really is. Bad though he is, he cannot love himself in his badness, he must blind himself to it and try to love the false self of his imagination. It is difficult to imagine a situation so far removed from reality as this; man whose self-love compels him to love a self that is not real.

Closely allied to the "fancy-dress" escape is the daydream which invades reality. This is very common. Orphans, illegitimate children, sometimes adopted children, and even children whose real parents fail to satisfy some psychological need in them, or whose inflation none *could* satisfy, have daydreams that they are the children of titled or royal people. The answer is that they *are* children of the King of Kings. I remember a little orphan girl in a slum whose daydream was that she was a queen's daughter. When she was brought into the Catholic Faith and saw the statue of Our Lady, her Mother, crowned Queen of Heaven, her dream was realized and translated into reality which transformed her life.

Man's patent longing for reassurance, for encouragement and applause from others, and his attempts to lose his individuality in a group, have an answer—far transcending any natural solidarity—in the communion of saints, the oneness of the Body of Christ in his Church. This is a oneness that is complete and carries man along in its stream of life, but more intensely because of his individuality, his *self* in communion with all other men. In it he has not only the encouragement of others, or anything so shallow as their flattery, he has the power of their sanctity and their love; it belongs to him, and his belongs to them.

The destructive drive towards self-punishment is a perversion of the Christ-given instinct for voluntary suffering and penance, and the life of the hypochondriac and the life of Christian austerity have much in common outwardly, though one drives from, and the other to, God.

The morbid wish to confess and to be reassured or exonerated in vice points to a necessity that God has given to man, sacramental Confession and Absolution.

The curious symptoms of guilt such as hand-washing and symbolic gestures of many kinds (the need for repetition, and so on) have their answer in ritual, with its ceremonial and symbolical hand-washing, its repeated words, movements and gestures, all deeply effective in human consciousness, and able to do in reality for man those mysterious things he tries in vain to do for himself by obsessional acts, remnants of magic and superstition, which become his torment. The astonishing mania, so common in neurotic people and even in some who are not neurotic, for counting and being ruled by numbers is connected with the need in man's soul for order, for mathematical precision and balance, which is something that dominates well-balanced, integrated personalities too continuously for them to be aware of it at all, though they are aware of its creative effects.

There is a tendency which is unlike counting, but really more closely related to it than is obvious: this is the wish or need to be swamped, to be lost, carried away by something stronger than one's own will, or one's own self. It shows itself in many ways—in drunkenness, lust, passions of anger, mob emotion, in religious hysteria, especially group hysteria with such practices as "testifying" and "conversion". It has some outlet in singing, especially hymn singing and community singing, and is one reason why when several people are drunk together, they usually sing and often sing and dance.

There is an answer to this; man was made to be caught up into the immensity of the Life of God, of the Blessed Trinity, the Life which is the cause of all other life and power. In God, man's individuality is not swamped and submerged, but it is marvellously released from its limitations, set free in the infinite life of Love and borne along on its eternal torrents of beauty.

Our life in God is the greatest of all mysteries, and here we recognize the homing toad again—in the pitiful madness which can lead a man to think himself Christ by his own virtue, a new messiah with a new message, or simply God. As the whole object of this book is to show that it *is* man's destiny to be "a Christ", it will be enough to quote here a definition which puts as clearly as possible in exactly what our *otherness* from Christ consists.

"The difference between the generation of God the Son and our generation from the Father lies in this, that the Son radiates from the Father from all eternity by necessity of his nature, while we are lifted into the mysteries of this endless life-stream only by a free act of God's overpowering love."*

No wonder the homing toad triumphs in man, dusty and pathetic though his triumph is!

No wonder man wants to be greater, holier, purer, more supernatural, more beautiful, more potent, more lovable and more loving, than he feels himself to be in his secret heart.

No wonder that he longs to lose the sense of his limitations and his slavery and impotence in immensity, to flood himself out of consciousness if necessary.

No wonder that in the midst of his sins, his confused glimpses of Heaven torment him, and yet draw him as irresistibly as a strong current in deep water.

Surely there can be few if any honest men and women who have the smallest vestige of self-knowledge, who have not, at some secret moment in their life, echoed from the depths of their soul the poignant cry of the poet Rimbaud, whose youth was a "Season in Hell":

This moment of wakefulness has given me the vision of purity.
The mind leads one towards God. Heartrending Calamity.

* Julius Tyciak, *Life in Christ*, Sheed and Ward (London), p. 22.

VI

CONFESSION

Nihil aliud sumus quam voluntates: "*We are nothing else but wills.*"
                                                        ST AUGUSTINE

But though my will is not yet free from self interest, I give it to thee freely. For I have proved by long experience how much I have gained by leaving it freely in thy hand. ST TERESA OF AVILA

WE HAVE SEEN that the means by which relief from feelings of guilt is most often sought is self-accusation and confession—a confession sometimes of real and sometimes of imaginary guilt. We have seen too how diverse are the people who come under this curious compulsion, ranging from the morally depraved to the timidly pious. There can be no doubt that the compulsion to confess is rooted in a real necessity of human nature, and is a manifestation of the homing toad struggling to get back to his own place of happiness.

Nevertheless, outside of sacramental Confession, confessing does not bring lasting relief. In fact confession and self-accusation, used to escape from the suffering of the feeling of guilt, disintegrate and destroy personality. When it is habitual, as with those who confess all their moral lapses to their friends, it has the effect of weakening the will more and more, until ultimately the whole character crumbles.

It is equally true that all the means used to escape from guilt destroy personality, because they are all acts of self-love. Every attempt to avoid the responsibility for guilt is an attempt at self-protection, self-delusion, self-gratification, or self-aggrandizement.

The man who fosters self-love is indeed his own executioner, for self-love grows like fungus in a dark, damp place, and the bigger it becomes, the smaller is that which causes suffering to

the one who fosters it. The more precious a man supposes himself to be, the more convinced does he become that he is beset
by dangers on every side. There are those in mental institutions
who think that they are made of glass that will be shattered at a
touch. In the same way, the more important a man supposes
himself to be, the quicker he is to see slights and insults in unintended trifles, and the more a man pities himself, the more
easily he will be bruised by the blows of fate that glance off less
self-centred people.

The more a man loves himself, the more inordinately he will
crave to be loved, and the less loved he will be, and, still more
tragic for him, the less capable will he be of loving anyone else
but himself.

It is not surprising, then, that when the compulsion to confess
and to make accusations against the self is inspired by self-love,
though it may be disguised self-love, it brings not relief or healing, but more and more distress and ultimately a collapse of the
whole personality.

Yet confession itself *is* something that is vital to man's happiness, and it is an essential part of the supreme remedy for real
guilt which has been given to man by God: the sacrament of
Penance, the sacrament which is nearly always spoken of simply
as "Confession".

Outside the Catholic Church there are few people who do not
cherish wholly mistaken ideas about what sacramental Confession is. Many think that it is a substitute for psychoanalysis and
that Catholics use it for the same purpose for which psychoanalysis is often used, namely to rid themselves of the *feeling* of
guilt, the reality of guilt being something which many people
fail to recognize. If this were true, those egocentrically scrupulous people already described, who are driven by self-love and
vanity to torturing introversion and repeated confessions in
search of relief, would all be cured, or at least changed to the
extent that medical treatment could change them.

Psychoanalysis and sacramental Confession are two completely different things.

Psychiatry is an experimental science for the treatment of
mental, nervous and functional disorder. A psychiatrist who
approaches a human being reverently as a person, a whole

human being who is both soul and body, and not merely an intricate assembly of materials or a frustrated sexual urge, has a humble and yet magnificent service to offer in simplifying man's response to grace.

Man is made in the image and likeness of God; even in his physical nature he bears the imprint of God. When he is true to the pattern that his human nature is created in, there is the balance and harmony, the order and rhythm within him that is in all created things, and his balanced personality is the ordinary channel through which grace can flow most easily. A disturbance in the working of the mind or body—such, for example, as the mind's being so flooded by emotion as to hinder the judgment of the intellect or the free choice of the will—can put obstacles in the way of grace, though it is not inevitable that it should.

Psychological illness can be the means to sanctify as much as any other illness can be, but also, in common with all other chronic and painful illness, it can be demoralizing and destructive to the soul.

It is the work of the psychiatrist to restore an unbalanced, disturbed personality to the sweetness of order that is true to human nature, and so to prepare the whole man for the inflowing of grace. The ideal psychiatrist is a St John the Baptist in the wilderness of the modern world, whose mission is to "prepare the way of the Lord, make straight his paths".

Sometimes a priest who recognizes that one of his penitents is neurotic or bordering on neurosis will advise him to seek the help of a psychiatrist, and with healthy results, but there are cases which psychiatrists fail to help. The result depends largely on the skill and the personality of the analyst, but sometimes the greatest skill and the most persuasive and sympathetic personality are unavailing to remove or mitigate the patient's mental suffering, or even to diagnose it correctly.

The sacrament of Penance has a purpose wholly different from that of psychiatry and one which far transcends it. It is one too which can never fail unless the penitent himself deliberately frustrates it by an act of sacrilege.

It is not limited to a certain kind of person, but is for everyone; it does not depend on the personality or the skill of the priest; it fulfils its purpose whether he is a man of the deepest understanding of human nature or of none at all.

It is not something experimental which may or may not be effective in a given case, but something absolutely certain which will be effective in every case. It is never an experiment; it is always a miracle.

The purpose of sacramental Confession is atonement—at-one-ment—with God. What happens in Confession is that man, who has separated himself from God, becomes one with him again. It is an unimaginable impact of love between God and man in which Christ gives himself to the sinner. To the soul that is dead in sin, Christ's life flows back, and in that sinner's life, Christ rises again from death. To the soul that is devitalized and nerveless from habitual sins of weakness, Christ gives an increase of his life, flooding the soul with his vitality and love and changing it as he changed the water into wine at Cana.

The sacrament of Penance is the sacrament of joy. It is not only the sacrament of joy for the sinner who returns to God and is restored to life and made one with Christ, but (and this is a mystery far beyond any joy or glory of man's) it is also a sacrament of joy for the eternal Father. He rejoices as the father of the Prodigal Son rejoiced. He sees in the Christ-redeemed sinner, risen from the death of sin and living again with Christ's life, his only beloved Son coming back to him, clothed in the red robes of his Passion.

The sacrament is not intended to be, and is not, a form of healing for mental or nervous disorder, though incidentally it may sometimes have that effect, as well as its primary one of removing the guilt that has come between God and man, and making them one. Just as the touch of Christ's hand or of the hem of his garment sometimes healed the physically sick on earth, his touch in Confession may sometimes heal the sick mind miraculously. Extreme Unction, the sacrament for the dying, sometimes restores the dying to health; but the sacrament of Penance will *always* do very much more for the incurable neurotic than remove his mental suffering. It will, while forgiving whatever sin he has really committed, change the suffering of his mind into the suffering of Christ's mind, infusing into it the redeeming power of *his* suffering.

By restoring his own life to man in the confessional, Christ changes man's heart, which is constricted by self-love, to his own heart, which expands to include the whole world in his love. To the suffering mind of the neurotic he will give his own suffering—in his temptation, in his contact with Satan, in his failure to make himself understood, in his knowledge that his love was rejected, in his fear and feeling of guilt in Gethsemane, in the humiliation of his nakedness on Calvary, in his utter loneliness and his sense of having been forsaken by God on the cross.

The purpose of sacramental Confession is to remove sin, not to remove suffering, though sometimes it does that too. But *always* it does something far more, and for all suffering, not only psychological suffering: it gives it a meaning, a purpose, and a power. It changes it from being destructive to being creative. By giving Christ's life, the sacrament gives the redeeming, healing power of Christ's love to the suffering that the forgiven sinner must experience.

For *ego*-neurosis, the disease of *self*-love, the sacrament contains everything necessary for a cure. This is not surprising, because this great remedy for guilt is not something which man has discovered, but something given to him by divine Wisdom, by him who "knows what is in man's heart".

When self-love is a deliberate choice for which someone is fully responsible because he knows what he is choosing, and knows also what he is rejecting, it is quite simply a sin; but there are many people in whom self-love is a psychological illness of which they are not conscious and which has taken possession of them through no fault of their own.

Early circumstances, to give only one example, may have started the disease in people before the age of reason was reached, and it may have grown with them and in them, buried so deep that they were never aware of the real cause of their suffering.

A child who has been treated cruelly and so put on the defensive may grow up with an attitude of self-protection that absorbs him to the exclusion of all else; a child who has, on the other hand, been spoilt and who has not been taught to know God may have had it instilled into him that *he* is the centre of the universe, that his feelings are the one thing that matters; and nothing may have ever happened to challenge or break down this delusion. Worst of all, a child may have been brought up in the Catholic Faith, but with the yet more disastrous delusion, instilled by cowardly and doting parents, that God exists for him, not he for God—that the whole fabric and structure of religion is intended only to give him pleasure, just as the world with its flowers and birds and animals is a plaything for him. He may even have been impressed by the idea that it is a sweet and consoling and very fitting thing, that Christ should have suffered for him, but unthinkable that he should suffer for Christ! Can such a child be held responsible, if he grows up seeking nothing else in religion but his own gratification, and when, as it will sometimes do, religion changes from a nice feeling to a nasty feeling, he either abandons it or becomes neurotic about it?

There are many causes of ego-neurosis as a disease, and many people who would be astounded and incredulous if they were told that their "sensitive" conscience, their horror of imperfection, their tormenting anxiety in approaching the sacraments, all spring from self-love that is blinding them to the love of God. Neither could these people be safely told to make a direct attack on their self-love and uproot it—for no one, not even the sufferer, knows how much fear, how much buried pain and grief, and even how much twisted courage, is wrapped round that kernel of self, and what might be the result if all the mechanism of defence were suddenly struck off.

It is precisely here that the sacrament of Penance in its secondary aspect as a means of curing ego-neurosis could be effective. But the reason why so much ego-neurosis is *not* cured by frequent Confession, as it could be, is that few ego-neurotics understand how to approach the sacrament, how to use it to cure themselves. Instead of allowing it gradually to heal their psychological infirmities as well as absolve their actual sins, they go to the opposite extreme and make of this sacrament of mercy and life and joy an instrument of self-torture.

The whole process of going to Confession, which is a quick and simple process if it is rightly used, is ordered and controlled by the wise and gentle discipline of the Church. It is safeguarded by the restraint of the sweet yoke of Christ, laid upon the emotions that swamp and obsess self-centred people. Every ego-neurotic who does go to Confession could make certain of a cure for his own misery, if he would learn to understand and accept this inward discipline.

The conditions asked of the sinner to obtain forgiveness and reunion with God are *contrition*, which is sorrow for sins for the love of God, and which includes, as of its very nature it must do, the intention not to sin again; *confession*, which is accusing one-self of some definite sin or sins to a priest to whom God has given the power to forgive in his name; and *satisfaction*, which means saying some prayers which the priest prescribes as a penance.*

After the Confession it is wise but not necessary to say the penance at once (unless directed otherwise), and there should be a thanksgiving. So far as psychological peace is concerned, apart from other more important things, the thanksgiving has incalculable value, but it is usually scamped, forgotten or omitted, except by those rare sinners who are both really devout and perfectly sane. The normal, un-neurotic person, who is not religious by temperament though he is by conviction, is usually so relieved when he has delivered himself of his sins that he is apt to forget to say Thank You, and the ego-neurotic has usually fallen into new quagmires of anxiety before he gets round to the thanksgiving.

All this sounds simple, but it is not simple at all to the person —a woman, let us suppose—who is concentrated more on self than on God.

She will doubt the sincerity of her contrition because she does not think that she *feels* sorry, or sorry enough, or sorry for the right reason. She will doubt the sincerity of her purpose of amendment because she thinks it likely that in spite of her good intentions she may sin again. The examination of conscience, her greatest bugbear of all, will present insurmountable diffi-culties. She will either think that she has not done *anything* sinful, or that *everything* she has done is sinful, or that she has forgotten what she has done that is sinful. If she ever reaches a decision about what she has or has not done, she will proceed to the torment of trying to assess the gravity of the sin, to decide

---

* Added to this, if some injury to another person is confessed, the penitent must undertake to put it right, if it is within his power to do so.

whether it is mortal, venial, deliberate, sin at all, or imperfection. When she has at last made her confession she will fall into fresh anxiety about how she made it, whether she forgot, left out or misrepresented something, even whether the priest understood what she said. Next, she will bring to the saying of the act of contrition, and her penance, the same anxiety which she does at home to whether she has switched off the electric light or not. She will worry about whether she really remembers what penance she was told to say.

All these difficulties come from concentrating on self instead of on God, and on not really believing in the goodness of God. A little reflection could dispel them all.

Going to Confession is an act of love for God. Like all love it is an act of will. Feeling may or may not enter into it.

In the love between two human beings there is not always, all the time, emotional feeling; there is something that is much more—union. The two are united by their will. They are so made one by love that they seem to live in each other's life, they know each other in themselves. Nothing can separate those who are made one by love like this.

This applies even more to the love between God and man. On God's side there is, of course, perfection of love. His love holds man in existence, man only *is* because God wills him to be. Man's response to God's love is his will that nothing shall mar this union, that no shadow shall come between him and God. Sin does cast a shadow between him and God. Grave sin separates him from God, just as death separates a man from his own life, for God is life and sin is the soul's death.

When man is conscious of sin, he cannot, as we have seen, be happy in God's presence. If he loves himself more than he loves God, he will try to get further away, to break the union which has become painful to him. But if his love of God is stronger than his love for himself, he will be willing to suffer anything in order to return to the joy of his conscious union with God.

Contrition is proved to be genuine, to be sorrow for sin for the love of God, by the fact that the repentant sinner *returns* to God, comes into his presence of his own free will, and deliberately seeks that which Adam fled from, self-knowledge in the penetrating light of God, and the consciousness of being seen, literally seen through, by God.

The reason why the contrition, apparent but not always real, of those who testify and make public confessions at revivalist meetings is frequently demoralizing is that it depends entirely on being able to stimulate *feeling*. The feeling when it has been achieved is not a feeling, much less a knowing, of the unutterable goodness of God, but a certain excitement and morbid pleasure in exposing one's own sores (such as school children experience) and in discussing one's operation (which many women enjoy), coupled with the relief of a violent and sudden discharge of pent-up emotion felt by some women on being able to scream out loud after the temporary paralysis of the vocal chords caused by seeing a mouse at close quarters.

If it is impossible for someone to experience contrition for the love of God—which, if they have not yet become aware of the mystery and wonder of God within themselves, and do not know God, it may be—attrition suffices for Confession. This is sorrow for sin, or perhaps one could more truly call it deep regret for sin, for the fear of Hell and the desire of Heaven. This is a motive closer to self-love, but this time it is the kind of self-love that man is told to have, when he is told to save his own soul. It implies a desire to come to love God and to return to him, and at least a remote will to love him perfectly.

The examination of conscience presents a yet greater difficulty to the ego-centred. This is often because the woman we have been discussing sets out to examine her conscience without having the faintest idea of what it is she is going to examine. She is not really trying to examine her conscience at all, but her feelings. If she has no uneasy *feeling* about anything, she is worried because she cannot discover anything to accuse herself of. If, on the other hand, she has a tormenting feeling of guilt but her memory does not recall any definite sin that she thinks bad enough to account for it, she probes and probes at the sore spot in order to find something, which probably is not there.

Once again the old stumbling-block of feeling crops up! Nearly everyone thinks that conscience is a feeling which tells us infallibly when we have done or are doing right or wrong. We have seen, in the peculiarities of the guilt feeling, that feeling is *never* a reliable guide. People can easily be induced to feel that it is wrong to be happy, right to destroy life. There are individuals incapable of feeling that *anything* that *they* do is wrong, others who feel that *everything* that *they* do is.

If feeling were conscience certain people would have no conscience at all.

But every sane person has a conscience, though many, from having ceased altogether to use their minds, have lost the use of it, for conscience is the judgment of the intellect concerning wrong and right. It is the use of reason. Even our reason would fail to guide us were there not a revealed law, had God not cleared up the confusion in our consciousness brought about by sin. We have, however, the commandments of God and the voice of Christ in the Church giving us the law of love in which there is life. We *know* with our minds that when we break that law we are sinning.

The preliminary to any examination of conscience is to pray for the light of the Holy Spirit. In our own darkness we none of us know ourselves; we can know ourselves only in God's light.

I remember that as a young child, overwhelmed and sick with feelings of guilt, I used to pray, not that I should remember all my sins, but that God in his mercy would allow me to forget some of them!

The prayer for the light of God is the beginning of real self-knowledge. It is not through trying to assess ourselves by our own morbidity that we know ourselves, but by putting ourselves into the blazing ray of that divine light. Examination of conscience should not be turning our minds inwards to our feelings, but flinging them out to God—it should be, as it were, a going out from ourselves to God, to look back at ourselves only from his side, through his penetrating light; and, having looked back once, and seen, as in his light we cannot fail to see, the sin disfiguring our souls, we must turn back to God again and concentrate on him. Thus our very sorrow for sin will become joy in the contemplation of God.

The other worries and torments of anxious and ego-neurotic people would disappear if, instead of concentrating on them, they concentrated on God—because they all derive from not knowing God, from having a total misconception of him.

The scrupulous ego-neurotic supposes God to be a monster of cruelty—one who, seeing his child coming to him in sorrow, and ready to make an effort that is very hard to her nature in order to be taken back to his heart, waits eagerly for an opportunity to trip her up and cast her into the outer darkness—and he watches, not for anything which she could do deliberately, but for some trifling lapse of memory or some failure in exactitude through fatigue or nervousness!

There are many who complain of the formality surrounding Confession, of the almost extreme measures used by the Church to make it easy for the weakest. For example, that *any* words expressing sorrow suffice for the act of contrition, that venial sins need not be confessed at all, that forgotten sins are included in the forgiveness anyway, that it practically never happens that a confession made in good will need be, or should be, repeated.

How strange it is, many decide, to surround a sacrament with so many little rules. But it is sufficient to spend one hour with an anxious and over-scrupulous person, to realize that these are the rulings of divine mercy. They are the balm poured into the wounds, the calm and rest insisted upon by the divine Physician.

If the sinner would look away from self to God, repentance could only lift her up into joy, for she would find herself contemplating, and in the end absorbed to the exclusion of self, in contemplating, the mystery of divine love and goodness.

The Father who longs more for the return of the lost child than does the child himself, who makes the way back as easy as he can and comes halfway to meet the child, who asks not for a microscopic, dreary history of his misdeeds, or for a trembling, broken expression of sorrow—but only for an expression of the child's love and trust in *his* love.

Like the father of the Prodigal, God wants to make the sacrament of Penance a feast. He wants to pour out his gifts on the sinner, to clothe him in his Son's radiant humanity, to put a ring on his finger sealing him his own, for evermore.

It is in this light too that the purpose of amendment should be made: that is, the determination to sin no more.

There is a growing tendency among wishful thinkers to doubt man's free-will. It is argued that, even if a man is not a monkey or a "libido", he has many unfathomable elements in his nature which are outside the control of his will. He has an "unconscious" as well as a conscious mind, he is subject to vast invisible influences, he is a slave to heredity and environment and so on. Catholics do not consciously doubt that they possess free-will, nevertheless there are some of them who, without putting this into words, do secretly doubt their own individual free-will. They have made and broken too many resolutions—they have been to Confession literally hundreds of times and they have not changed at all; they really have very little hope that they ever will.

For ego-neurotics the case is even worse; they attack themselves—verbally—more violently. They make sweeping resolutions, and they feel that God ought to change them from weak, vulnerable creatures to the very reverse in the twinkle of an eye.

We know too that people are able positively to violate themselves by onslaughts on their own will: attempts by sheer will power to overcome fear or acute shyness, or the shrinking from life that is characteristic of many neurotics, frequently result in a breakdown, while similar attempts to overcome sins of weakness, such as drunkenness or solitary vice, not infrequently result in increasing the frequency of the sin by making it a nervous obsession. Psychologically this is easy to understand: repetition of "I will" or "I will not" is again a concentration on self, and this time one that is a continual reminder of something that it is desirable to forget; "I will not do this" is a suggestion to do it—such acts of will become a strain, and tiring too; and for nervous people fatigue is an added danger.

By way of a suggestion for those who do not suffer so much as this from doubt of their own free-will, and yet in the light of experience find something a little ironical in the sweeping promise, found in some Acts of Contrition, never to sin again: it is advisable not to focus upon that but to stick simply to the purpose of amendment, pray that one may not sin again, and concentrate upon some way of avoiding some one sin. It may be a negative way—to give up a place where the temptation always lurks, or the company that provokes it; or it may be a resolution of humility that will help—for example, the irritable could decide to take more sleep, the censorious to make fewer voluntary acts of self-denial.

But for these people and all others the secret of using the will as God wills us to is, first, to *surrender* our will wholly to his, which means to accept the pattern of our nature as he made it, to accept ourselves as being fallen men, and with that to accept the certainty that we shall always be obliged to wrestle with ourselves. To accept God's word, that is his law—and above all, to accept our destiny to be Christ-bearers.

In this we have the example of the Mother of Christ, and we are in fact called upon to share her experience in a mysterious way. To form Christ in ourselves, or more exactly to give ourselves up to Christ that he may form himself in us.

Our Lady's *Fiat*—"Let it be unto me according to thy word" —meant that she gave herself, soul and body, to be made into Christ. She gave him her eyes to be his eyes, her mind to be his mind, her heart to be his heart; and before she gave birth to him, before his human body was fully formed from hers, she knew the impulses of his love, who lived secretly within her. She was driven out by his charity to her cousin Elizabeth, his presence in her lifted her voice in an expression of joy in God that rings down the ages; through his presence in her she became conscious of the unborn generations that would know him, and she exulted in his mercy to them. "My spirit has found joy in God who is my saviour."

She accepted too the suffering that he would inevitably bring into her life, and that too began before he was born, in Joseph's misunderstanding, and in the added hardship of obeying the law and journeying to Bethlehem when he, her life's sweetness, was also her heavy burden.

If we echo this *Fiat*, our whole attitude to God changes from being one of knowing *about* him, to one of *knowing* him. We begin to realize, not from hearsay, but from our own experience, what God's love and goodness and beauty really are. We begin to understand what is really meant by that union in which the heart of the Beloved beats in our own.

In this realization we get the real incentive to resist sin, which alone can separate us from God, the incentive that makes our free-will always, at all times, the will to love God. Once this surrender is made and we become more and more continually aware of the inexpressible beauty of God, the pain of resisting evil or of returning to God's presence if we have sinned will pale beside the incomparably more terrible pain of being separated from him. Our will grows strong in the measure in which we realize the reality of God, and in the surrender echoing in our lives from the *Fiat* of our Lady, all those mysterious and unexplored and unconscious elements in human nature are drawn in, and carried along on *God's* will.

It may be, however, that the change which takes place in us as the result of surrendering our will to God in many Confessions will not be visible. Christ grew secretly, imperceptibly, in Mary, and he grows secretly in us. The sign that he is growing in us is not that life becomes effortless, but that faith, which we live by, grows brighter, and hope and charity increase in us.

Repentance and the sacrament of Penance are then the remedy for guilt. In this remedy, short and simple and often almost formal as going to Confession is, is contained the whole psychological process by which fallen man can be restored to God and live in the fulness of his nature.

In contrition he admits himself a sinner. In the examination of conscience he knows himself in God's light. In his purpose of amendment he surrenders himself to God and discovers the power of his own will—but in absolution more than all that is achieved. In that stuffy, dark little box we call the confessional, every one of the ceaseless drift of human beings of every kind and description who kneel uncomfortably, listening to the whispered words of absolution, is made one with God.

PART TWO

GUILT, SUFFERING AND
CHRIST

VII

CHRIST AND GUILT

Each mortal thing does one thing and the same;
Deals out that being indoors each one dwells;
Selves—goes itself; myself it speaks and spells,
Crying Whát I do *is me: for that I came.*

I say môre: the just man justices;
Kéeps gráce; thát keeps all his goings graces;
Acts in God's eye what in God's eye he is—
Christ—for Christ plays in ten thousand places,
Lovely in limbs, and lovely in eyes not his
To the Father through the features of men's faces.

GERARD MANLEY HOPKINS

THE KEY to human nature is Christ. He is the pattern in which man was originally made, and by becoming one with him, man can be restored to that pattern and become whole.

From all eternity he was with God and was God, having one Nature with the Father, but a distinct Person, all the same, the Person of God the Son. He is known too as the Word: "At the beginning of time the Word already was; and God had the Word abiding with him, and the Word was God. He abode, at the beginning of time, with God" (John 1.1,2).

When the Son, the Word, became man, he uttered his Father's love to the world, but from all eternity in the silence of the eternal peace of God, every possible expression of his own Goodness that God would create was known to him in the unspoken Word.

In his Son, the Father knew every man whom he would create. In Christ each one of us was with God eternally, each one of us was loved with the Father's love for his only begotten Son.

"It was through him" that all things came into being, and "without him came nothing that has come to be". All creation—men, and even animals and material things—was to find fulfilment in him. But human beings above all. The human nature of

Christ was the absolute fulness and perfection of human nature, human nature as God wanted it to be, for it was made for a person who was God. Therefore it was the design, the idea, the origin of every man whom God would create. Looking at Christ's human nature, we know what God wants ours to be.

Christ was to be the Light of the World, and it was God's decree that his light should be reflected in every man whom he would create—all should radiate Christ and shine before God with his light, as the light of the sun shines back to Heaven from the countless drops of dew that receive its brilliance. It was God's plan that every man would be alive and live fully with Christ's life, that every man would be one with Christ and live in the life of the Trinity, glorifying God in unimaginable joy.

God created the world to be the womb and the cradle of Christ. It was a foreshadowing and symbol of Christ's human birth, and of his birth in us. First there was darkness and the waters of birth: "And the earth was without form and void; and darkness was upon the face of the deep. And the Spirit of God moved upon the face of the waters. And God said, Let there be light and there was light" (Gen. 1.2-3).

When the earth was ready, the Spirit of God breathed over the world again, and made man out of the dust, in his own image *and in the pattern of Christ*. There before God, made from the dust of the earth, was the man for whom the world was created, who was destined for perfect joy: the man to whom Christ's life was given.

We have already spoken of Adam's sin and its effect on man, his loss of the Christ-life, the supernatural life, his separation from God; now it is its effect upon Christ as man that we are considering.

Christ is man's destiny. There are theologians who teach that he would have been incarnate, even if man had not sinned, in order that man should glorify God. But because man sinned, when Christ did come into the world he came as the world's Redeemer, taking the suffering of the world's guilt on himself, making all the pain of mind and body, which sin had brought into the world, his own.

He came to redeem, and he came to show men how to become whole again, he came to show them how to cope with guilt, he came to give them back his life, the life that was to illumine theirs and to be the fulfilment of their humanity.

Man had made the world a place of darkness. Therefore in the perfection of his humanity, the perfection of love, Christ plunged his light into the darkness of the spirit of men. "And the light shines in darkness, a darkness which was not able to master it" (John 1.5).

At that moment in time predestined from eternity, the Spirit of God again descended upon the darkness and moved upon the waters, and Christ was conceived in the womb of a Virgin. For nine months the Son of God was hidden in the Virgin's womb, his human body forming from hers. He was voiceless, sightless, powerless, his presence in the world secret. He was born in a stable, among animals, in dirt and discomfort, and he experienced the things that all infants do, cold and heat, hunger and thirst.

He became immediately the object of the jealousy and, therefore, the hatred, of Herod; he was hunted into exile and hiding. He spent his babyhood as a refugee in a foreign country, his boyhood in his foster-father's workshop, learning a carpenter's trade. He was obliged, like other boys, to labour to acquire his skill. We may safely assume that some of his customers found fault with what he made and haggled over the price of the work of the Son of God.

He grew to manhood and his passage through adolescence was unhindered, as every adolescence should be. At twelve years old, the age at which a Jewish boy assumes the spiritual responsibilities of manhood, when he remained, unknown to his parents, in Jerusalem among the temple priests, he showed his independence and his determination to do the work God had sent him to do; he showed too that though he was a son who loved his mother deeply, indeed with love unequalled by any other son, he could not be tied to her by the childish dependence or twisted emotions that cripple so many boys psychologically: "... his mother said to him, My Son, why hast thou treated us so? Think, what anguish of mind thy father and I have endured, searching for thee. But he asked them, What reason had you to search for me? Could you not tell that I must needs be in the place which belongs to my Father?" (Luke 2.48-9).

Grown to manhood, he went out to meet and wrestle with evil, to come face to face with Satan. He had taken our guilt on himself, and acted as a *guilty* man should in the fight with evil, although he was innocent. He began to fight evil by wrestling with his own human nature, blameless though he was. He went into the wilderness and fasted. He lived with the animals for forty days, fasting. In the wilderness he was tempted by the Devil. For the second time in the record of Christ's life, angels and animals are brought together by Christ's presence. The first time was at his birth; now ... "the Spirit sent him out into the desert: and in the desert he spent forty days and forty nights, tempted by the devil; there he lodged with the beasts, and there the angels ministered to him" (Mark 1.12,13).

There followed the short time of his public life, three years of preaching, healing, tramping the roads, working miracles, training his disciples, and making both friends and enemies by the uncompromising truth he taught. After that his Passion, beginning with the Last Supper and the institution of the Blessed Sacrament, the giving of himself to men in Communion, and passing swiftly to the Agony in the Garden, the betrayal by Judas, the crowning with thorns, the unjust trials, the carrying of the cross, the nakedness and the death on the cross.

And after three days in the tomb, he rose again, spent forty days on earth, and then ascended into Heaven.

Those facts are, briefly, the story of Christ in his human nature on earth.

There is a startling paradox in this, that he who came, as he said, to give life to men, to fill up the measure of their joy, to show them the way back to the wonder and peace of living in God, he who is known by names that are radiant with joy, light, life, love, is known also as "the Man of Sorrows". At first sight one would be tempted to say that he had fallen in love with our suffering. He made himself subject to our limitations—to discomfort, poverty, hunger, thirst and pain. He chose to experience fear, temptation, failure. He suffered loneliness, betrayal, injustice, the spurning of his love, mockery, brutality, separation, utter desolation of spirit, the sense of despair, and death.

But it was not with our suffering that Christ fell in love; it was with us. He identified himself with our suffering because he identified himself with us, and he came not only to lead his own historical life on earth, but to live the life of every man who would receive him into his soul, and to be the way back to joy for every individual. He took our humanity in order to give us his, and since guilty man must, as a very condition of his own ultimate joy, and even for his fullest measure of earthly joy, "make" his soul through expiation, through personal atonement, Christ chose to atone for mankind as each man must do for himself: through suffering. "He who was without sin was made sin for us."

Christ is "the Way". He taught the way to wholeness, showed it in his historical life, and he *is* the Way in the life of every individual who does not refuse his destiny of Christhood.

There is no nerve or fibre of man that he does not know.

The secrets which the psychologists wrestle for with angels and devils, the secrets they toil and labour to wrest from the heart of man, the means to the healing of the suffering mind and to human fulfilment, were told, two thousand years ago, by Christ, to the motley crowd of poor, ignorant and suffering people who flocked to hear him speak.

The modern psychologist thinks that it is he who has discovered that the way back to mental peace is the way back through childhood, that man must become a little child again and re-live his earliest experiences with his father and mother to discover the cause of his present suffering, and that some must even go through something like a psychological rebirth in order to overcome the fear of life, and incidentally the fear of death.

But it was Christ who first taught these things. He who said that the way back to Heaven is the way back through childhood, that man must become a child again to know God through a child's response to an infinitely loving Father. The one cure for anxiety, for humiliation, for fear, is the trust of an unspoilt child in the Fatherhood of God. To the uncontaminated child's heart, the secrets of divine love are given.

"At this time, Jesus was filled with gladness by the Holy Spirit, and said, O Father, who art Lord of heaven and earth, I give thee praise that thou hast hidden all this from the wise and the prudent, and revealed it to little children" (Luke 10.21).

"I tell you truthfully, the man who does not accept the kingdom of God like a little child, will never enter into it" (Luke 18.17).

"You should not be asking, then, what you are to eat or drink, and living in suspense of mind; it is for the heathen world to busy itself over such things; your Father knows well that you need them. No, make it your first care to find the kingdom of God, and all these things shall be yours without the asking" (Luke 12.29-31).

"Why then, if you, evil as you are, know well enough how to give your children what is good for them, is not your Father much more ready to give, from heaven, his Holy Spirit to those who ask him?" (Luke 11.13).

It was Christ who first puzzled men by telling them that they must actually be born again: "Believe me when I tell thee this; a man cannot see the kingdom of God without being born anew" (John 3.3).

The human race as well as each individual had to be born again, to be twice born, in order to be restored to its heavenly Father. In Christ this happened; the birth of Christ was the rebirth of Adam. To give life to man, God himself was born as an infant, and in order that man should know the Kingdom of Heaven in his heart, God became a little child!

Every man is born again when he is baptised. Once again the Spirit of God breathes upon the waters of birth as it did at the creation of the world and at the conception of Christ in the womb of his Mother. Now in the souls of the newly baptised, Christ is conceived, that from their life he may be born into the world again.

Everything discovered by science or by psychology can be tested by the words of Christ. It is quite true that a man's life can be crippled by some flaw in his earliest relations with his father and mother; this is because the father and mother stand in the place of God to the little child, he forms his first emotional —and usually unconscious—conception of God from them. Their love for him must be God's love for him. If it is not, if it is selfish love, or if they disillusion him or betray him, his conception of God will be awry. His journey back through all the confusion and conflict of adult life and experience as well as through the broken, cynical, unchilded childhood will be a long and a difficult one; but he *must* go back to the true childhood that finds the perfect Father and is restored by him to a child's trust. This is the absolute condition for him to possess the Kingdom of Heaven.

We have seen that in general guilty man has, through trying to escape from guilt, formed a false conception of God. Everything Christ said or did on earth was designed to show men what God is really like, and especially to show them his Fatherhood and their childhood.

The touchstone of the effect of guilt upon man is his awareness or unawareness of God—or again whether, even when he realizes that God is present to him, this makes him more conscious of God or of himself.

After he had sinned, the presence of God did not make Adam more aware of God's love and goodness, but of himself and his own humiliation. Men have not changed since Adam. The more a man looks into himself and probes the sores of his own sin, the more self-conscious he becomes; the more he feels the pain of his own wounded vanity and remorse. And the more aware he becomes of himself, the less aware he becomes of God; the more he loves himself, the less he loves God.

The beginning of human happiness, and even of human sanity, is to begin to know God.

The mainspring of Christ's life was his love for God, his heavenly Father. His first recorded words were about him— "Could you not tell that I must needs be in the place which belongs to my Father?" (Luke 2). So too were his last words, spoken literally with his last breath—"Father, into thy hands I commend my spirit; and [he] yielded up his spirit as he said it" (Luke 23.46).

It is a commonplace now with psychologists that it is a psychological necessity for a child to know his father as great and good, and if his father is not what he longs for him to be, he will go in search of a "father substitute". If he has no father he will invent one in his own mind and invest him with every adorable quality, as well as a profound tenderness for himself. Some go so far as to see this deep-rooted need of the great and good father as a proof that God is not real—they say that man has invented God to satisfy his own necessity. It would be equally convincing to tell a hungry man that bread is only an idea which he has invented to satisfy his hunger.

Christ, who knew everything that is necessary to man, and that only what is real is necessary to him, knew that the most profound secret of psychological healing for guilty men is to know the Eternal Father: "Eternal life is knowing thee, who art the only true God; and Jesus Christ, whom thou hast sent" (John 17.3). The Gospel is woven together from beginning to end by Christ's continual awareness of the Father and his continual awareness of his own Sonship.

He used everything around him to try to make men realize the Father's love for them. Everything should remind them of his tenderness, even the sparrows and the daisies and the grass. In that wonderful discourse before his death, in the hush of the Cenacle, he makes it clear that being at one with God is the utmost happiness man can know, and that it is his own happiness and glory.

Just as he spoke continually of his Father to make him known and loved, he continually reiterated the fact that his human will was wholly surrendered to him. His work in life was to do his Father's will: "I came not to do my own will but the will of him who sent me". Every act of his was done through him by his Father's Will: "... and the Father, who dwells continually in me, achieves in me his own acts of power" (John 14.10).

Every word that he spoke was a word that it was his Father's will to utter through him: "... it was my Father who sent me that commanded me what words I was to say, what message I was to utter. And I know well that what he commands is eternal life; everything then, which I utter, I utter as my Father has bidden me" (John 13.49,50).

It was this surrender to the divine will that allowed the Holy Spirit to sweep him on to his Passion and the consummation of his love.

It is in the garden of Gethsemane that the surrender of Christ's own human will comes to its climax; here too, that the drama of the culmination of his fight with the shadow, a fight that had been going on all through his life, comes to the final crisis; and here that in Christ the struggle every man is faced with is fought out, ending in his accepting the suffering of the guilt of mankind.

In Gethsemane Christ faced the crisis which so many millions must face when they are challenged by love—will they be stripped of all pretence, and be naked, themselves, before love? Will they consent to the revelation of the secret of self, and the mystical death of love? Will they take up the cross of daily hardship and poverty and sacrifice of self, and carry the burdens of life, for love of others? This is the challenge which comes in turn to everyone—"Can you drink the chalice that I must drink?" It came to Christ in Gethsemane, and his consent led on to the consummation of his love on the cross.

Above all, it is in Gethsemane that we see the climax of Christ's acceptance of guilt, which began with the first pulsation of his human heart, and dimly, from centuries and centuries away, realize what mental suffering it involved him in. "My soul, he said, is ready to die with sorrow" (Matt. 26.38). For he was seeing what he was to take upon himself—the guilt of the whole world. He saw all the sin of the world for all time in all its naked evil, and he saw all the results of sin on the soul and body of man, and all the results of it in suffering.

He saw all the disease and corruption, and festering and swarming and seething of sin. For the second time in his human life he saw "all the cities of the world and the glory of them"— the blasphemy of luxury side by side with slums, the rat-infested brothels hidden away in mean streets in London, flaunted almost on the steps of the Shrine of the Blessed Sacrament in Montmartre. He saw the black industrial cities with their back-to-back houses, and the stunted and twisted little children forced into the factories; he saw all the battlefields of the world with all their mutilation and suffocation and agonized dying, he saw all the secret dungeons and prisons where men rot away, and all the concentration camps with their starvation and corruption and their piles of corpses and their gas-chambers. He saw all the persecutions that would destroy the souls and bodies of men: the persecution of Christians by heathens, of Catholics by Protestants, of Protestants by Catholics, and, most bitter of all to the breaking heart of Christ, the persecutions of Jews by Christians, carried out in his own name.

All this and more and more and more. And incomparably more terrible than any of it, the sheer elemental evil that was the cause of it all.

But worst of all he felt himself to be bearing the guilt of it all, felt, as he lay there on the ground exposed to the eye of God, that all that guilt was on him.

Adam was the first sinful man, and he tried to repudiate guilt; Christ was the first sinless man, and he accepted the guilt of all sin. Adam was the first man to hide from God; Christ was the first man to expose his soul, covered in the wounds and ugliness inflicted by guilt, to the fierce blaze of God's light.

His human will shrank from this, and from the death that measured evil hung up naked in the sight of God, covered from the crown of his head to the soles of his feet with the blood and the filth and the spitting of sin.

"When he had gone a little further, he fell upon his face in prayer, and said, My Father, if it is possible, let this chalice pass me by; only as thy will is, not as mine is" (Matt. 26.39).

As he prayed, in agony of mind, Christ experienced in himself the struggle of our whole race—with the accumulation of guilt from which nearly every individual, except the saint, tries to escape, and for which nearly everyone repudiates all personal responsibility. There was no escape for Christ. For the last time his human will surrendered to the will of God, and the man who had a few moments before been lying on his face on the ground, oppressed by all the fear and dread and depression of all mankind, was comforted by an angel, and rose up, self-possessed, majestic, to go out to the consummation of love.

Very aptly, that night, Christ was crowned with thorns.

Soon he was stripped of his garments. Adam had covered himself and hidden. Christ was exposed to the crowd, and lifted up naked before those who ridiculed him and those he loved. And there, on the cross, in that tremendous surrender of self, love was consummated.

It is a tenet of modern psychology that for his own happiness man must accept himself whole, not as he would like to be but as he is. He must reconcile the conflicting elements, the opposites in himself. He must accept joy and sorrow, conflict and peace, darkness and light. He must realize that the shadow, the dark side of his nature, cannot be projected outside himself, or be buried and ignored inside himself, but must be acknowledged and accepted, though this acceptance involves lifelong conflict. He must realize too that the good in him and his loveliest spiritual aspirations must be fulfilled; he needs to adore, to pray, to open his mind and heart to the world of the Spirit, to hear the "still small voice of God" in the depths of his own being. He is soul and body; he must accept this fact too, and know himself as man, a soul and body which are inseparable in this life and affect each other by every single thing done by either.

In Christ every opposite is reconciled. This principle of paradox and reconciliation runs all through his teaching, in all that he does, in what he *is*. The only thing that Christ taught must be cast out of the whole man is sin: "If thy right eye is the occasion of thy falling into sin, pluck it out and cast it away from thee; better to lose one of thy limbs than to have thy whole body cast into hell" (Matt. 5.29). For the rest, the tares and the wheat must grow together until the final harvesting. The sorrow for sin, the travail and sadness it has brought to the soul, the never-ceasing wrestle with temptation, all these must be reconciled with the soul's peace, even with its joy, while this world lasts.

> Christ is God and man.
> He is Lord and servant.
> The Man of Sorrows is the source of joy.
> The Life of the World dies to give life.
> The Light of the World shines in darkness.

The secret of this reconciliation of opposites in Christ is love. In him is God's love for man and man's love for God: "God so loved the world, that he gave up his only-begotten Son, so that those who believe in him may not perish, but have eternal life" (John 3.16).

> Love made it joy to Christ to suffer man's sorrows.
> Love made it peace to Christ to wage man's war.
> Love made it fulfilment for Christ's humanity to die to give man life.
> Love made it glory to Christ to illuminate man's soul.
> Christ's whole teaching is love.

Men are beginning to discover now that they have largely lost the power to love, and in this is their failure as human beings. In Christ is the whole secret of love. Only by living Christ's life can men find the way to love, and so to the fulfilling of their human nature again.

Man's life in Christ is the life of the risen Christ, but it must be lived by men still taking up their cross daily. Christ has told us what kind of life it is to be, in his last discourse on the night before he died. He has shown us *how* it is to be lived, in his own risen life on earth during the forty days between his resurrection and his ascension. It is to be a life of love; but that love which will lead to the consummation of man's human nature, as it led to the consummation of *his* human nature, is to be *like his* love.

"Your love for one another is to be like the love I have borne you" (John 13.34).

"This is my commandment, that you should love one another, as I have loved you. This is the greatest love a man can show, that he should lay down his life for his friends" (John 15.12, 13).

To man as he is now, this seems at first sight to be an impossible ideal.

A great deal of nonsense is written and spoken about love. It is said to glorify man in itself, to ennoble him, to justify anything whatever that he does. It is made the excuse for endless self-gratification, sensuality, possessiveness, and cruelty. In the name of love crimes and murders are committed, as well as many beautiful and heroic acts.

Christ's love is creative, it is the love which transmits life. It is love which puts no limit at all on self-giving, which excludes no one, includes everyone; it reaches to the ends of the earth, it is communion with everyone. It is the love which even in a world of suffering can fill up the life of each one with its full measure of joy.

Our Christ-life is the life of the risen Christ. He who lives in us (to use St Paul's phrase, which repeats our Lord's words at the Last Supper) has suffered all that any human being can suffer now, and has overcome it all. He has overcome temptation and manifold sorrows, hardship, complete poverty, anguish of mind and body, and even death.

If it were possible for anyone to write the story of Christ's

PETER KÜRTEN

mind, he would write the story of every man, and he would discover the incommunicable secrets of every man's soul. And from coming to know the inward lives of men, we learn more and more of Christ. For every experience which men suffer or rejoice in, except that of sinning, is an experience already lived through in Christ's earthly life and one which he is living again in all those in whom he lives.

This is the secret of man's capacity to fulfil his human nature through love, to atone for guilt by his suffering, to experience joy in a world that is overburdened by sorrow. He has been given back the life of Christ—Christ's mind to adore with, Christ's love to love with, Christ's sacrifice to atone with.

Christ lives on as an infant in infants, as a boy in adolescents, a man in men, a worker in workers, a poet in poets, a friend in friends. He has experienced the particular sufferings of every age including our own, and he is experiencing them now in his members.

Many people who are physically and mentally helpless, dependent, hidden away in prisons, unheard, inarticulate, voiceless, live the advent life of Christ. They seem to be helpless to help the world, but in their lives is the secret pulsation of Christ's human life, which healed the world.

Among those who wrestle with the fear of life, and the shrinking from the adult world that offers its wealth and success on Satan's terms, some go with Christ into the wilderness to see the cities of the world and their glory and to choose the humility and uncompromising way of Christ in the world.

The neurotics and psychotics who suffer continually from fear and from a tormenting sense of guilt, as well as those who accept their own perfectly real shame and the grief for their own sins, go with Christ into Gethsemane, and those who surrender themselves in these bitter trials to God's Will, as Christ did, are crowned with him with his crown of thorns. In many men Christ is crucified: some crucify him on themselves by their sins; and some, those hundreds and thousands who give their lives in battle for the love of their fellow men, die his life-giving death with him, with him they rise again. Sinners whose sins are seen by everyone, those who are found out and put to shame, are stripped naked with him—those who shrink from being known

G

but accept his will are exposed in his nakedness, and in his nakedness the lover's surrender of the secret of self is consummated.

When Christ had risen from the dead, he no longer had the limitations of human nature which he had accepted in taking a real human nature to himself. There was nothing now to stop him from dazzling the world with his glory. At the first glance, one would expect him to do so. His apostles were still dazed and shaken by the shock and horror of Calvary, they were in fear of their own lives, and still brokenhearted by the seeming loss of Christ and of the promised kingdom.

He could have made his voice heard and his beauty visible simultaneously all over the world, bringing his enemies to their knees, restoring those who, in spite of their weakness, loved him, to immediate joy and certainty. He could have made himself loved by the whole world, and have swept away the threats that overshadowed his little flock, as they would overshadow it all through time.

He did none of this. Indeed he seemed to be as intent on proving himself to be really man after his resurrection as he had been on proving himself to be God before it. The news that he had risen from the tomb was entrusted to people who still had their tears for his death upon their faces. They were to tell it, it was to be given by one to the other, and the first messenger, known to be an emotional woman who would hardly be credited, was sent to convince the first Pope that Christ had risen.

Without being under any necessity to do so in his glorified body, Christ did ordinary things. He walked and talked and ate with men, built a little fire and cooked for them, comforted them and renewed their faith, but not by compelling them to be shocked into faith—even by a shock of joy—but by approaching each one individually through the individual's own mentality and temperament. He used the same means as before—words, kindness, going on a journey, setting his pace to the pace of the others, accepting their invitations, preparing food for them with his own hands, and that most wonderful and yet simplest way of all, the breaking of bread, the giving of himself sacramentally.

He was showing men how they were to go on living his risen life all through time.

They were to give him to one another, and as simply as he gave himself, through words and kindness: through their work and friendship, through learning one another's mind and heart and approaching each one separately, through accepting what each one had to give, and giving too: by comforting one another and leavening the sorrow of the world by the interchange of their Christ-love. Above all, by sacramental Communion with him, in which they are made one.

Christ knew man's need to learn how to love as he loves, and so to fulfil his human nature; he knew man's need to atone for sin, and so be able to rejoice in the source of joy, the uncreated light of God.

He had already told his apostles at the Last Supper what the world in which men would lead his risen life would be like. A world such as we know now—a world of unbelief, of persecutions, of hatred and contempt for the purity and truth of Christ and for those who live his life; yet, for those in whom Christ lives, a world in which they will be restored to the wonder and joy of the Kingdom of Heaven in their own hearts. And all their living with one another would be an interchange of his life.

"If the world hates you, be sure that it hated me before it learned to hate you. ... They will persecute you just as they have persecuted me; they will pay the same attention to your words as to mine" (John 15.18, 20).

"I have said this to you, so that in me you may find peace. In the world, you will only find tribulation; but take courage, I have overcome the world" (John 16.33).

"You have only to live on in me, and I will live on in you ... if a man lives on in me, and I in him, then he will yield abundant fruit; separated from me, you have no power to do anything" (John 15.3, 5).

"I have bestowed my love upon you, just as my Father has bestowed his love upon me; live on, then, in my love" (John 15.9).

"All this I have told you, so that my joy may be yours, and the measure of your joy may be filled up" (John 15.11).

And so, the heavenly paradox is to go on in man. But there are yet more mysteries of divine goodness to be accepted, concerning *how* it can be, for every man could well echo the words of the Mother of Christ, when her destiny and that of the whole world was told to her by an angel—"How can that be?" and the answer to every poor broken sinful creature is the same as it was to the sinless Mother of God: "The Holy Spirit will come upon thee."

Christ lives in man through the descent of the Holy Spirit into his soul, the Spirit of wisdom and love and light, who gives men understanding and patience, fortitude and peace, who brings the seed of Christ to them, and to its full flowering in them. And this thought of the coming of the Spirit sweeps us back on the great wings of the Dove of Peace to the unimaginable wonder of the love of the Blessed Trinity in eternity, and God's decree of perfect joy for man. For the Holy Spirit *is* the love between Father and Son, the burning light in which from all eternity each man has been with God in his only Son.

An unborn child forming in his mother's womb is conditioned by her love for him. Before he draws his first breath her love for him is forming his character, is disposing him to be aware of love as his true environment and the glad source of his life, to be drawn towards it almost irresistibly, to respond to it as the condition of his being, to accept it as he accepts the air that he breathes.

We human creatures, each one known to God from all eternity, are formed by God's pre-creational love, as children are formed by the pre-natal love of their mother.

Because this is so, and because Christ has given back his life to us, we are drawn towards our true happiness in spite of all the evil that is in us. Goodness draws the human soul as a tide is drawn by light.

VIII

THE REAL REPRESSION

We have all of us to continue the Incarnation.

ABBÉ GODIN

THE GREAT REPRESSION of our age is the repression of Christ in man.

If Christ in man were simply an idea, or something contrary to human nature which man could acquire and somehow add to himself by his own efforts, this could not be true; we can only repress that which is so much a part of us that we cannot cast it out or get rid of it, but can only repress or inhibit it.

If we inhibit something, we succeed in burying it so deep, pushing it so far out of sight, that we are completely unconscious of it, and it is not able to function in us at all. If we repress it, we are consciously holding it back and trying to frustrate it, even if we do not recognize it for what it is. Those who are repressed are always conscious of a strain; they live in a state of nervous tension and frustration without being aware of the fact that they are causing the trouble themselves.

Very often people are said to be repressing their sexual instincts; sometimes they are said to be repressing their aggressive instincts; but most often they are said to be repressing *themselves*; we speak of a *person* being repressed, meaning presumably his whole personality.

The fact of the matter is that if anyone represses himself, he does so, and can do so, only because he is repressing Christ in himself.

It is only the full flowering of Christ in a man that can give him the willingness to suffer strong enough to lead him out, as Christ was led out by the Spirit, to face the shadow: to be tempted and to wrestle with temptation, to be afraid and to overcome fear, to see the world and all the "glory" of it challenging him, and to overcome the world. It is only his surrender to his destiny of Christhood that can enable any individual to dare those experiences in life which lead to the fulfilling of his human nature, and only this that uninhibits his capacity for love, so that through the power of love his life may bear fruit and be a communion with all other men.

Man was created by God after the pattern of his Son and in the sense explained later.* The image of Christ is woven into every man's being. Man cannot know this, save by God's revealing it to him: man has no innate knowledge that God exists, still less that he has a Son and that this Son became man. But the fact that man is made in the pattern of the Son and that Christ's image is woven into his very being has certain consequences: in the merely natural effort to be more fully himself, to be all that he should be, he collides, so to speak, with Christ, not knowing what he is in contact with, but stirred all the same, by shadowings of that unrealized Presence. Feeling his own imperfections, he is *in fact* feeling the defects in his resemblance to Christ: trying to imagine himself restored, it is Christ that his imagination is feeling for, though he does not *know* it.

Every man is born with Christ in this sense present in the unconscious depths of his being, and sometimes entering his consciousness as a dream enters the consciousness of a sleeper, flooding his mind with its secret and possessing him. And just as it does in a dream, it comes often in the form of a symbol.

It comes to him too in myths and fairy-stories and those recurring, irresistible fantasies that motivate his inner life.

Intuitively man reaches out to God in the created world and listens for his voice in the wind. He trembles at the sound of his anger in the storm and the blaze of his glory in the lightning, he hears the tender voice of his love in the gentle wind that stirs the grass. This secret presence in man's soul hovers on the fringe of his consciousness, possessing him and yet evading him, like a memory which is just out of his reach and yet saturates his thought with its warmth and colour, as the sunlight saturates the thin green leaves on the trees.

Because it is *knowledge of Christ* that is innate in man, it reaches out, seeking for the Father. Man is close to truth in the error that leads him to discover many gods in nature, some

* See p. 187.

fiercely potent and masculine, seeding the earth with life, some feminine and tender, maternal goddesses in whom life grows and becomes fruitful, some virginal as the first light of dawn on the shallow waves on the shore, like Aphrodite, the beloved, and Goddess of Love, born of the living waters. For in the one God all these abide. In him is all potency, all life, all paternity, all motherhood, all virginity, all love and all life, and the created world is the expression of the love of the one God.

Men have always turned to God, though in the form of many gods, to bless the sowing of seed, to make the earth fertile with the bread of life—even before Christ came to sow the seed of his blood and to be the Bread of Eternal Life.

Before he came who is the Light of the World, they worshipped light in the sun. Sometimes one arose among them, pure enough to receive truer intuitions than the others. Thus Akhnaton, Pharaoh of Egypt in the fourteenth century before Christ, lifted the worship of the sun to the worship of the *one* god who lit the sun, and knew the tenderness of God for his creatures, as if he had heard it from the mouth of Christ— "Thou art he ...," he sang, "who createst the man child in woman—"

> Who makest seed in man
> Who givest life to the Son in the body of his Mother,
> Who soothest him that he may not weep,
> A nurse (even) in the womb,
> Who givest breath to animate everyone that he maketh.
> When he cometh forth from the body....
> On the day of his birth,
> Thou openest his mouth in speech—
> Thou suppliest his necessities.*

He tells the secret of his prophetic intuition in one line of his great hymn—"Thou art in my heart".

Water is the Christ-symbol of life, and all through the ages the mystery of water shines in man's soul. Before John baptized in the Jordan, water in the mind of man was the symbol of the birth of the spirit. The journey of the dead into everlasting life was across the dark birth waters of the river Styx. Before Christ

* Arthur Weigall, *The Life and Times of Akhnaton*. Thornton Butterworth.

himself rose from baptismal waters, primitive peoples initiated
their young men into adult life with ceremonies of immersion,
and so they were born into manhood. Those who are familiar
with the dying know how often death comes to them in the
symbol of water bearing them gently on its flood into life. In our
over-civilized, over-specialized modern world, it is water that
wells up in the soul of the dreamer or stretches out before the
awakening eyes of those who seek psychological healing, at the
moment preceding their psychological rebirth.

The secret knowledge of Christ which comes to man out of the
turgid darkness of his own unconsciousness cannot come
through in its purity. It is stained by man's touch, mixed with
his sensuality, twisted by his ignorance, contracted by his littleness, and, like the symbols in his dreams, confused with the
superficial things of his conscious life.

Since the human race is a fallen race, man's innate knowledge
of God is confused. He fumbles in the darkness like a blind man
trying to learn the divine features through the touch of his
finger tips; but the mystery of Christ, of the Trinity, and of
man's place in that unutterable dispensation of love, can only be
known by faith, through the revelation of the Word.

That revelation is realized in the Mystical Body of Christ, and
in each member of it. "I pray for those who are to find faith in
me through their [the apostles'] word; that they may all be one;
that they too may be one in us, as thou, Father, art in me, and I
in thee; so that the world may come to believe that it is thou
who hast sent me. And I have given them the privilege which
thou gavest to me, that they should all be one, as we are one;
that while thou art in me, I may be in them, and so they may be
perfectly made one. So let the world know that it is thou who
hast sent me, and that thou hast bestowed thy love upon them,
as thou hast bestowed it upon me" (John 17.20-24).

Christ in us *is* our supernatural life, on which the fulfilling of
our human nature depends. When we repress Christ we repress
self.

Those people who are quite convinced that what they are
repressing is their sexual life are really repressing Christ.

For this reason there are far more sexually repressed people among those who suppose themselves to be living a full sexual life than among those who are enduring enforced sexual starvation. Sex is a glorious medium of life-giving love, but it can only be lived fully if the love it expresses meets with no hindrance.

The love between man and woman, in its perfection, is a more visible showing of the imprint of God in human nature than any other. They know the ineffable joy that shines straight down on to them from the eternal love of the Blessed Trinity; the natural end of their love is to generate life in their own likeness. In their child the man and woman see themselves and one another; they see the proof of their oneness in love. Yet their child is not just a projection of themselves, he is a separate person, because God has breathed a soul into him, which no man could generate, and this soul has been known to God eternally. It is the child's soul that makes him an individual.

We think with amazement of the privilege given to those craftsmen who are entrusted with the work of making the chalice to hold the Precious Blood of Christ—or to those who make the bread that is to be changed into the Body of Christ; but husband and wife share the privilege, they make the children of flesh and blood, to be changed into the Mystical Body of Christ on earth.

Sexual love does not only give natural life, through procreating and bearing children. Christ has made a sacrament to empower this love with his own. Through the gift of this sacrament, husband and wife give a continual increase of Christ's love and life to one another.

Sex is only fulfilled when it becomes the expression of love that gives supernatural life or natural life or both. In this it is a living of Christ's life, for Christ came to give life. Those who frustrate and destroy natural life by destroying their own unborn children, or supernatural life by destroying the life in their own and one another's souls—by using their sexual powers sinfully, in or out of marriage—are those who are really repressing sex, which can only be lived fully through the life of Christ in the man and woman, unhindered, fulfilling the intent of love of the Blessed Trinity.

Many people suppose that the members of religious orders are either repressing or "sublimating" sex. They are doing neither.

Every religious knows the consummation of love between God and his soul, which is, just as marriage is, comparable to the marriage between Christ and his Church, and gives, as that gives, *supernatural life* to the world. And in living his Christ-life every true religious develops and fulfils the instincts of manhood or womanhood to the fullest capacity. Every life lived in religion is life-giving, every one bears Christ into the world, brings a continual birth of Christ and a continual resurrection of Christ into the world, and in doing that brings the manhood or womanhood of the religious to its own perfection.

The same thing applies to unmarried people who forego the physical expression of sex in the world—supposing, of course, that their reason for doing so is not selfishness or fear of responsibility, but some circumstance in which there is a clear indication of God's will. If they allow what will almost certainly be a cause of loneliness and suffering to them to corrode and embitter their natures, and refuse to look for that aspect of Christ's life which it really indicates, they may indeed wither up their sex. Women may become hard, bitter, and unmotherly, men effeminate, dependent and incapable of taking responsibility; in that case they will repress their sex, because they are repressing Christ. If they surrender their will to the intent of Christ in their life, they will fulfil their human nature and their sex as completely as married people, and sometimes more completely. They will not *sublimate* sex, for sex *is* sublime in its proper expression, and cannot be made more so.

It is the curious idea of those who, while being greatly agitated about sex, have not given much thought to its purpose, that anything which uses up superfluous energy or distracts the mind "sublimates sex"; thus football, arts and crafts, community singing, keeping rabbits, and countless other things of the same kind, are said to be "sublimations of sex"!

Most people do repress Christ, not only in their sexual love, but in all their human relationships. Man represses Christ in himself because he is ignorant of the fulness of joy in this mystery of Christ-life, and still more because he is afraid of "the shadow". He is afraid to face the reality of his individual share in the guilt of the world, but naturally even more afraid to accept the limitless sorrow and shame of the agelong guilt of all mankind. Surrender to his destiny of Christhood must include both these. There is no way of discovering, except by surrender, that in accepting the darkness we also accept the light: that in accepting the universal experience, the collective experience of all men, through our surrender to the one Man in all mankind, we accept simultaneously all the loves of all men, and all their power of love: that in accepting the burden of the earth, we accept the joy of Heaven.

If we dare to surrender, our infinitesimal experience becomes the experience of the whole world. We live in the past, the present, and the future; we receive the sorrow of Eve and all the children of Eve, and also the sorrow and the joy of the second Eve, the Mother of Christ and of the Mystical Body of Christ.

Deep in the heart of everyone living is the longing to be in communion with other men. It is this longing which gives even selfish people an instinctive wish that they were of the fibre that is willing to bear its share of the common burden of effort and hardship. Of all the sufferings of the insane, none is so terrible as isolation, and the cruellest conflict that torments the neurotic is the conflict between his fear of humiliation, which makes him withdraw from other people, and his longing to be one with them.

In Christ, all those who are members of his Mystical Body are one in a way that our generation, divided and torn as it is, can hardly imagine. It is a far closer oneness than that of husband and wife, of a mother and her unborn child—of a man with his own thought.

We are one as the different parts of a human body are one because in them all there is one life. The bloodstream that flows through the human body gives life to the brain and the heart, to every limb and organ, to the tips of the fingers—not a multiplication of lives, but one.

The cause of this oneness is that all the members of Christ's Mystical Body *live with his life*.

Here is a description of the union between Christ and those who belong to his Mystical Body: "Thus our relation to Christ is closer than the natural relation of brothers to a brother or even of children to a parent. It is that of cells in a body to the person whose body it is. It is therefore closer than *any* natural relationship that one human being can have with another. By membership of the Mystical Body we are more closely related to Christ Our Lord than Our Lady is, simply as His mother in the natural order .... Each one of us is more closely related to every other member of the Church by this life of grace than to his own mother by the life of nature. 'And you are Christ's body, organs of it depending upon each other' (I Cor. 12.27). This is easy enough to say. But if we were ever to let ourselves look squarely at it and really try to live by it, its immediate effect would be a remaking of ourselves so thorough that nature shrinks from it; and the ultimate effect would be to renew the face of the earth."*

Perhaps it is because of the tremendous implications—and sometimes terrible implications—of this mystery that many pious people prefer to shrink into themselves and their own devotions, rather than to allow the whole wonder of their life in Christ to break down every barrier to the uncompromising charity which it commits them to.

It means that nothing whatever that one member of the Church does is without its effect on all the others.

If one member—like the "Monster of Düsseldorf", who was a Catholic—commits the most hideous series of murders, the shame is shared by all the others, they all owe penance, they all owe reparation.

It is time that Christians put aside the self-protective type of religion, with its interminable formalities and pious exercises and its careful exclusions and respectable cliques, and recognized *Christ and themselves* in the disreputable members of the Church; the socially ostracized, the repulsive, the criminals, the insane; the drifting population of the streets and the doss-houses, the drug addicts and drunkards; the man waiting in the condemned cell to die—and the tiresome, thankless and dissolute members of a man's own household. It is time that Christians answered Cain's question, "Am I my brother's keeper?" by more than an affirmative: "I am more than that, *I am my brother.*"

To *each* man who lives in Christ, *all* men belong, all love and wisdom and joy, all suffering and fear and atonement, all power

* F. J. Sheed, *Theology and Sanity*, pp. 228-229.

and beauty, all living and dying, all childhood and manhood. Because Christ is whole in each member of his Body on earth now, each in a sense is the Mystical Body. He is in a sense all humanity. Each man owes his tears for his own sins to every other man, and each owes the joy of Christ to every other. The Christian in whom Christ lives has in himself all men; the child in him is capable of understanding all the dreams and fears and mystery of all childhood, the lover in him the love of all manhood.

The responsibility of *all* sin is upon the shoulders of each Christian man.

We cannot escape from Christ, the destiny of our being. We can open our minds, abandon our will to the mystery—or refuse to do so, and live in conflict with Christ, and therefore in conflict with our own life, struggling, as the majority are doing today, to repress Christ in our souls, to dam up our life, and to doom the human race with the doom of a city divided against itself.

To accept, to abandon ourselves to our destiny as "other Christs", is not only to allow all the grief and suffering of the world to flow through us, but also eternal love, love that has no beginning in time and does not end in time: love that has no limitation of place, or act, that does not depend upon the accidents of our lives, though it can be expressed through them too.

The responsibility of all the love of all the ages of the world belongs to each one, through each one flows the whole torrent of life that is given from generation to generation by love: love, which through the miracle of the Incarnation is made tangible and audible in us, so that its music is heard in our voices—in the plighting of our troths, in our marriage vows, in our words of comfort and pity and joy, in our laughter, in the songs beside our cradles, in our choirs of adoration; love, which we transmit with our touch, with the work of our hands, with the labours and pains, the ecstasies and the embraces of our bodies, in the act of procreation, of giving birth, in nursing and serving, and in closing the eyes and bathing the limbs of our dead; love, which holds the timelessness of God in a moment of time, which —with the sacramentals of our flesh and blood, our hands, our voices, our hearts, our minds—forgives, redeems, heals, generates, adores.

To attempt to repress Christ in ourselves is to attempt to hold back the river of life, to stop the bloodstream of the Son of God that is the lifestream of all mankind.

The man in whom Christ is not repressed is a channel through which the life and love of all humanity flows back to God. And as the bloodstream in a man's body is purified by the air he breathes, his supernatural life is purified by the breath of the Spirit that perpetually renews the life of Christ in man. It flows through the divine Mind and through the heart of mankind, continually purifying human nature of the poison that has infected it, perpetually renewing the life of the world.

IX

THE HUMAN DESTINY

*And yet I tell thee, if thou shouldst ask Me who these are, I should
reply (said the sweet and amorous Word of God) "They are another
Myself. ..."*
Dialogue of St Catherine of Siena

THE SAINT is the only person who makes no attempt whatever to resist his destiny as a human being, the destiny to be a Christ.

This is the explanation of everything that causes us to wonder in sanctity, of everything that puzzles us in it, and even of everything in it that startles or horrifies us.

It explains the saint's attitude to his own sins. The saint has become one with Christ. His sense of sin is Christ's sense of sin. Christ took all sin upon himself, from the first sin of Adam to the last sin of the last man to live in the world. "Him, who knew no sin, *God has made sin for us*" (II Cor. 5.21).

Christ identifies himself with every sinner, and—yet more astonishing—God identifies every sinner with Christ. The saint, who is in fact a sinner and the natural heir to original sin, stands before God covered in his own guilt, but he also stands before God as Christ, covered by all guilt. He knows each sin as all sin, and himself responsible for it all. Christ in him is the explanation of the saint's attitude to suffering, both of his willingness to suffer and his desire to suffer.

Any man's will to participate in the lives of other men can be measured precisely by his willingness to suffer to gain this object. Christ wills not only to take part in other men's lives, but to be *one* with all other men without exception; consequently there is no limit at all to what he is willing to suffer. Suffering is the means by which Christ chose to redeem sin; logically so, since it is the direct result of sin. For this reason Christ and suffering are inseparable for so long as there remains one jot of unredeemed sin, or one sinner, on earth.

It is not for the love of suffering that Christ chooses it in his saints, in whom he lives on, but for the love of men, because it is their redeeming and his communion with them. "It is a joy and a bliss," we have heard Julian of Norwich say, "an endless liking to me, that ever I suffered passion for thee; and if I might have suffered more, I would have suffered more."

In man Christ does suffer more, and he will suffer more until the end of time; and in the saints, simply because they love men as Christ loves them and with his love of them, it is "a joy, and a bliss, an endless liking" to suffer too.

When we are scandalized by the voices of the saints we must listen, beneath the crude and clumsy expression, for the undertone which is the voice of Christ.

Those who accept only a material explanation for man's psyche are right in one thing at least: suffering is a man-made thing, it is in fact the only man-made thing that there is. We *do* make our own and one another's suffering, by actually co-operating with Satan's hatred of us, by consenting to his temptations to sin. Suffering is not only something we have given to one another, it is also something we have given to God, in the person of Christ.

Christ came to give life to humanity. For answer, humanity gave suffering to Christ, and Christ accepted it and gave suffering the power of his love. That is why no Christian can be without suffering, and every saint—that is, every man who does not resist his destiny to be a Christ—is destined also to suffer, to the limits of his human capacity not merely for suffering, but—and this is so much more—for love; and more yet, not merely of his own capacity for love but Christ's.

This means that in surrendering himself without reserve to his destiny of Christhood, the saint surrenders himself to suffer *all the suffering of the world*, he takes all the sin of the world upon himself as his individual responsibility. "He who grows in love grows in grief": these words of a saint (St Catherine of Siena) are a tremendous understatement, for he who grows in Christ's love opens his heart not only to grief but to all the suffering and terror and sorrow and pain of the whole world.

Christ has given suffering the power of his love; this power is now inseparable from it, and this is why suffering is never ineffective. It can do appalling harm and it can do unimaginable good, but it *cannot do nothing*. It has become the one thing which because of this infusion of love is never negative.

Christ has given suffering a sacramental quality, and like any sacrament its effectiveness for good or ill depends upon the man who receives it. Man can receive suffering sacrilegiously, he can resent it and do all in his own puny power to resist it; he can desecrate it, and desecrated suffering is destructive. It corrodes the man who has inflicted it on himself and turns him sour; in the end it destroys him. In the measure that we accept the suffering God allows to come to us individually, we accept the power of God's redeeming love, which we can use to heal mankind as well as to be healed by it ourselves.

The stoic's attitude to suffering is just as destructive to his humanity as the coward's. In him, pride puts up a tremendous sham of indifference, which sometimes really becomes indifference to others, but never *really* indifference to self. Self merely sets in a mould of callousness as painless—or painful— as a tooth stopped over an exposed nerve.

The saint's desire for suffering is not the expression of a morbid mind, but of the love of Christ for the world. The saint's desire to suffer is Christ's desire to heal.

Satan, whose craft it is that has induced man to make his own suffering, can use it for his own ends. This is a mysterious and terrible fact, and it is comforting to know that the ultimate control of it is in God's hands, even when he allows Satan to make use of it. To find proof of this we have only to turn to the Book of Job. There is a difference between Job's suffering and ours, in that Job suffered before the Incarnation, and so before Christ had consummated his marriage to human suffering. Moreover, Job's sufferings came straight from Satan's hand. Today Satan, jealous of Christ's Incarnation, unable to become man himself and so unite evil to humanity, makes use of men who give their wills up to him to inflict suffering on others.

The misuse of suffering is sacrilege, a misuse and violation of something in which the redeeming power of Christ's love is hidden, not unlike a sacrilege committed against the Sacred Host; in fact a sacrilege against the Mystical Body, against Christ in man. Our age has proved itself an age of Satanism.

There has never been any time in history when such diabolical cruelty has been inflicted by men upon their fellow men, or when it has been inflicted with such indifference and in such magnitude.

There has never been such blasphemy against suffering, the true expression of Christ's love, as we have seen in our times. Modern man has made a multitudinous holocaust of human beings to evil. Europe is the altar of a black Mass, the whole world a witches' sabbath of suffering.

Whenever great evil breaks out among men, evil which expresses openly Satan's hatred of the human race, it is answered by great love, expressing God's love for human creatures, through man's immolation in Christ, by the saints. The suffering which a saint seems to choose for himself will often be one which is a direct answer to some tremendous sin which is either characteristic of his own generation or yet to come.

Thus St Benedict Joseph Labre chose the apparently useless life of a wandering beggar; he was destitute and he was dirty, he ate scraps of refuse picked from garbage heaps, he was homeless and verminous, he died from starvation and exhaustion. He was the answer to the sensuality and gluttony of his own generation, but he was much more, he was "another Christ" living through and atoning for the horrors of our concentration camps, Christ taking *that* sin upon himself, overcoming *that* torment in each one of its victims, in the person of the strange misunderstood beggar. And the life which St Benedict Joseph chose exactly foretold the suffering of those who were to come, those victims of the concentration camps, who would be homeless, destitute, half naked, verminous, starving, glad to find scraps of refuse to eat, and, when they were not herded into gas-chambers, dying by hundreds and thousands of starvation and exhaustion.

The self-inflicted suffering of a saint, which seems unreasonable, fanatical and even repellent, is in reality an absolute necessity if the whole world is not to perish, a necessity springing from the Crucifixion.

I have spoken of the suffering which a saint *seems* to choose, because in fact the saint very seldom chooses anything: he merely surrenders to his destiny, which as often as not he understands as little as we do. In every circumstance, even such a matter as his own temperament, he sees the will of God, and because he is "a Christ" he does, not his own will, but that of his Father. As Christ too, he is led by the Spirit, driven on by an inward compulsion to acts which seem ludicrous to utilitarian Christians. There is nothing cold and calculating in sanctity.

Because he is inlived by Christ and makes no resistance to Christ's action in himself, the actions of a saint are prophecies. Christ took upon himself not only the past, but the future of suffering and sin; not only the memories of the ages streamed through him, but everything that was to come. And so it is that if we had eyes to see, we could read the future of mankind in the earthly lives of saints now long in their glory.

Some of the saints have in fact prophesied, foretelling future events, but more often the saint is one who does not know the meaning of his own life; his actions are prophecies, but he does not interpret them. He is usually unconscious of their prophetic character and, far from wishing to reveal the secrets of his life to the world, he wishes to hide them. The tongue of the prophet Isaiah was cleansed by a burning coal; the tongues of the saints are often incoherent or dumb, but their hearts are purified in the crucible of love.

Some of the saints, like St Francis of Assisi and St John of the Cross, have been poets in the literal sense; all the saints have been poets as Christ was—in everything that they did, in their attitude to life, in their total surrender to the Spirit, who is the fire and the light of God and the wind of Heaven.

Because the saints are Christ led by the Spirit, all that seems illogical and grotesque in their lives is in fact the living out of Christhood in the world. It is above all else a giving battle to evil, even when they seem to be withdrawn from the world.

The madman who is really mad is alone, isolated in the midst of men, because he is aware only of himself, he lives to and for himself alone. But many people, even on the natural plane, enter into communion with men by withdrawing from them. Madame Curie, the discoverer of radium, dedicated her whole life to the healing of human pain. Withdrawing from men, she suffered profoundly in the intense sacrifices she made in the cause of science. She was not led to work long hours behind locked doors, and to live a hard, austere life, either by a masochistic love of suffering or by a neurotic desire to escape from life. She was consciously driven by a passion for science. In God's plan she was driven by the Spirit, to bring healing to men. Her solitude was her communion with the world.

An artist is driven by the nature of his work to a solitude which is often irksome to him; it is, in God's plan, the condition of his gift to the world.

In the same way the saint is led by the Spirit, by an inner compulsion, to a life of contemplation, or a life of activity and "usefulness", or even a life of apparent uselessness and offence to the worldling and the fastidious. But, in whatever the saint does under compulsion of the Spirit, Christ's plan is shown. In him Christ faces the evil in the world and makes reparation for it. Through him, however mysteriously, he becomes one with all men again. He faces guilt, led by the Spirit, as he was led in his historical life to face Satan in the wilderness.

It need hardly be said that the diversity among the saints is without limit, for Christ wills to utter his love for men and to enter into communion with them through every possible kind of human creature. It follows that it would be very difficult to like all the saints.

In spite of the fact that Christ inlives them all, they retain their own characters, and they are even more varied than other people, because whilst other people are limited by anxiety and fear and self-love, the saints, driven as they are by the Spirit, have no limitations other than their natural ones; they are not hindered by fear, or any form of self-love, from living fully, from any experience offered to them. And unlike other men, who tend as they grow older to be set in rigid grooves and incapable of change, the saints are able to pass from one way of life to another with astonishing mobility. The changes in their lives often read like fairy-stories. St Joan of Arc went from the life of a shepherdess to that of a. general in the French army; St Catherine of Siena, from a recluse to being the most effective figure, man or woman, in the international affairs of her stormy world; St Ignatius, from being a soldier, became a scholar among little boys, and afterwards a priest. The two brilliant little princes, Aloysius and Stanislaus, went from magnificence to be novices in religion. St Peter began his life as a fisherman and ended it as a Pope.

There must be, among the diverse multitudes of the saints, some whose personality we do not like. In this event we are apt to try to compromise by saying that one must get underneath the accidents, such as the particular saint's way of self-expression, to the kernel of the sanctity, to the essential character which, we are usually able to persuade ourselves, must prove to be the kind of character which fits our own preconceived idea of what a saint should be like.

No one has suffered more from this kind of dishonesty than St Teresa of Lisieux, especially among the English (the French have stronger stomachs for sanctity). The average Englishman requires a special grace to love Teresa Martin *as she is;* mercifully, he usually gets it. When he *has* got it, he will actually be able to think of it, without nausea, as a "rose petal".

Before receiving the rose petal he will concentrate as exclusively as he can on the hardness of her hidden life, the iron that was driven into her soul, and very likely he will flatter himself that by his own insight he has discovered things which she was not able to tell him herself. He will go so far as to say that the exterior things of her personality tell him nothing about her, and might well be suppressed. He imagines that he is scandalized by her, but the fact is that he is scandalized *by Christ*, for choosing to become Teresa Martin, because Teresa Martin had a suburban mind, and was true in every detail to what she was, a very sentimental little French bourgeoise.

The imagery which she uses to describe her life of contemplation is not like that of St Teresa of Avila, descriptive of the gorgeous passion of a mature woman, but rather of the immature romanticism of a genteel French girl, for whom a marriage to which she willingly consents has been arranged by an adored father. When it is realized that she did in fact endure almost unbroken, lifelong aridity, and that on her side the surrender to divine Love was really a countless multiplication of acts of will, it seems to suggest that her life *was* an arranged marriage with Heaven.

These things are baffling to the mediocre, and we try to ignore them by saying that they tell us nothing of the essential saint. Their tremendous importance is, however, not what they reveal or conceal about Teresa Martin, but what they tell us about Christ.

Not that Teresa wills to become Christ, but that Christ wills to become Teresa.

Satan refused to bow down to the Son of God in the Incarnation. Now Christ asks a great deal more than our adoration of himself as the perfect man that he is in his human nature; he asks for our recognition and welcoming of him in every kind of imperfect, unlikely, and—assessed by our own vanity—unsuitable human creature.

We need to remind ourselves often that the likeness between the saints and certain neurotics is not accidental, but is part of God's plan, of Christ's identification of himself with all kinds of men, with *any* man who does not resist him.

The compelling fact is not that a suburban-minded girl or a verminous tramp, or anyone else, will become Christ, but that Christ will become the one or the other, and that through that one he will utter the Word of God in language that Satan's unconscious little imitators shut their sensitive ears against.

The fact that Christ's choice in personalities brings home is that there is *no* kind of person through whom Christ will not love the world. If we dislike certain kinds of saints, it is simply because we dislike certain kinds of people. There are many kinds of people from whom the mediocre shrink: borderline psychotics, insane people, people in whom suffering is stripped naked in all its ugliness, and whose suffering cannot be cured by our charity, but is a perpetual challenge to the much more difficult self-giving, called compassion—people who are in fact suffering the anguish and loneliness of Christ in Gethsemane, and from whom the chalice may not pass. Like the disciples in the garden we prefer to shut our eyes rather than to enter into this suffering without being able to hide or alleviate it.

The charity of Christ on earth will not be filled up ("those things that are wanting to the suffering of Christ") until Christ is accepted and contemplated in every kind of human being that allows him place in itself.

We are reminded of our failure by the fact that there are saints for everyone to dislike.

The Christhood of sanctity explains, as we have seen, the saint's attitude to sin and suffering. His words, which sometimes jar our feeble minds and embarrass us, are not inspired by morbidity, they are simply the expression of Christ's love for us

It is also the saint's willingness to suffer which measures and liberates his capacity for love. The saint has the capacity to love *with Christ's love*. He has exchanged his heart for the heart of Christ, his will for the will of Christ: in that is the secret of his tremendous surrender to his destiny as man—Christhood.

St Catherine of Siena has uttered the last word on this human destiny of Christhood:

"But in no way does the creature receive such a taste of the truth, or so brilliant a light therefrom, as by means of humble and continuous prayer, founded on knowledge of herself and of God; because prayer, exercising her in the above way, unites with God the soul that follows the footprints of Christ crucified, and thus, by desire and affection, and union of love, makes her another Himself."*

"Another Himself"!

* *Dialogue of St Catherine of Siena.* Kegan Paul (London, 1896).

X

GUILT AND SUFFERING

Just as there grows no herb which can keep away death, so there exists no simple means which can make a hard thing, as life assuredly is, an easy matter.

C. J. JUNG, "Love Problem of the Student",
*Contributions to Analytical Psychology**

QUITE SIMPLY, suffering is the result of guilt, for guilt means that we have broken the law of our being, we are in collision with reality, and suffering follows inevitably. A man's attitude to suffering is therefore an estimate of his attitude to guilt. Again and again people who have no personal conception of God, and therefore no real sense of sin, or of the common guilt of mankind, are heard to say, with genuine bewilderment, "Why should I suffer?" or "Why should my child suffer?" They declare that they have done no harm to anyone, thereby unconsciously proclaiming that if they believed that they *had* done some harm to someone, and were guilty, there would be justice in their suffering, or even in the suffering of their children.

On the other hand, the man of faith, who knows God, sees suffering as something which he can use to expiate his own sins and so come into closer union with God; and besides that he sees in it a means of a closer communion with other men, for through Christ who abides in him he can use his suffering to ease that of mankind in general. Through offering himself in his suffering, of whatever kind it is, he can be a "Christ" to the world, that knows so little of Christ. He can reach out far beyond the stretch of his own short arms, to the stretch of the arms on the cross, and bring down the tender pity of God upon men who are far out of the range of his vision; perhaps outside the reach of his imagination. Through this self-offering of Christ, through his individual suffering, man, who lives the life of the

* Kegan Paul (London, 1928).

risen Christ who has overcome death and suffering, can in a spiritual sense do what a risen and glorified body can do in a material sense. He can cross the seas, walking upon the waters; he can pass through prison walls and the walls of hospitals, institutions, asylums, concentration camps: and wherever any man is in need, is forgotten, isolated, seemingly out of reach of human mercy and love, he can reach him with the love of Christ crucified. The individual man is not the helpless creature he often supposes himself to be. Often through what seem to be his limitations, his crippling circumstances, his frustrations, he is able to extend the arms of love illimitably. Again and again in human history those who are lived in by Christ have been able to heal because they could not be healed: and those who were immobile, tied down to one room, one bed—prisoners, cripples, old, bedridden people—have been in all places, everywhere, at once: present in Christ's love.

Since men have covered their eyes from the light of God, and, in so far as they could, have shut their hearts against the entry of Christ into them in order to escape from their destiny of Christhood, there are few who realize the possibilities of suffering, and many who repudiate it absolutely, at least as an idea. Few people now have a clearly defined attitude to suffering, but those who have are seldom so consistent in it as they think that they are. Usually there is a big discrepancy between practice and theory.

Although it is the creed of mediocracy that the only sane and healthy object of life is material well-being, in practice most people impose a great deal of suffering and even austerity and unnecessary suffering upon themselves. They do so, of course, without realizing fully what they are doing. If they could be compelled to face the facts and to discuss a subject so distasteful, they would probably say that they do not resent suffering or even self-denial when it is for *some purpose*, used as a means to an end, but they abhor "useless suffering".

They consider that all the suffering of the saints is useless, and above all the voluntary austerity and self-denial of contemplative saints. They have less condemnation for those who ministered to the sick or the destitute, such as St Vincent de Paul, but it is difficult for them to understand why *he* found it necessary to give up his own little property and to *share* the suffering of those he came to help. Why not have kept his small income and provided a few more loaves, instead of one more mouth to feed!

The modern mind, besieged though it is on every side by conflicting invisible forces, is a utility mind, and consequently able to realize the effectiveness of suffering (as of anything else) only when it shows material results. But for material results, what sufferings man will endure!

Those business magnates, so envied by their clerks, who have changed from office boys to millionaires, did not change with just that sleepy inactivity with which the chrysalis changes into a butterfly. There were, on the contrary, years of early rising on cold, dank mornings; wearisome journeys in the rush hour, packed together, straphanging; nauseating lunches in steamy, greasy, overcrowded tea-shops; extra study at night, books brought home from the office, and countless sweet and lovely and, to most people, even necessary distractions forgone. And when the man who has given up so much to be rich—such things as lying on his back in a sunny field, reading poetry at his leisure, listening to music, talking with friends, and so on—has achieved his ambition, how much petty suffering will hinder his enjoyment of his riches, because in acquiring them he will have acquired a habit of worry, of suspicion, of insomnia, of dyspepsia, and probably a gastric ulcer!

Again, there is social success, a peculiar ambition more common to women than to men, and one which demands, especially from the type of woman to whom the very idea of mortification is repellent, a quite frightening degree of self-denial and austerity.

She must be attractive, or at least she must conform to the fashionable conception of attractiveness. I remember as a hideous little child how a dressmaker, while gaily (but of course unconsciously) snipping a little piece of flesh out of my neck while fitting a dress, declared *"Il faut souffrir pour être belle."* The society woman must deny herself the most tempting dishes at table, must allow her face to be drawn taut and stiff in packs of mud, her body to be pinched, slapped, boiled, pummelled and rolled, her head to be fixed to a hot electric machine by the hair, for hours on end. All this and more, not only occasionally, but regularly and continually for years on end, and with the haunting certainty of ultimately losing the battle.

But both the successful man and the society woman would be surprised if anyone commiserated with them on their suffering lives, and affronted if it were further suggested that their suffering revealed a strain of morbidity in their thinking. They would justify their choice of endurance by pointing out that it is for an end, and it attains the end. Provided that suffering attains a man's object, it is considered to be respectable; the fact that the object itself may be selfish, base or foolish, is of no consequence, provided only that it be of this world.

Examples of this kind of motivated suffering could be multiplied indefinitely, but there are others which are embraced even more readily, indeed eagerly, which are much more bewildering to the onlooker, for the very object achieved seems to be suffering too. In sport, it is difficult to decide where the pain ends and the pleasure begins. There are certain sports which are beautiful to watch and exhilarating to practise, such as cricket or skating or horsemanship or sailing a boat—about these there is no mystery, but there are others which are baffling. Amateur boxers are as ready as professionals to be beaten and pummelled about the body, and to have their faces smashed and pounded to pulp. On sweltering summer days, hordes of cyclists race for hundreds of miles, parched and panting, on their one day's leisure in the week. Even in St Paul's day, athletes were overcoming their appetites and denying themselves the joys of life to win at the games—and St Paul remarked that the end attained seemed hardly worth the effort: "Every athlete must keep his appetites under control, and he does it to win a crown that fades."

However, man's readiness to suffer goes deeper than the superficial motive, and if we probe, we meet the homing toad again.

In his heart of hearts, even the sophisticated and cynical man knows that suffering is a common burden, a load laid upon the backs of all mankind, and one which is lightened for everyone when anyone lends a willing shoulder, and made heavier for everyone when one man shrinks back from the effort. This explains the anger which enters into the attitude of hard-working men towards those who are too nerveless and supine to welcome the commonly accepted tests of manhood, even when these tests are silly.

It explains, too, why those for whom life is made too easy at the beginning, feel humiliated, and why, quite apart from the possibility of superficial envy, other men often feel a grudge against those who seem to them to have been given on easy terms the things that they must get by the sweat of their brows.

Men want to prove themselves able to endure, even if they must prove it in a way that on the surface seems absurd, and they want to do this because even when they have lost sight of the whole meaning of communion with others, they do want to participate in other men's lives, they want to be accepted and esteemed and loved by their fellows, they are eager to prove that they have the right to be one of them.

Even when a man's values are all wrong and his ideals are awry, he wants his money or his power to be got by his own struggle: or a woman wants her social success or artificial beauty got by her own endurance, in order to be entitled to her place in the solidarity of the human race. A man may strive for a communion with men which is made almost a sacrilegious communion by his personal dispositions; but nevertheless what he really wants, and is compelled by his nature to want, is communion.

In the degree in which the willingness to suffer, which is innate in normal men, becomes un-selfseeking, it unites men with one another and is the beginning of the communion which is fully realized only in the saints.

There are professions and trades and labours which are vocations to suffering in union with, and for, other men.

First there is the priest, whose life is a sacrifice offered for all men. Then there are the doctor and the nurse, both of whom are always ready to give up sleep or comfort or rest, to go to those in need—ready too to risk any infection and to face any terror or mutilation in the service of mankind. There are those who must live, as it were, in other men's hands; whose success, even if it be of a spiritual order, must be paid for in a suffering of poverty far more terrible than material poverty, a poverty of not having themselves, not having anything of their own—not time, or solitude, or their thoughts, or even their senses: their hearing

filled always with other men's troubles, their eyes with the face
of other people's sorrows, all their words given to others without
stint for their comfort, their touch the perpetual touch of healing
and blessing.

Such a life of willing privation was lived by St Francis de
Sales, of whom a modern writer says: "But the most revealing
thing about him is the description to be found in every life ever
written of St Francis de Sales—'he was accessible to all'; when
he became a Bishop, and an extremely popular Bishop, this
meant that there could not have been one moment of an
eighteen-hour day which he could claim for his personal delight.
It is somehow more difficult to imagine life on these terms, than
one of splendid miracles."* It is on these terms that every
modern Pope must live.

But in order to embrace humanity, a man may be obliged to
withdraw from humanity. Scholars, poets, artists, scientists, and
contemplatives, whose lives are lived in terms of universal love,
will usually have to pay their debt of suffering to the world and
enter into communion with men through detachment, as well as
through work. To give oneself to the world, to take all mankind
to one's heart, may be the loneliest of experiences.

Among those who follow the humblest trades and whose lives
are filled up by manual labour, it is almost universal to take
hardship and suffering for granted, and everyone sees that the
suffering of such men is useful to others, though few realize its
effectiveness in the supernatural order and its power to redeem.
If everyone realized that Christ is in himself, and offered his self-
sacrificing life of work and hardship that is taken for granted, to
expiate guilt, how swiftly the face of the earth would be changed!

Every day the miner goes down into the great caverns hewn
under the earth, and there with the sweat pouring down in rivulets through the grime on his stripped body, he risks his life
from moment to moment. The ship's stoker sweltering at his
furnace in the tropical seas: the crews of submarines, firemen,
and divers, and all those whose service is hard and dangerous,
touch the point at which the ordinary suffering which is taken
for granted, and hardly recognized as such, becomes sacrifice,
a mysterious participation in the priesthood of the human race,

* G. B. Stern, *Man Without Prejudice.*

through which God is glorified in men. This too is taken for granted in the life and the death of the soldier:

> Yes. Whý do we áll, seeing of a soldier, bless him? bless
> Our redcoats, our tars? Both of these being, the greater part,
> But frail clay, nay but foul clay. Here it is: the heart,
> Since, proud, it calls the calling manly, gives a guess
> That, hopes that, makesbelieve, the men must be no less;
> It fancies, feigns, deems, dears the artist after his art;
> And fain will find as sterling all as all is smart,
> And scarlet wear the spirit of wár thére express.
>
> Mark Christ our King. He knows war, served this soldiering
>   through;
> He of all can handle a rope best. There he bides in bliss
> Now, and séeing somewhére some mán do all that man can do,
> For love he leans forth, needs his neck must fall on, kiss,
> And cry 'O Christ-done deed! So God-made-flesh does too:
> Were I come o'er again' cries Christ 'it should be this.'*

On the whole, it can be said truly that even though the most widely professed creed of mankind today is to seek for personal happiness and to avoid suffering, nearly everyone who professes this creed takes upon himself a good deal of voluntary suffering, and admires other men for their powers of and willingness for endurance.

He justifies himself by the plea of usefulness, but there is no such thing as useless suffering.

Suffering does something *to* the man who suffers, not merely something *for* him.

It is quite impossible to suffer anything, no matter what it is, and not be affected by it. The effect may be good or it may be bad. One man will be made new and whole by suffering; another will be destroyed by it. In its turn, the character given to a man by suffering will affect everyone with whom he comes into contact. It leaves a stamp on the soul, a seal, as if it were the sacramental of some mysterious force, like the chrism in Confirmation; but a sacramental which can be used by the evil spirit as well as by the Spirit of Love. It may disfigure; it may make beautiful; one or the other it *will* do.

No one ever lives who has not at some time or other the

* Gerard Manley Hopkins, "The Soldier".

possession of suffering; it is the one thing man possesses by his own right, and it is certainly essential for any achievement or success that he desires. It seems, too, that he cannot have anything else essential to his happiness, unless he has suffering with it—above all that greatest essential of all, to be able to love. Directly a man loves, he suffers.

No matter what joy is granted to a man on earth, suffering will balance the scale that weighs it out to him. If a man imagines that he is experiencing joy, but without any accompanying suffering, the answer is that he does not really know what it is, or can be, to experience joy.

No man is ever unaffected by suffering. It goes to the roots of everyone whom it touches; it either embitters him or enlarges him with divine compassion. It makes him hate, or it makes him love, and equally, the seal it has set on his soul makes him either hated or loved in return. A man's strength and his power to strengthen other men can be measured by how much he can suffer well.

By suffering a man is either made a slave to himself or he is set free—suffering has a germ of effectiveness in itself, as virile as the germ of life in wheat. This germ of life is Christ's redemptive love. In itself, suffering is without value; worse than that, it is destructive. But Christ used suffering to redeem the human race. He did not try to escape it, though he could have redeemed man without it. On the contrary, he gave himself to it from his birth to his death; he gave his body and mind and his soul to it; he literally took it to his heart; he sowed it with the seed of his redemptive love. That is the germ of life in suffering.

Man, who is sinful, and who inherits original sin, cannot escape from suffering. His attempts to do so add to suffering. His futile struggle to resist must break down sooner or later. It succeeds, if it succeeds in anything, only in the tragedy of his refusal to receive the seed of redemptive love into the dry dust of his heart.

The widespread neurosis of our days is largely caused by the attempt to resist suffering, because it involves an attempt to resist the redemptive love that is in it.

The man who tries to resist suffering succeeds only in frustrating that power of love. He makes a futile attempt to resist that in which it is concealed and given. He lifts his puny little arms to try to hold back the torrent of divine love, in order to avoid the one thing that he can never escape, and which hides its own healing within itself. It is not surprising that in such an impact man is broken.

Suffering is a mystery. Not one to be dismissed or to remain unexamined. It is man's only achievement, his only contribution to his own life. Yet it can be a creative thing, not only a destructive one. Evil is its cause, but because Christ has given it the power of his redemptive love, it can redeem evil.

To understand what we can about this it is not enough to gaze stupefied at the wounds it has inflicted upon men, or to consider its effect on those who neither wholly repudiate nor accept it. We must go much further, we must see what happens to those human beings who try to escape altogether, who have a definite will *not* to suffer; and on the other hand what happens to the saints, who, without conditions or reservation, are in the fullest measure willing to suffer.

XI

FRUSTRATION

To love belongs the depth and loyalty of feeling, without which love is not love, but mere caprice; true love will always engage in lasting, responsible ties. It needs freedom only for the choice, but not for the accomplishment. Every true deep love is a sacrifice. A man sacrifices his possibilities, or to put it better the illusion of his possibilities. If the sacrifice is not made his illusions hinder the realization of deep responsible feeling, and accordingly the possibility of experiencing real love is also denied him.

C. J. JUNG, "Love Problem of the Student",
Contributions to Analytical Psychology.

I T IS the reiterated complaint of ego-neurotics that life has frustrated them. There are two words which are always hovering on their tongues—"Fulfilment" and "Satisfaction". They are obsessed by the idea that they have been prevented by an unkind fate from "satisfying" their deepest emotions, "fulfilling" their humanity. In the details as well as in the broad sweep of life, they have, so they believe, been frustrated at every turn. They have been denied the opportunity of revealing, let alone developing, their talents. They have been passed over at work, and in any case have never been able to obtain any suited to their temperament or their ability.

For some mysterious reason, all their human relationships are unsatisfactory and invariably bring them more distress than happiness. Above all, they think, they have been denied the opportunity to love. While they imagine that their capacity for love is deeper and more sensitive than that of others, its fulfilment has been denied to them. In short, life has frustrated them at every turn.

Their real tragedy is not that life has frustrated them, but that they have frustrated life. Not that love has been denied to them, but that they have denied themselves to love.

To discover what is at the root of this kind of human unhappiness, we must look for symptoms common to all the sufferers. They are easily found—hesitation, anxiety, indecision —all pointing to one thing, fear; all means to one end, self-protection. The ego-neurotic never takes a risk that he can possibly avoid; therefore, he never willingly goes out of himself to meet life; he shrinks back from every adult experience. By constant delays, by never being able to make up his mind, by magnifying all the real and imaginary difficulties in every possible course open to him, by putting off every decision until too late, he is able to avoid the minimum of risk involved in taking any positive action at all.

We have seen that everyone is willing to suffer in the measure of his desire for communion with other men. But anything which involves co-operation with others, let alone communion, is precisely what ego-neurotics cannot face. It is often said of them that they "dare not face life", and that is both literally and metaphorically true; they do not want to show their face, they do not want to show themselves to the world. They are tortured by a painful self-consciousness, a wish to be hidden, if necessary even by becoming part of the faceless and voiceless mediocrity, drifting through years of accepted defeat to the grave.

At the core of this tragedy is this: the ego-neurotic is haunted by a deep inward humiliation, which is not thought but *felt* in the roots of his being, and consists in a profound doubt of his own potency as a human being. He does not want to put himself to the test because he is afraid to be found wanting. He is afraid to know himself and to be known, and if he cannot overcome this fear, he does at last become in reality what he imagines himself to be, impotent before life, helpless in the face of conquest, incapable of loving, and so unable to win love for himself. A failure as a human being.

The person who will not take any risk to enter into contact with others, to pay his part of the debt of human conflict and suffering, inhibits his capacity for love, until it actually becomes so weak from sheer inanition that it is no longer a power in his life at all, and cannot be his driving force to experience.

Each step forward in life, with the risk and the self-giving involved in it, strengthens the emotional sinews of a human creature and is the remote preparation for the supreme surrender to love. This process, and it is a process of self-revelation as well as of co-operation, begins at the first children's party, if not before, and it is significant that the game which extroverted children delight in and introverted children dread is hide-and-seek. It is only one example of how children's games, like children's stories and fantasies, show us the secrets of human nature.

There are two ways of playing hide-and-seek. In one of them all the players hide excepting one, who remains, with closed eyes, in the place chosen as "home" while he counts a hundred, and then starts seeking. When he finds one of the hidden players, that player must try to escape from his hiding-place and to run home before he is caught by the seeker. The first who is caught becomes the seeker next time.

The other method is played in a dark house, without lights. One only hides, and all the other players seek. As they find him, one by one they join him in the hiding-place, remaining quite silent. The one who is the last to be left seeking will be the first to hide next time.

Those who are not able to imagine the feelings of a child who shrinks from hide-and-seek—feelings ranging from acute shyness to actual terror—would do well to read Graham Greene's short story in which a little boy dies of fear during the game of hide-and-seek at a party, while his twin brother holding his hand in the darkness experiences the other's terror in himself, and it lives on in him when the brother is dead. Could we experience one another's fears and doubts through the compassion of our human brotherhood, we would go a long way towards healing the neurosis of the world; we should at least know its reality.

After the children's party there is school, and at school the fear of *being* afraid, as well as of showing fear, develops into an acute suffering. Already the process that is going to be repeated all through life begins; the child is asked to stand up to things which are more than he *can* stand up to unafraid. He is asked to hide every natural feeling, and to bring a good face to the world—the horrible little world into which he has suddenly been flung, while he is still quivering inwardly from the separation from his home, his parents and his babyhood. All the "tests" are designed expressly to show what he is trying to hide —that he is a milksop and a coward; and because he already believes the falsehood that to be sensitive and to be afraid is to be a coward and a failure, it becomes his great object to hide the shame of being himself.

The same pattern goes on when the child must go into the world of adult life. In our civilization, entering into manhood means again being put to a test which is far beyond a test of nature, and demands unnatural qualities. The young man or woman is faced now with his personal conquest of the materialism, the callousness and the false values of the world; and he is still crippled by his delusions—his fear of being afraid, his fear of being unable to shoulder responsibilities, his fear of failing in the drastic tests that must come to every man and woman who fall in love, and above all his fear of being stripped of his garments and revealed as he imagines himself to be, impotent in the face of life, incapable of the fullness of living which is the expression of love. The ego-neurotic shrinks from life and refuses to take risks, because he is unwilling to put himself to the test.

Until he is put to the test, terrible though his doubt is—his secret lack of self-confidence and self-esteem—it still is a doubt; it is not a certainty. He prefers to forgo the fullness of life, rather than risk the final humiliation of knowing himself as a failure for certain.

He is afraid to know himself and to be known. To this fear love is the ultimate challenge. For the first condition of love is the total surrender of the secret of self. To love is to know and to be known. Love reveals to himself, and to her whom he loves, exactly what a man is; it reveals also his potentialities, his power to suffer, his capacity for responsibility and for joy, his ability for self-sacrifice.

The attempt to escape from the self-revelation and self-knowledge of love is the key to countless human tragedies and wasted lives.

It is often an instinctive self-protection against the risk of falling in love that keeps young men, and even old men, fixed in adolescence. There are women who, rather than risk proving themselves unable to attract love, will adopt a dowdy way of dressing and an anti-social attitude to the world; they do not "make the best of themselves", because if the *best* of themselves failed, they would taste the humiliation of certainty. It has been said, and I believe truly, that a woman's hat, the hat that she *dares* to wear, is a fair criterion of her secret estimate of herself.

There are many forms of this sad escape from the perils of love. Sometimes it takes the form of an abuse and misuse of religion, and women who have no religious vocation (*that* involves the most complete self-surrender of all) invent for themselves a kind of pseudo-companionate-marriage with the Lord in the world, or an extraordinary mission in life, which precludes fulfilling their ordinary obligations, but eludes definition which might commit them to any self-surrender at all, and is itself a lifelong delaying action.

Many women who dare not surrender themselves to the love of a man find it necessary all the same to have a man or men in their lives with whom they have emotional or intense relationships, which are rendered safe for themselves by some circumstance. There are women, for example, who invariably fall in love with married men, and among the pious there are those who foster a merciless devotion to a sympathetic priest.

Timid men are more afraid of love than women are. What is more pitiful than the middle-aged bachelor facing the depression of a lonely, homeless and childless old age, because he always set his standard of living—with a wife—too high for there to be any serious risk of his ever reaching it?

There are women who make a hobby of making and breaking engagements, and others who, for so long as the man's patience holds out, invariably postpone their wedding when the date draws near.

Sometimes the fear of impotence translates itself quite crudely and simply onto a physical plane, but with the most baffling intricacies of mental, spiritual and hereditary forces behind it, not to mention complications of environment and education. Thus we have those young men who, without an *obvious* motive, commit suicide on their wedding eve.

Again there are many homosexuals who have become so because they were unable to risk the self-sacrifice which is involved in meeting the far greater responsibility of natural love.

Homosexuality, like scrupulosity, is a very big and complicated subject, which it is impossible to explore thoroughly in any book that is not devoted solely to it. The belief which used to prevail that there is what Edward Carpentier described as an "Intermediate Sex"—made up of persons in whom the sexes are so intermingled that they may be said to be, psychologically, both man and woman—is denied by most modern schools of psychology. They insist that homosexuality, like other abnormalities and neuroses, can always be traced to early, perhaps infantile, experience, and therefore can usually be cured by psychoanalysis. There is a surprisingly high number of recorded cures to support this theory, but it is nevertheless not yet proved.

I am inclined to the view that there are many causes of homosexuality, and that there *are* rare, very rare, cases when sex is so intermingled that—though this is an unnatural thing in itself— it may be a particular individual's nature to combine the two sexes in himself in the way that makes him homosexual. I do not mean merely that the man and woman are both in him, for this applies to everyone; everyone who is normal has ingredients of both man and woman in him, usually well balanced against each other. The type of homosexuality I speak of is one in which the psyche, the whole invisible part of the person, his or her mind and character and emotions, belong to one sex, and his or her body to the other. Thus one meets a woman who has unquestionably a man's psyche; or the reverse, a man with a woman's psyche. It is true that in this case there are usually masculine characteristics in the woman's body, and feminine ones in the man's; but I think that these are largely developed through the influence of the psyche, and of course accentuated by the manner of dress. Just as a neurotic may attain to sanctity *through* his neurosis, a homosexual may do so through his homosexuality, for he is fated to a life of great loneliness, and not infrequently to one of very great love, which he can never satisfy; to attain sanctity he would have to deny himself the physical expression of his love altogether, and to some extent *any* expression of it which would disturb the life of another or impose too great a strain on himself.

Even if the homosexuality is not innate, but has a cause in

infantile experience, if it is established it can still be accepted as a neurosis and sanctified; and as many homosexuals of this kind have a great power to love, it may be their vocation actually to be power-centres of selfless love in the world.

But there is another kind of homosexual far more numerous— the self-lover, who seeks not to give but to get from every human relationship; the sensation-hunter, the man or woman who understands love only in terms of sensuality and self-gratification on a physical plane.

Natural love points to marriage; marriage, not only to daily small, sometimes big, acts of self-denial, but to great acts of self-giving, tenderness and restraint in the expression of love. It leads on to imparting life, one's own life, and then to the whole responsibility of family life.

Not surprisingly, the homosexual whose perversion springs from self-love is nearly always mean as well as cowardly; he not only does not want to give anything, but he does not want to share anything, even his sensual pleasure. There are no inescapable ties or obligations in a homosexual relationship; no risks of unwanted children.

It is true that there are many homosexuals who do marry, but the story of their married life is usually one of failure, for the reasons I have mentioned, and for another—namely, vanity. Homosexuality, whatever the cause, is often complicated, in the case of men, by physical impotence, and this deepens the bitter inward humiliation of all ego-neurosis. To be impotent before a woman is more than most men can bear, and even though homosexuals may have procreated children, they usually go through long and humiliating periods of impotence.

The usually quite unbalanced response to them (at first) from other men with whom they enter into homosexual relations, is a tremendous salve to their aching vanity, as well as to their inevitable physical obsession with sex, which they cannot satisfy.

Self-love is pitifully apparent in the stormy relationships which always result when a marriage has been broken by homosexuality. Each side demands from the other unnatural excitement and sensation, which they both crave as the drunkard craves for alcohol. There are always sordid quarrels about money, incessant demands for it from one or the other; and the relationship, sunk as it is in self-love, a mental and physical mutual masturbation, breaks up in acts of violence and spite, and sometimes insanity.

There are the examples, sufficiently well known to cite, of Verlaine and Rimbaud, of Oscar Wilde and Alfred Douglas—stabbed and pocked with hysterical scenes, quarrels, spite, partings and reunions, orgies of drinking, of gluttony, and of almost unbelievable bursts of conceit; and finally, between Verlaine and Rimbaud, shooting!

But in addition to the cases in which there are definite "liaisons", there are the homosexuals who ask for no "love" at all on the spiritual plane, and simply regard other human beings as a means to physical pleasure or relief for themselves. Those of their own sex are safer and cheaper than those of the opposite sex. Not only do they in these casual relationships demand little in the way of material recompense, but less still in the ways that demand personal effort, courtesy, manners or refinement.

There are men, too, who deny themselves friendship with women altogether, because their company is a challenge to their manhood which makes many small demands on them involving effort, as well as the menace of a potential emotional demand, to which they feel unable to respond.

There are many of these unhappy, hesitating people, who do manage to avoid all intimate relationships throughout their lives, and with them not only all responsibilities and some kinds of suffering, but also all the delight and lasting joys in life.

But this is not the case with every ego-neurotic. Sometimes ego-neurotics do marry or form other human contacts in spite of themselves, but they do not find happiness in them, and they certainly do not give it. The same sense of being frustrated and unfulfilled haunts them as that which haunts the obviously lonely. They are in fact equally lonely.

The reason for this is twofold; it is because the ego-neurotic, though unable to give love, makes an unreasonable demand for it, and he demands it on his own terms—not from God, who alone could give it in the measurelessness that he wants, but from other human beings, who are as helpless as he is to give love at all unless they give God's love.

He demands love and esteem in limitless measure, and "for myself alone." The need to be loved and encouraged is an obsession, and this because the inward shame and humiliation, the profound and never finally tested doubt of self, causes a continual need of reassurance. Without reassurance from one hour to the next, life becomes a torment.

This terrible need for reassurance translates itself into many forms. There is the boaster and romancer, constantly blowing his own trumpet, who in the absence of anyone else to do it for him, tries to reassure himself of his own worth. On the other hand, there is the person who is always disparaging himself, always apologizing for his existence, and so extorting reassurance. The more aggressive sufferer demands open and blatant flattery and spends his life provoking it. Aggression is very often the expression of the inward helplessness of ego-neurosis. For not only does the sufferer feel the need for love and esteem, but he feels all other people to be competitors; he cannot hold up his head if he does not feel that he is the *only* one who is loved, or the *only* one who is esteemed; so weak is his grasp on life in the psychological sense, that he cannot bear—or does not dare— to share love and esteem with anyone, in case there is not enough for himself.

Sometimes, feeling that he is not getting the love and esteem that he hungers and thirsts for, the ego-neurotic becomes openly aggressive; he feels anger and even hatred for the person who, as he imagines, by not giving him what he needs in the impossible measure in which he demands it, causes him to suffer—the one thing he is trying to avoid.

In extreme cases he imagines that in everything the other person says or does not say, there is an expression of the contempt which he really feels for himself. It is noticeable that nearly every persecution-mania begins in self-persecution.

Almost more pitiful is the person who always tries to placate; who, in order to be liked, always flatters others; who makes himself servile in order to be indispensable.

Once the suffering that is hidden in this need for reassurance is understood, many things that seemed ludicrous and grotesque in human nature are seen in their real pathos. It is very often the cause of promiscuity and immorality. Your Don Juan who attempts to seduce woman after woman is not necessarily the great lover he would like to be; he may well be the man who cannot love and who is driven by his tormenting fear that his power of attraction is failing too.

Girls and women who secretly doubt that anyone could love them for themselves are often willing to have "love affairs" with as many men as they can, only to keep the illusion that the physical pleasure they can offer wins them some kind of love, and is some salve to their vanity.

A further peculiarity of humiliated human beings is that they are unable to believe in the reality of another's love if they have it, and while on the one hand they are continually asking for reassurance, on the other hand they refuse to believe it when it is given. Once again aggression creeps in, for convinced as they are that they are in fact unlovable, unesteemable, they attribute ulterior motives to those who proffer love to them.

Thus the person who has forced his service and his flatteries on another, will turn on him in the end and declare that he is exploited; the girl who has used her body to attract will upbraid the man who has succumbed to her, on the grounds that he has treated her as an unpaid prostitute; and equally, married ego-neurotics will declare that their husband or wife has just such motives and no real love. In plain words the humiliated egoist wishes to give nothing at all, for the inordinate love that he demands.

There is yet another aggravating cause for the sense of being unsatisfied of which the person who has failed in his human relationships always complains: he imagines that being satisfied by life is being *sated* by this life.

He is conscious of the terrible emptiness of emotional starvation, made all the more intolerable by the fact that it was originally self-induced; and, as in physical starvation, the starving person is too weak to be able to digest the food he needs. Most boys pass through a phase in early adolescence in which they consider that they have not been fed unless they are stuffed, sated and sickened. People who, through fear of adult responsibility, remain psychologically adolescent, ask the same from their emotional life. They want to be replete, filled, even sickened, and in this they imagine they would be "satisfied"!

But while the ego-neurotic's appetite for emotional satisfaction grows bigger and bigger, his emotional capacity grows smaller and smaller and he seeks to satisfy it with less and less. While his craving to be loved grows, his power of loving shrinks. There is always a hierarchy in love; in the human failure it is a descending one; when the nearest anyone can approach to loving at all is only to need to be reassured, and to be unable to give love, it is tragic to watch this descent. From the supernatural plane, which means the love of united body and soul, it descends to merely the body, and from that sometimes to the possessions of the supposedly beloved. Women who have failed in their human relationships are often seen giving the highest love of which they are still capable to dogs; and men sometimes give it to food. It is not only in direct personal relationships that love operates; it is the one means to fulfilment in any life, whether that life is lived for one other person or one little family, or for multitudes—perhaps of people who will not be known in the body in this world.

The tremendous challenge of love, the challenge to surrender to the stripping of Christ, to know and to be known, comes on other planes as well as the emotional; it is equally the problem of the celibate and the dedicated artist, the contemplative, and everyone else. The surrender of the secret of self is the condition for the potency of every kind of human giving and taking of love.

Fear of risk, of self-surrender and self-revelation, operates in the same way on intellectual, spiritual and artistic levels as it does on emotional levels. Many pictures are not painted, many sculptures are not made, many books are not written, because the men and women who could have created them cannot bear to face themselves stripped naked in their work, or allow others to gaze upon the humiliating secret of self.

Again and again they escape, just as the victim of scrupulosity escapes from self-seeing, through a destructive passion for self-perfection, or a paralysing state of indecision.

The world is full of brilliant people whose brilliance comes to nothing, of naturally spiritual people whose spirituality comes to nothing; of people who spend their whole lives searching for a motivating ideal or faith, but who, in order that they may delay their surrender to it indefinitely, cultivate and foster a never-ending series of intellectual doubts and difficulties, because belief inevitably weds thought to action, commits the believer to the risk of love, and forms in him, as the flower is formed in the bud, a pattern of irrevocable decisions for the future.

Pierre Janet writes:

"We have within us special forms of activity whose precise purpose it is to constitute new tendencies competent to function in the future. Thus the realistic tendencies which comprise will and belief, organise tendencies to action. To take a decision is to organise a particular grouping of actions and words, to organise it so strongly that it becomes capable of functioning regularly for years to come.

"To believe something is nothing else than to form the decision that we shall act in a certain way when certain circumstances arise."*

The real cause of frustration, of the lack of fulfilment and the failure of human beings as human beings, is the will not to suffer.

In proportion to our willingness to suffer we succeed as human beings; we fail in proportion to our will not to suffer. This, because it is the will to accept suffering which liberates the capacity to love, and on the capacity to love, and on that alone, our fulfilment as human beings depends.

This seems to suggest that the will to accept suffering, far from being a symptom of morbidity, is the primary condition of psychological life.

Even a mediocre person may come to realize that willingness to suffer, to make efforts and to overcome self-consciousness, is a *condition* for joy, so that to accept one is to accept the other; similarly, the saint's willingness to suffer includes his acceptance of joy. He in no way resembles the morbid type of pious person who tries to exclude the joys of religion from his life; on the contrary, life for the saint means welcoming both the fasting in the wilderness and the feast with the bridegroom.

There is a tiny episode in the life of St Teresa of Lisieux when she was a child, which sums up the saint's attitude, and it is shown up more vividly by being compared to a contrasting

* Pierre Janet, *Psychological Healing*. George Allen and Unwin (London).

episode in the childhood of an ego-neurotic. The latter I can vouch for, for I was the ego-neurotic. Let it come first.

Christmas parties were always a torment—above all, the moment when the gifts were distributed from the Christmas tree, for this meant being called out before all the others, made the centre of attention, and being obliged to raise one's voice and face to the hostess to thank her. In vain, on this occasion, did I hide behind the others, hoping to escape. I had fallen in love with the fairy doll on the tree and longed for it, but I had reason to think that if I had it I might be obliged to give it away to a relation who was ill. Better to forgo the joy of possession than first to go through the ordeal of shyness, and after that, the suffering of loss. When my turn came and I was asked what I would like from the tree, I said, "I don't want anything."

St Teresa of Lisieux was also brought, when she was a small girl, to choose one from a display of presents. How differently she answered! "I choose everything," she said.

How well this illustrates the difference between the ego-neurotic and the saint. The ego-neurotic really means, "I want only what I can have without suffering"; but the saint means, "I will accept everything, the suffering that is inseparable from the joy, and the joy that is the crown of suffering."

The picture of those in whom the capacity for love is feeble is a depressing one, but there is the tremendous comfort that though it may be so feeble as to seem dead, the capacity for love is not really dead in any living human being, for every human being is made in the image of God, who *is* love.

The complaints of discouraged people are never heard on the tongues of the saints; not one of them has ever exclaimed that life had cheated or frustrated him, however much it may have seemed that it had to the onlooker. Circumstances do not frustrate saints. The universal circumstance of guilt does not frustrate them. Different though they have been in every external detail, there is no saint in Heaven who did not fulfil his human nature on earth.

That which countless millions of unhappy, frustrated people long to achieve and cannot, every saint has achieved, and for every broken human failure, there is a saint like enough to himself to show him his own way to glory.

XII

ACCEPTANCE

*Love has more than one element in common with religious con-
viction; it demands an unconditioned attitude and it expects complete surrender. Only that believer who yields himself wholly to
his god partakes in the manifestation of divine grace. Similarly,
love reveals its highest mysteries and wonder only to him who is
capable of unconditioned surrender and loyalty of feeling. Because
this is so hard, few indeed of mortal men can boast of achieving it.
But just because the most devoted and truest love is also the most
beautiful, let no man seek that which could make love easy.*

C. G. JUNG, "Love Problem of the Student"

Asaint is one who is continually and always aware of
the being of God, even when his awareness consists in
a sense of having lost or been abandoned by him. It
is this objective love of God and this continual awareness of his
being which makes the saint's attitude to guilt different from
that of all other men, and which makes his realization of it an
incomparably greater suffering to him than it is to any other.

This suffering as it is experienced by a saint is unimaginable to
those who know it only as the misery of scrupulosity, the obsession of wounded vanity, or the slow festering of remorse. Yet it
is only the saint who accepts the realization and responsibility
of guilt and is not broken by it.

He makes no attempt to escape. He *wishes* to participate in the
world's sorrow; not only in those exquisite refinements of suffering which may be peculiar to sanctity, but in the common
suffering of all mankind: in the whole world's fear and labour
and pain: because knowing himself to be a sinner, he acknowledges his personal responsibility for the suffering of mankind.
He knows that every sin of his adds to the total of human
misery. He knows that every man owes his tears for *his own* sins
to every other man. He acknowledges his debt, which must be

paid in the coin of suffering. The rest of men refuse to acknowledge *a debt* at all.

On the purely natural level, there is a type of man (one not far from megalomania) who is prolific in generosity, who is never more exalted than when he is providing sparkling entertainment and lavish hospitality, who grudges nothing that he spends on buying alleluias for himself, but who at the same time ignores his obligations, and leaves those people to whom he owes money, or for whom he is responsible, to be in want.

Such a man has his counterpart in those pseudo-saints who, though spiritual by temperament, have not taken one step on the stony road of sanctity with their shoes off. It is because a genuine saint among them all unwittingly reminds these people of their *debt*, that they hate and persecute him. They are willing to bear suffering which seems to come straight from God's hand, and they are willing to bear that which they inflict upon themselves as a means of escape from consciousness of personal guilt, and a prop to their complacency. But they will not confess themselves to be as other men, sinners, and therefore will not humble themselves to accept suffering at the hands of other human beings. They are willing to suffer in condescension but not in participation.

The saint's attitude is in complete contrast. When he suffers at the hands of his fellow men he bears no resentment; indeed he considers, if he analyses the situation at all, that he is receiving an alms from them with which to pay his debt to mankind for his own sins. He thinks it mere justice that he should suffer.

Obviously these two opposite attitudes have a profound effect on the characters of these two kinds of men.

Nothing so aggravates suffering as a sense of its injustice. Even the pin-pricks which most people accept as the fair wear and tear of life fester in those who feel it to be an affront to their egoism that they should suffer anything at all. Their resentment swells to exactly the size of their self-love, for self-pity measures self-love.

The bigger a man's self-love is, the smaller is the thing which can make him suffer. He sees slights and insults to himself in everything, not only in everything that other people do and say, but in everything that other people have and are. If they have more wealth than he has, or more talent or charm, if they have the indefinable quality which makes them popular; above all if, without having any of the things which might attract others through self-interest, they have something in themselves which makes them loved, the egoist who lacks these qualities becomes infected by envy.

Envy is literally a poison, not for the mind only, but for the body too. We are not merely using a figure of speech when we speak of evil passions making bad blood. They do. A great deal of neurosis is accelerated by physical fatigue, resulting from blood poisoned by envy.

The man who is warped by ideas of injustice and persecution is profoundly irritated by sanctity. Above all, he is irritated by the saint's attitude to suffering. In him, he sees a man who is not humiliated by contempt, who is not degraded by poverty, and who even rejoices in suffering. Worst of all, he rejoices not in spite of, but *because* of his personal suffering.

The selfish man, who cannot even be resigned to the ordinary adverse circumstances of life, cannot hide from himself or others the humiliating fact that he is a failure as a human being, unless he can rationalize his own nerveless inability to wrest some good from adversity. Consequently the saint is a complete denial of everything that could save his face. To the egoist sick with self-love and self-pity, the irrepressible joy of a saint in the midst of suffering seems to be an irresponsible burst of laughter at his own expense.

When the sources of a neurosis are exposed, the sum total of them will often seem to be so petty that it is difficult to believe that such trivialities could have twisted a human life into the grotesque shape they have. Childish jealousies, superficial criticisms, thoughtless, unintended snubs, trifling humiliations will suppurate in the darkness of the subconscious until they grow into running sores of self-pity, which poison the whole personality.

It will be explained that these trifles are not in themselves the cause of the disaster, which cause rather lies in their effect on emotion, appetites, instincts, needs, already in conflict. So differently do the saints react to the same things, however, that we are compelled to look for some other explanation. All the more

BENEDICT JOSEPH LABRE

so, because the saints have the same emotions, appetites and drives that other people have, the same universal inheritance, the same burden of racial memories and dark and terrible impulses, the same reasons for being in conflict with themselves.

Moreover, history shows that no saint has ever been canonized who did not suffer, in an overwhelming degree, those very things which twist and warp others; yet these same things have had precisely the opposite effect on their personalities. I speak of canonized saints, because although there are many saints in Heaven who have not been canonized, and many saints on earth who will not be, they are not helpful to this enquiry because we do not know anything about them.

A canonized saint, on the other hand, can have no secrets. He has become almost cruelly the possession of all men. He has been submitted to the most thorough and gruelling examination that has ever been devised, one beside which trial by the O.G.P.U. fades into pastel shades. His actions, his words, his motives, his supernatural experience have been subjected to microscopic examination, by theologians, scientists and specialists of every kind. No Freudian psychiatrist ever brought such withering cynicism to the visions and ecstasies of the saints as the Devil's Advocate brings. No secret agents have ever competed with those who remorselessly search out every secret of the saint's life for the Vatican.

The canonized saint has been well and truly stripped of his garments, weighed and measured and sifted. He has been dissected, reconstructed, buried, dug up, shown up, and even cut up. In short, we know something about him. There is no canonized saint whose mind is not laid open before us. No case history of a psychological patient exists which tells more about his conscious and his subconscious mind, his motives, his drives and impulses, his words and his reservations, his fantasies and dreams, his thoughts, his actions and his will. And there is certainly no "case history" so free from guesswork, so little coloured by any one theory, so honestly factual and realistic, and so amply confirmed by the test of time.

Consequently, while there are many secret files hiding the dark stories of disintegrity, which are seen only by a few

G   K

specialists, there are thousands of detailed stories to be read of human integrity and of how it has been attained.

The most striking thing—and it is one of the very few things that people so diverse as the saints have in common—is the willingness to suffer. This might truly be called the basic quality of human integrity.

By a curious paradox, the willingness to suffer is the key to natural happiness and balance in a world of universal suffering and neurosis. The willingness to suffer is not the explanation of sanctity, but it is the explanation of the *sanity* of the saints. Because of it, that which contracts the selfish man's heart expands the heart of the saint. That which enslaves the selfish man sets the saint free, that which humiliates the selfish man dignifies the saint, that which embitters the selfish man sweetens the saint, that which hardens the selfish man is the source of the saint's gentleness. That which drives the selfish man in onto himself in lonely isolation is the saint's communion with all other men.

Nevertheless, the saint is not only a stumbling-block to vain and egocentric people, but to many sensitive, intelligent and unselfish people who, inspired by a generous love of humanity, see in suffering not the results of evil, but evil itself. These are compassionate people, who have been wounded by the agony of the world, and nauseated by the cruelty with which men inflict wanton, apparently useless suffering on one another. Every fibre in their being calls out for happiness for mankind here and now, and every instinct that they possess repudiates suffering and shrinks from the sanctity that seems to be a willing magnet to it.

To these people the saint's attitude to suffering, and indeed to life generally, seems neurotic, morbid, and unhealthy, sometimes even vicious. Among the more aesthetic of these critics the word "masochism" is used freely, and usually wrongly; they mean, when they say that a saint is a "masochist", that he enjoys suffering for its own sake. This word masochism is used very loosely nowadays; like so many words that are passed to and fro in discussions of psychology, it has lost its original meaning and gained others. Masochism really means deriving sexual satisfaction from having pain inflicted upon one.

The followers of Freud who maintain that *all* human experience is derived from sex, whether through the repression or expression of sex, would maintain that even when it is not apparent, the enjoyment of mental pain, which some people *do* experience, is in the true sense masochism, because the mental state is sexual too; others have come to use the word as simply meaning to enjoy suffering for suffering's sake, or for no earthly reason at all! Even those people who are really moral masochists do not enjoy suffering for its own sake, but in common with all other neurotics they choose (often unconsciously) among various sufferings, that one which may protect them from another which would be more intolerable.

This process was well and crudely illustrated by the conscious deliberate choice of a schoolboy friend who, in order to avoid the boredom of spending Christmas with an over-severe guardian whom he disliked, gave himself a stomach-ache, severe enough to prevent his travelling to the guardian's house, by taking a tremendous number of pills. I have known other boys who require no stimulant but their own wish, to develop fever on the day of return to boarding school. And I know at first hand from the doctor concerned, the amazing story of a patient of his (an insignificant, lonely little woman, in whom no one seemed interested) who, fearing when she was restored to health to lose even his professional interest, filed great raw patches on her own flesh with a wood rasp, preferring the pain of this to the feeling of being nothing to anyone.

It is characteristic of the saint's willingness to suffer that it includes no choice, he does not choose *what* he will suffer, or take one suffering to avoid another, or as an indirect means to pleasure. On the contrary, in his attitude in this, as in all else, is a tremendous surrender of self. He does not *choose* suffering at all, but he accepts it without conditions, because he surrenders himself to life and his personal destiny and makes no conditions.

The sanity of the saint begins in that tremendous *Fiat;* "Let it be unto me according to thy word"; while the insanity of selfishness begins in another *Fiat;* "Let it be unto me according to my vanity."

It is—one cannot repeat too often—possible for a neurotic to be a saint, and possible that a neurosis or a mental illness, as much as any other illness, may be the means by which someone may sanctify himself. On the other hand, sanctity and neurosis are not the same thing. No one ever became a saint *because* he was neurotic, though anyone could become a saint through the truly heroic means of sanctifying his neurosis. The difficulty here, which puzzles the outside observer, is that whilst sanctity and neurosis in themselves are two different things, the outward symptoms of both are often alike.

Nevertheless it is not surprising that many people confuse sanctity with neurosis, for superficially, and even to a certain extent on deeper levels, saints and neurotics have much in common, much that makes it difficult to distinguish one from the other with certainty. There is a reason for this that goes deeper than the obvious one, which is that in spite of the fact that every individual is uniquely himself, there are certain basic factors which all human beings have in common simply because they are human beings; but this deeper reason will be explained in a later chapter.

To begin with the most superficial thing of all, and yet an exterior thing which expresses what is hidden in a man: appearance and dress. There are saints in every grade of society, from kings and courtiers to beggars and monks, and therefore saints who are dressed in scarlet or in rags, or even in black coats and tweeds. But it is the ragged sanctity which stands out in the imagination of those who know the saints only from a distance, and therefore know only those who are outwardly most conspicuous.

Now put Benedict Joseph Labre, who is a saint, by the side of Arthur Rimbaud, who is a degenerate; they are both in rags, they are both unwashed, it might be very difficult to know at a glance which was the saint and which the sinner. More so because both are consciously in revolt against society, and choose their rags.

Or compare the depressing description of St Gemma Galgani, in her dowdy black dress and hat, which made her a joke to the Italian street urchins, with one of those morbidly shy women who dress in just such a way because they secretly dare not put their charm to the test.

We cannot spot our saint by his clothes, but neither is it

always easy to know him by his way of thought, or by what he does or says. There are many things commonly done both by neurotics and saints, things which we would regard as hysteria, or even vice, and certainly would be unwilling to tolerate in members of our own family, and in this we should seldom differ from the saints' own relations in their time. There is, for example, flagellation, self-starvation, vagabondage. It is true that the average hagiographer would give different names to these peculiarities, but those are the terms that might well be used if it were not presupposed that we were speaking of saints.

It is not always easy to distinguish between the ways of thought of saints and lunatics. I have myself been given a most edifying explanation by a lunatic of how his life was modelled on that of St Teresa of Lisieux. In "offering up" (he told me) every detail in life for the glory of God, he sanctified every "indifferent" action. Thus he had on three separate occasions been able to make even so simple and indifferent an act as the swinging of a club, holy (on three occasions he had swung it down on old ladies' heads).

Perhaps most bewildering of all are the saints' own words concerning guilt, sin and their willingness to suffer. Not only is their way of expressing themselves often repellent to those who hear them, but it is not always easy to believe that their words can even be sincere, unless we are allowed to think that the saint who utters them is unbalanced.

After years of self-conquest in the religious life, St Teresa of Avila asserts: "I realize how numerous are my imperfections and how unprofitable and how dreadfully wicked I am." And again: "I am sure that nowhere in the world has there ever been a worse person than myself."

And listen to St Catherine of Siena, to whose unflinching intellect self-knowledge seemed to be the beginning of all supernatural love: "And with a great knowledge of herself, being ashamed of her own imperfection; appearing to herself to be the cause of all the evil that was happening throughout the world, conceiving a hatred and displeasure against herself, and a feeling of holy justice, with which knowledge, hatred and justice, she purified the stains which seemed to her to cover her guilty soul, she said: 'O Eternal Father, I accuse myself before Thee, in order that Thou mayest punish me for my sins in this finite life, and, in as much as my sins are the cause of the sufferings which my neighbour must endure, I implore Thee, in Thy kindness, to punish them in my person.' "*

But we know that the young woman who is speaking is innocent. She is not a converted sinner, she has been a saint since she was a tiny child, there is no flaw in the crystal purity of her mind, she is known to the people of her little city, who are intimate with her and who idolize her, as "The Lily of Siena".

We have already considered the ego-neurotic who declares in almost identical words that she is "the greatest sinner in the world". Why should these words be symptomatic of something totally different when they are spoken by a saint? Above all, by a blameless saint! Why, if they spring from colossal vanity and self-love in the case of the egoist, should we suppose that they spring from humility and the love of God in the case of the saints?

It has already been suggested that the sufferings which ego-neurotics bring upon themselves by deliberate but unconscious choice are not accepted as those of the saints are by their willingness to suffer, but by the desire to escape from some other, and to them intolerable suffering, against which they offer a defence. But why does not the same thing apply to the saints?

It must be repeated, the saint's willingness to suffer can be distinguished from the egoist's disguised will *not* to suffer, by the different effects of suffering itself on the two kinds of people, on their personalities, and on their lives.

The three commonest results of the will *not* to suffer are these: it produces an unbalanced, sometimes even a disintegrated personality: it impoverishes life by limiting and narrowing experience; and it paralyses the capacity for love.

On the other hand, the saints' willingness to suffer results in an integrated, balanced personality; it is the doorway to a limitless variety and magnitude of experience; it liberates the capacity for love.

Sanctity is the only cure for the vast unhappiness of our universal failure as human beings.

* *A Treatise of Divine Providence.* Kegan Paul (1896).

XIII

THE CAPACITY FOR LOVE

Thy friend put in thy bosom: wear his eyes
Still in thy heart, that he may see what's there.
If cause require, thou art his sacrifice;
Thy drops of blood must pay down all his fear:
But love is lost, the way of friendship's gone,
Though David had his Jonathan, Christ his John.

GEORGE HERBERT, "The Church Porch"

THE ONE ESSENTIAL for sanctity is the capacity to love. Certainly this means, first of all, the capacity to love God. But because it is impossible to love God without loving man simultaneously, it necessarily includes the capacity to love other people.

Sanctity is a genius for love. This is why the saint never complains of not being "fulfilled". No matter what the circumstances of his life are, the saint loves to his fullest human capacity not only supernaturally, though this is what really matters, but naturally too; and it is on the degree of his capacity for objective love, and on nothing else, that the fullness of any man's life depends.

It does not depend upon circumstances or chance, on whether he is gifted or not, on whether he has a happy or a melancholy temperament, on whether he is rich or poor, married or single, on whether he has a magnificent vocation or a humdrum one, on whether he travels the world over or is restricted to the same few streets for the whole of his life, on whether he is good-looking or plain, on whether he is healthy or unhealthy; it depends upon one thing and one thing only—whether he has or has not got the capacity to love.

The one thing which all the saints have in common is the capacity to love. There are many people who think that they have almost every other characteristic *but* this in common, that they are all turned out, as it were, in one mould, and that a very inhuman one. They believe that the saints are not subject to the ordinary weakness of human nature but are free from the temptations and difficulties of temperament which assail other people. Further, they think that they are not obliged to struggle for their immunity but are born as saints, just as small children sometimes imagine that nuns are born as nuns, complete with religious habit, rosary and boots.

The saints are and have always been people of every imaginable type and character, born with every possible heredity and temperament into every possible environment and circumstance. They have been people of every class and race and colour. They have been legitimate and illegitimate children, they have been born to riches and to poverty, to honour and contempt. They have been ugly and beautiful, crippled and whole. They have belonged to every trade and profession, followed every imaginable vocation. They have been priests and monks and laymen, contemplatives, labourers, poets, artists, kings and queens and peasants, and servants. They have been doctors, soldiers, fishermen, tradesmen, husbands and wives, mothers and fathers, celibates, virgins and penitents.

Some have already been sanctified in childhood and kept their integrity, others have been sanctified and died, complete human beings, while they were still children; others have begun to be saints in their youth, others only in their maturity. Some have become saints slowly and after years of perseverance, others have become saints suddenly and after living dissolute and sinful lives; one at least became a saint only in the last moment of his life—the thief upon the Cross.

There is no type, no pattern, which predisposes to sanctity. Spiritually minded children are not more likely to become saints than wilful and mischievous ones. Simple, uncomplicated people are neither more nor less probable than introverted and complex people. Piety is as full of pitfalls as impiety.

The saints have exactly the same problems as everyone else. They have to overcome temptations, to control passions, to accept themselves. Their family relationships are as difficult as our own; there is no special privilege given to the saints, when they are striving towards sanctity, which either saves them from the results of clashing temperaments or, on the other hand, saves their long-suffering families from being bewildered and sometimes exasperated by their ways.

The only thing that distinguishes a saint from other people on earth is his capacity for love.

The personal, natural loves of the saints are the illuminated pages of history; the friendships of the saints are the epic friendships of the world. It would be a heavenly task to write a book that was only an anthology of the human loves and friendships of the saints, but that would have to be a far bigger book than this one, and here I can only speak briefly of a few of them.

Very close to most ordinary people is St Thomas More, because his home was a home built upon genuine family love. His second wife did not understand the brilliance of her husband's sanctity or of his mind, and tended to nag, but his affection and humour even overcame that, and his was a household of joyful children, of wit and laughter and happy learning. But between him and his daughter, Margaret Roper, there was a yet deeper love, the natural blossomed into the supernatural; she was the one human being who encouraged him in his long imprisonment, and who suffered most and yet rejoiced in his martyrdom.

The love between St Monica and St Augustine, who were mother and son, is known to everyone, but not everyone knows of his deep *love*, as distinct from the sinful lust which he had also had, for his mistress with whom he lived for many years faithfully and who was the mother of his son. Augustine was a passionate and a sensual man to whom, until he received extraordinary grace to overcome his lust, a woman was an absolute necessity. But she was not simply "a woman" to him, as a mistress often is to men of his type. The pain manifest in his own description of their separation, brought about (bafflingly, to me) by St Monica, who planned a marriage for her son, tells its own story of genuine love accompanying but transcending the passion that enslaved him.

"Meanwhile my sins were multiplied. She with whom I had lived so long was torn from my side as a hindrance to my forthcoming marriage. My heart which had held her very dear was broken and wounded and shed blood. She went back to Africa, swearing that she would never know another man, and left with me the natural son I had had of her. But I in my unhappiness could not, for all my manhood, imitate her resolve. I was unable to bear the delay of two years which must pass before I was to get the girl I had asked for in marriage. In fact it was not really marriage that I wanted—I was simply a slave to lust. So I took another woman, not of course as a wife; and thus my soul's disease was nourished and kept alive as vigorously as ever, indeed worse than ever, that it might reach the realm of matrimony in the company of its ancient habit. Nor was the wound healed that had been made by the cutting off of my former mistress. For there was first burning and bitter grief; and after that it festered, and as the pain grew duller it only grew more hopeless."*

As for his son, he is remembered over all these hundreds of years, though he died still a boy and had achieved nothing. But he is remembered as a uniquely lyrical personality, very brilliant and pure and shining, the impression given by his father in words that are lit up by love.

Lyrical too the romance, for romance it was, of the marriage of St Elizabeth of Hungary and her crusader, Louis, whom she would kiss on the mouth before all the crowds when he came home from the crusades.

Surely St Catherine of Siena was the most effective woman in history, yet it is not for that that she is so cherished in the minds of thousands of people today, but because of her friendships, romantic friendships on their side, with courtiers and poets and soldiers, and her deep affection for her devoted women friends.

St Teresa of Avila smiles warmly across the centuries in her delight in her little pocket-man, St John of the Cross, while the love between St Clare and St Francis of Assisi is both the most intensely realistic love that there has ever been between a man and a woman and sheer poetry. It could be a story told by Hans Andersen, for it is told in the shining of snow, in miraculous roses breaking upon the snow-covered trees, that Francis might gather them for Clare in midwinter, and told in water and moonlight, when God granted Francis the vision of Clare's

* *The Confessions of St Augustine*, trs. F. J. Sheed, p. 119.

lovely face, that the saint pined to look upon, shining up to him from a well of moonlit water.

We could go on for ever—the saints and their mothers, the saints and their husbands, the saints and their friends. But the saints' capacity for love, while never growing tepid in its natural expressions, reaches out beyond them, perhaps radiates from them, and we find them loving the unlovable and the repulsive.

The same man who loved the Lady Clare and gathered her roses of snow, who was a troubadour and fastidious, took a leper into his arms and kissed him. And that is typical of all the others. Wherever human misery is, the love of the saints finds it. St Vincent de Paul was driven by love to fight the rats on the dust heaps of Paris to rescue and save the illegitimate babies flung there by their mothers; St John Bosco gathered the delinquents around him and gave them his home—we can go on for ever in this strain.

From the love of the saints all the mercy and healing in the temporal world has sprung—hospitals, orphanages, shelter for old people, help for the wounded in battle. From their love all mercy has come, and from it too the spiritual healing of mankind. It is the saints who find and enlighten the ignorant, who teach the poor and the ragged children as well as clothing them, who go out from their own homes to find and teach the heathens and savages and to save them from the satanic cruelty that is mixed with their religious practices. It is the saints who penetrate secretly into Soviet countries, and for the sake of shriving an old peasant or catechising a little child, die gladly.

We may well ask what, in a practical sense, gives the saints this unlimited capacity for love, this capacity for love which is uniquely theirs in that it does not exclude anyone at all. For the saints love sinners as much as they love saints, they love both the rich and the poor, and their friends and their enemies.

There is *one* exclusion from their love, which explains something of their huge gift, namely self. In a saint there is no self-love as that word is ordinarily used. It is self-love which has given a false ring to the beautiful word charity, a false sound and a false meaning for modern ears, for the characteristics of self-love are its sharp limits and its strong instinct for self-protection.

The lover of self does indeed appear to love those who love him, and those who he would say belong to him; he loves those who help him to keep his self-esteem, who give him a sense of security or who minister in some way to his pleasure, but every one of these affections is subjective. He sees no one, knows no one, as a distinct human being, separate from himself, with his own life to live, his own work to do, his own soul to make, his secret self. No, everyone is known to the self-lover only in relation to himself, only through his relationship to self: "*My* husband (or wife), *my* child, *my* mother, *my* friend"—and so on.

The self-lover further limits the radiation of his love by self-protection. It is impossible to love self and not live in fear; everything is a threat to self—disease, poverty, death. Even in those subjective loves that he admits, there lurks the threat of suffering or loss; he may be bereaved, demands may be made on him of a nature that will threaten his own well-being. He may be asked to give, he may be asked to serve, he may be asked to forgive; he may be asked for sympathy.

All those things may deprive himself or bring him suffering which he need not have had. If he gives too much, he may find he is in want of something. Service may tire him or, if it is to the sick, contaminate him; forgiveness may force him to see something through the eyes of another and disturb his complacency; and sympathy is the worst of all, as this means sharing in another's sorrow, a real self-giving. Anything else can be given without involving self, but sympathy *is* giving self to suffer someone else's suffering.

The person who really loves self exclusively almost invariably suffers from an unresolved guilt conflict, guilt which he has never faced squarely, never admitted to himself, done nothing at all to expiate; and consequently guilt seeps into all his emotions and poisons them. Even those subjective loves that he allows himself are likely to prove distressing both to himself and the subjects, because the threat of suffering or the demand they make will bring an element of dislike into them. The mere fact that his happiness has become, to some extent, dependent on another, who may bring suffering to him through something beyond the control of either (such as death), or who makes him feel that since he is no longer heartfree he has lost something of his emotional independence, can turn his affection to resentment and dislike.

The complete lover of self will in extreme cases develop hatred for anyone to whom he has a natural obligation, such as parents, husband or wife, or even his own children, and because such hatred makes him feel guilty he will abandon them, or neglect them in order not to be reminded by their presence of the duty which, because it makes a demand on him and limits his freedom, he repudiates and detests.

Fear above all will be aggravated by self-love, so that the very existence of suffering, illness and poverty will become hateful to him, not because it is the outward showing of universal guilt, not because he has compassion for others, but because it is a personal threat and a depressing reminder of the things he wishes to forget, particularly his own responsibility to a race whose common guilt he shares.

For these reasons, this word charity rings so false, and self-lovers at the same time are often said to be very charitable, because they are only too willing to give, from a distance, to institutions, in order to do what they can to have sickness and misery of all kinds kept under control, kept out of sight, and as far as possible decontaminated. Their unexamined motive is not to heal suffering, but to disinfect it.

Now in contrasting the attitude of the saint, something can be discovered about his capacity for love. The saint's love is objective, he does see others as themselves, and he sees them as equally important as himself, or more so. But he too has a certain kind of subjectivity in his love for them, for he sees one thing about them which he realizes as part of himself. He sees his own guilt as a contributory cause of the suffering of the race and so cannot see any man's suffering as no affair of his. This is one reason why he cannot see suffering and not be driven to help to alleviate it, why he must give to the poor without counting what he gives, and must tend the sick with his own hands, and why he cannot see pain or grief on the face of a little child and not make that little child his own, for whom his own interests, and if needs be his own life, must be given up. He has in himself Christ's heart to love with, he loves with his love, it is Christ in him who loves.

But also it is Christ that he loves in them. Man's soul is created by God in his own image and likeness. But within the Godhead, the Son is the image and likeness of the Father, so that man's soul is created by God in the pattern of his Son. Not only that; God the Son became man, not merely a human soul, but wholly man. Because he is the perfection of manhood, the manhood of all men can but be modelled upon his, so that his image is woven into our very being as men. Our destiny is to preserve that image and to develop it into the closest possible resemblance to Christ. In that sense, Christhood is man's destiny. We may by sin distort the image, but not out of all recognition. God, looking at the worst of men, can see in them what image it is that they have distorted. So can the saints. Saints cannot see men primarily as sinners; in sinful men they see Christ on the cross. And they cannot see men as derelicts, useless, having no worth if they do not and cannot give something to the state or community; they can only see them as Christ, down on his face in the dust under the weight of the cross, needing another man to help him carry it.

"I was thirsty and you gave me not to drink ..." When we refuse drink to the thirsty, we are not consciously refusing it to Christ; we do not see Christ in them. The saint does. The saint's love is a cradle and warmth for the infant Christ in every needy infant, haven and peace for the child Christ in flight in the refugee children, the orphaned and lost. It is food and drink for the hunger and thirst of Christ in the destitute; a cloak for the naked Christ in the shamed and exposed; silence for Christ derided and mocked in the persecuted; myhrr poured over the dead Christ in the reprobate and the lost.

It is the vision of Christ in man that enables the saint to do what the lover of self can never do—devote himself to those whose suffering he cannot relieve. Even love in these materialist days is utility for the self-lover. If he can derive the immense satisfaction of seeing results, it repays him for his efforts, and he will go on, but where there are no results, he soon finds he cannot go on, for he has nothing to give. For those whose suffering is incurable, the only thing anyone can give is compassion—the self-giving which is entering into communion with another by sharing his passion.

This applies to so many forms of suffering in the world today —there are so many survivors of the worst horrors of our wars who cannot be comforted, and so many sick who cannot be cured, so many unstable who cannot be changed—and most of all, so many whose suffering is in their mind, and so cannot often be even alleviated. In all these the saint sees Christ. He sees Christ in Gethsemane, the Christ who asked in vain, not for his friends to take his suffering from him (that they could not do), but that they would watch with him, simply be there with him and give him themselves in compassion.

The fact that the saints do relieve such suffering as can be relieved, that they clothe and nurse and feed and illuminate and shelter, is incidental; it is the overflowing of love, and its inclusiveness and dauntless quality is that they go to suffering people because in these people they see Christ and must be with him. When they cannot relieve a man's suffering they must suffer it with him. That is illogical, it is foolish, it is improvident, it is fanatical—precisely—but that is love.

Knowing the weakness of human nature, it seems surprising that even the saints are able to sustain such love for the *suffering* Christ, and to pursue him in his suffering and dwell on it so continually; and this is all the more so in view of the fact that his suffering in men is, after all, a continual reproach to them, and that reproach felt, one presumes, as acutely as their sorrow for sin—which, as we know, far surpasses that of other people.

For the saint realizes, with the sharp realization of the lover, that it is sin that crucified Christ, and that all this suffering that continues in the members of Christ is the crucifixion going on in man. He cannot live in the world without seeing the crucifix wherever he looks, and he cannot see the crucifix, the living man, and not be pierced with the thought that it is he who crucified Christ.

This is why in contrast to the lover of self, who seeks only the company of those who help him to forget his debt to mankind for his own sins—the prosperous, the outwardly attractive, the healthy—the saint is constrained to seek those who are disfigured by the suffering that guilt has brought into the world and who bleed with Christ's wounds. It is the comfort of the saints to comfort Christ in man. It is precisely because of the character of a saint's sorrow for sin that his love for the suffering Christ is strong and lasting.

As we have seen again and again, subjective sorrow for sin, the sorrow of self-love, turns a man's eyes away from God, but the saint loves God objectively, with Christ's love, and his sorrow is not because of a wound inflicted on himself, but because of a wound inflicted on Christ. He does not turn in to himself to apply healing balm, but he turns to Christ and pours out his sorrow on *his* wounds. And instead of being dragged down and devitalized by the aching misery of his own sin-consciousness, the saint is lifted up into self-forgetting by the knowledge of Christ's joy in receiving his sorrow and the saving of his soul, as his own crown.

This love and joy of Christ on the cross it is that Blessed Julian of Norwich had seen in a vision, when she said: "This that I say is so great bliss to Jesu, that he setteth at naught his travail, and his passion, and his cruel and shameful death. And in these words '*If I might suffer more I would suffer more*' I saw truly that as often as he might die, so often he would, and love should never let him have rest till he had done it. ... He said not if it were needful to suffer more; but '*If I might suffer more*'. For though it were not needful and he might suffer more, he would. This deed and this work about our salvation, was ordained as well as God might ordain it; it was done as worshipfully as Christ might do it; and herein I saw a full bliss in Christ; for his bliss should not have been full, if it might any better have been done than it was done."*

It is this joy of Christ's love, *his* endless bliss in his Passion for love, that enlivens the saint and expands his own heart with great increase of love for him, and enables him to love him in suffering men, insatiably and even joyfully. Such love is without end, and is an ever increasing desire; the saint does not ask to be satisfied, he knows that love is illimitable desire, and says, not in sadness, but in the bliss of divine love, with Christ, "If I might suffer more I would suffer more."

* Blessed Julian of Norwich, *Revelations of Divine Love*. Kegan Paul (London).

PART THREE

INTEGRITY

XIV

CHILD, MAN, SOUL

It was not you that chose me, it was I that chose you (John 15.16).

MODERN MAN is obsessed by himself, and the obsession is an unhappy one, for it is really an obsession with his personal failure as a human being. He is acutely aware of his want of integrity. He longs to realize himself as a complete human being, but he does not know how to achieve this. Not unnaturally he is bewildered by the multiplicity of theories that are continually increasing about him—theories which contradict each other, and which impress him chiefly by their obscurity.

Psychiatrists, particularly amateur psychiatrists, have started to build a tower of Babel, and again the would-be builders are divided and frustrated by the confusion of tongues. The psychological jargon that has become part of colloquial speech has taken on so many different meanings, that for the majority it no longer means anything at all. The ordinary man has ceased to know what he is, or *why* he is. He has even ceased to know what man is; he may be a kind of monkey or he may be a kind of god, or he may be merely a wild confusion of tortured psychological processes.

He thinks that his bewilderment is caused by lack of knowledge about himself, but here man is wrong; the real source of his bewilderment is lack of knowledge about God.

It is true that in order to achieve an integrated personality man must have some true knowledge of himself, but he cannot get this knowledge by introspection, or self-analysis. Indeed the more an individual concentrates on himself, gazes into himself, the less does he know himself as he is. The only way in which any man can learn to know himself sufficiently to begin to achieve integrity is through coming to know God. It is only through his response to God that a man can begin to know what he is and why he is, and how to become whole, and only when he *has* become whole can any man fulfil his destiny as a human being.

Man is God's image. He is made in the likeness of God. There are three Persons in God, and if it would be fanciful to say that there are three persons in man, at least man may profitably be considered under three aspects. They are the child, the man, the soul. As I say, I do not mean that there *are* three distinct persons in man, but I do mean something more than a woman does when she says of a man that he is a "child at heart".

A child in years is of course a complete human being; he has his soul, the same soul that he will have as a man, if he grows to manhood. He is able to fulfil his human destiny of Christhood as a child, as child saints have done. It is a mistake to think of a child only as a potential adult, as many people do. This is an attitude which, if the child becomes conscious of it, may even frustrate the full flowering of real childhood, which must develop if his childhood is to attain its own perfection.

If he grows to manhood, the child that will persist in him is likely to keep the characteristics of his actual childhood. If he was never, spiritually, a child at all, he will have a hard way to get back to that real state that is essential for possession of the Kingdom of Heaven.

By saying there are these three elements in man, I mean that he remains the child of God when he is a man, and he has the character, the instincts and the needs of a child all through his life. He has, at the same time, the character and maturity and powers of a grown man, the potential or actual lover, husband, worker and father. And he has an immortal soul, with its own imperious needs.

The harmony of these three is the secret of man's integrity. Each of them must come to its own fulness of being; the child to the full flower of childhood; the man to the maturity of manhood; the soul must radiate the Spirit of God.

The child in man exists because there is a father in God, because God is a father. Man's childhood is the answer to God's fatherhood; it is the father's love in God that is the cause of the child's being in man. The child in man grows to the loveliness of complete childhood, just in so far as it responds to the father in God.

The man—that is, the adult—in every human being becomes mature only in the measure in which he lives in God the Son, and because God the Son became man, and is the very incarnation of love, the mature man is essentially a lover; man's maturity is love.

Neither the child in man nor the lover could live, as they do live, with God's life, were it not that the Holy Spirit, who is, in himself, the sign of unutterable love between the Father and the Son, breathes life into the dust to be the soul of man; only in the response of man's soul to the Holy Spirit in God can his childhood flower, his manhood bear fruit, his soul illuminate his personality.

Not one of the three elements in man is there by chance; they are dependent upon each other, and as we have said, on their harmony with one another man's integrity depends. The reason for this is perfectly simple; the oneness of these three restores man to his likeness to God, and that and that alone is man's wholeness.

The neglect of one of the three persons in man, or the repression or inhibiting of one of them, or the overdevelopment of one at the expense of the others, is the most usual cause of the unbalanced, lopsided personality which is the characteristic of our generation, as it must necessarily be of any generation that does not know God.

Equally certain is it that a generation that turns away from God will be a discouraged generation, and that we most certainly are. It is because modern man has an essentially discouraged personality that he tends to turn away from the idea of God, and to seek refuge from the effort involved in restoring the divine image in himself, by accepting, and even wallowing in, the squalor of his own unhappiness.

Discouraged as man is, he accepts his sense of human failure, because he believes that any effort to restore God's image in himself would inevitably lead to greater failure and greater humiliation. This is one of the legion of evils resulting from seeking self-knowledge by introspection—in looking at self, instead of looking away from self to God; trying to know self not only through self-analysis but even through the most distorting mirror there is, self-pity, instead of trying to know self through knowing God.

An infant knows its littleness through the largeness of its mother's lap, its dependence through the strong circle of its mother's arms. The fulfilment of its needs teaches it what it needs, its insecurity becomes its confidence.

In what we lack we come to know God's love.

When I say that in order to know ourselves we must know God, I do not, of course, mean that we could ever know God wholly through our intellect. We can know a little, a very little indeed, *about* God through it, but that is all. Heaven forbid that in saying this I should be thought to mean that we ought not to use our intellect to find God—too many people do think that; they even seem to think that we should not use our intellect at all upon God. The opposite is true; we ought to train and instruct our mind and consecrate it to God, but this is not the essential means to psychological integrity. That is come to not only by thought, but by *living* in God consciously.

The Blessed Trinity is illimitable mystery, but just because we are made in the image of the Trinity, we can know God a little through love, *not our love for him, but his love for us.* Through all that we lack, we can know something of what God gives, through all that we are *not* we can know something of what God *is*, and the most and surest that we can know about ourselves is that we are that which God wills, *we are that which God loves.* It is in this knowledge that there exists just that kernel of reassurance that is so desperately needed by the hesitating and faltering human beings that we are.

It is not by an impersonal study of theology that we come to this kind of knowledge of God, but by responding to his will to love us, by *not resisting his love.*

Although God lacks nothing and cannot need us, it is his will and his choice to *want* us, to want us to be the answer to his love. He who needs nothing, wills to have us to be the objects of his love, the creation of his love. God created us to want us, God created us to love us.

Once we realize this, it must become obvious that we have no need to be ashamed of our feeling of personal insufficiency, or to be surprised by the pattern of our neurosis, with its apparently insane egoism and unreasonable demands, or of our torturing sense of helplessness and nothingness, or of our seemingly inordinate and insatiable longing to be loved. Naturally, when these demands are directed to other human creatures instead of to God they cannot be met, and must become grotesque and ludicrous, but in themselves they are right and reasonable.

Man is constantly haunted by the fear that if he is not loved, he will cease to be; this is not a delusion, it is the truth. If he were not loved, he would cease to be; he exists only because God wills him to be, and keeps him in being, that he may be the object of his own creative love.

We should rejoice in our lack, in our nothingness, and in our excessive desire to be loved, because it is God's delight to love us, and to love us immeasurably and with the illimitable tenderness that our violent littleness craves.

The *child* in us exists and feels the clamorous needs of a little child, because it is God's nature to create, to make new, to sustain, to feed and to clothe, to see himself and to love himself in a little one. For his own delight he creates this child in us. He *wants* to clothe and to feed, and moreover to clothe his children extravagantly, to dress them more beautifully than he dresses the wild flowers: to feed them on living bread, grown from the seed that has been buried and has received the light of the sun in darkness, that has been gathered and bound in the splendour of the ripe ear of wheat, and threshed and purified in the fire; to feed them on his own life. God did not create woman, whose joy it is to feed her child at her breast, by chance; she is the expression of his own love that wills to feed his little children on himself.

It is not a matter for shame or fear to the mature *man* that he cannot contain the sweetness of his own life, that rises in him like the sap in the trees; that he is aware of the spring and the summer within himself, of the very shape of the bud and the leaf pushing towards the light. He must give life, and the glory of life is within him to give, only because God is the giver of life, and Christ the Son of Man, whose image he is, came to give life abundantly on the earth. Man is a lover because God wills to give life through man, and love is the giving of life.

Most mysterious of all is man's *soul;* it is not man who first desires all that he has through the possession of his own soul— that his life shall be a thing of beauty, that from it Heaven shall be radiated on earth, that his love shall be creative, that he shall have the faculty to know God and the possession of immortality. None of this or the desire of it starts in man; it is again simply that which *God wants.* The Infinite Spirit of Divine Love desires to descend into the dust, to breathe life into it, the life of God; *desires* to abide in man and to *be* his life, so that God may look upon himself eternally in this creature of dust whom he has made out of nothing to be the object of his utter love.

If you will think back to the first section of this book where we paused with man in his saddest condition, grotesque with sin, isolated by his own egoism, sometimes alone in society, sometimes in prisons and lunatic asylums, sometimes on the scaffold, and often trying to escape from God by making a god of himself, you will see now why I said in every man, even the derelict, the outcast who has cast himself out, there is a homing toad.

So absolutely essential to man's very being is the pattern in which God has made him, that when he has distorted that pattern by sin, even his abnormality, his neurosis and his madness struggle to get back to it; what appears as the most terrible contortion is the writhing and twisting of this mis-shapen thing trying to get back into its proper shape. Deny it as he will, frustrate it as far as he and Satan together can, there is deep down in man a craving to be that which God wants him to be.

When a man fastens this craving on to some other being, either because he does not know God, or because he does not know that only God, who created his need, can fill it, the result is neurosis.

It must be remembered here that many self-consciously "spiritual" people do not know God, because their spirituality tends to continual self-examination, which like all self-obsession blinds one to God. I am speaking not of theoretical knowledge of God, but of the direct knowledge which comes by living experience.

When a man fastens this craving on to *himself*, it results in grotesque and horrible shapes, leading sometimes to crime and sometimes to madness. In spite of these tragic facts, the nature of man's craving, which is stripped naked in neurosis and insanity, points straight to the basic realities of human nature, and to the secret of its healing.

What is it that the neurotic invariably demands? It is to be loved inordinately, to be the absorbing and exclusive object of someone's love, to be loved unreasonably and in fact illimitably, and for himself alone! Again, he asks to be treated like an irresponsible child, one to whom everything is given and from whom nothing is asked in return. And the most striking and frequent characteristic of criminals and of lunatics? Surely, personal aggrandizement.

It is only because his desires are not centred upon God that they wreck a man, for what the neurotic asks is exactly what man was created for; to be loved illimitably, to be loved not for any particular quality or act of his own, but because God made him only that he might love him with infinite, inexhaustible love. The only meaning and purpose of his existence *is* to be loved. The neurotic is broken, but he is broken on the rock of truth, for he is in fact infinitely loved. If he were not, he would cease to be.

Again, man *is*, and is meant to be, a child, to whom everything is given, and that certainly without return, for man *has* nothing and *is* nothing, excepting that which the Father gives him and makes him.

As to aggrandizement, the poor lunatic who thinks that he is God comes far closer to realizing what he is made for than the mediocre person who is resigned to snivel his way through life, preferring to be a poor fellow rather than make the effort or take the risk involved in being anything else!

Man was and *is* created to be like God. Satan, who sometimes persuades criminal men that they are like God because of their crimes, or through their own power, or who deludes the lunatic into thinking that he is God by virtue of his own nature, has not changed his technique of temptation in the least since he put this idea into Eve's mind in Eden, that by disobeying God, she would make herself equal to him—"and the woman said unto

the serpent, We may eat of the fruit of the trees of the garden:
but of the fruit of the tree which is in the midst of the garden,
God hath said, ye shall not eat of it, neither shall ye touch it lest
ye die. And the serpent said unto the woman, Ye shall not surely
die. For God knoweth that in the day ye eat thereof, then your
eyes shall be opened, and ye shall be as gods, knowing good and
evil" (Gen. 3.2-5).

Satan is, as he always was, subtle enough to work on a desire
which *must* be in man, and at first it is surprising that it should
have been a sin for Eve to want to be like God, since God made
her to be so.

The answer is this: when man thinks that he can *make himself*
like God, that it is in his power to make himself like God, he is
mad.

When a man tries to become like God by going against God's
will, he is bad.

When he surrenders to God's will, then he *is* like God,
because God wills him to be so.

But that is a great understatement; man is more than *like*
God; through his union with Christ he really does live in God's
life, he is in fact one with God. The difference between the Son
of God and Christ in man is that Christ is the Son of God and is
God by his own nature, but man is lifted up into the life of God,
to share in it, by a free act of God's love, which makes him one
with Christ.

The pathos of the madman's and the criminal's passion for
aggrandizement can only be understood when we understand
that man's true destiny is to be a Christ, and therefore that his
glory is not only not inconsistent with humility on earth, but is
crowned by it.

The beginning of integrity is not effort, but surrender; it is
simply the opening of the heart to receive that for which the
heart is longing. The healing of mankind begins whenever any
man ceases to resist the love of God.

XV

THE CHILD IN MAN

Like a child who has wandered into a forest
Playing with an imaginary playmate
And suddenly discovers he is only a child
Lost in a forest, wanting to go home.

T. S. ELIOT, *The Cocktail Party*

W E ARE all familiar with the child in man, the child who never leaves the adult. We are quick to see it in others and to rebuke it in them, and we are inclined to repudiate it in ourselves, to be ashamed of it and to do what we can to keep it out of sight, and not only out of other people's sight but our own. We try to banish the child in us from our consciousness, to send him away where he will not be seen or heard, much as many parents of the Victorian days banished their children to the nurseries of their great sad houses.

There are, however, a minority of people who indulge the child in them, at the expense both of their maturity and their soul, and are determined that he or she shall be recognized and pandered to by others. Who does not know one of those women who resort to infantile behaviour and mouth out baby-prattle when trying to extort money for their extravagances from their men? or those who use their own babyish character to avoid the responsibilities of womanhood and actually demand of their husbands, whom they condemn to childless and comfortless marriages, that they should treat them as helpless little children —and even play with dolls and stuffed animals with them? But this woman has her counterpart in the man in whom the child is so predominant that he is quite unable to fall in love and marry so long as his mother lives. His whole emotional life is knotted up in his relationship with her, and he is quite unable to face the adult responsibility of supporting a family. He may, however, marry when his mother dies, if he can find a woman content merely to take her place and to have no child but her husband.

It is the child, who, of the three elements in man, is least understood, who meets with the most inconsistent treatment, and not unnaturally becomes troublesome; sometimes not merely troublesome but terrible. This poor child in man has almost universally become a nasty child, and what is there on earth *more* nasty than a nasty child?

The child in the adult, just like the child in years, is largely the victim of circumstances. His character has usually been formed when he really was, physically, a child. There are a great many children in years, unhappily, whose essential qualities of childhood are twisted, or even destroyed, long before they grow to manhood or even to adolescence: children who are not children.

The first step towards adult integrity is to restore the child in man to the primal loveliness of essential childhood.

Perhaps the most decisive fact about the character of any individual child is his attitude to life and to other people. But in most cases, his attitude to life and to other people has been largely imposed on him, long before he was able to defend himself.

Keeping in mind the fact that what the child becomes in the nursery years is what he is likely to remain in the world (unless he deliberately sets about restoring his own childhood), we can learn much about the grown man from a study of the effects of the various kinds of emotional education meted out to little children. For it is certain that attitudes are caused mainly by feeling, and hardly at all by thinking. By "attitude" I mean the approach to other people and to life; it may be one of trust or cynicism, affection or hostility, gentleness or aggression, confidence or fear. There are three kinds of children resulting from wrong emotional education: the humiliated child, the cynical child, the negative child.

Obviously, from such a generalization there are countless variations—no two individuals are quite alike, and cut-and-dried definitions about human beings must always be faulty, but they will serve to start a train of thought. Of course, there are many people in whom attitudes to life are mixed, and are so partly because of inherent differences in the individuals, partly because of conflicting elements in the education; for example, a spoiling mother and a bullying father, or a doting father and a nagging mother—or a mixed marriage, parents with different, perhaps opposite convictions. We have only to think of any individual we know and to ask ourselves which type of child abides in him, to discover that in most cases we shall find that there are characteristics of more than one of them. Since human nature and human circumstances are inexhaustibly involved and complicated, this could be taken for granted.

Spoiling makes a child helpless. The child who is waited on hand and foot, literally spoon-fed for too long, whose every wish is granted without any effort being required on his part, and from whom, moreover, even the idea of suffering is hidden in so far as it can be, and the reality of evil and sin and their consequences buried under a flowery mound of pretty, wishful thinking, is quite obviously condemned to become helpless and incapable of loving. He is dependent on other people, he is unable to make the efforts of will necessary to become independent or to achieve happiness for himself. Inevitably, he must grow into a humiliated human being.

From wanting simple bodily necessities and pleasures, this child will soon grow to want abstract necessities; he will want the love of grown-up people, not because he appreciates what love is, but because it is the only guarantee of his security; unless someone is wholly concentrated on him, his needs and wishes may not be seen and immediately gratified. For this reason he will see all other people, children and adults, as dangers to himself, competitors for the love which is his surety. He will resort to a number of transparent devices to keep his mother's attention strained upon him, and very soon he will discover that his strong suit is to keep her in constant anxiety— what power this gives him! He starts his tyranny by refusing to eat, he continues by refusing to sleep. He is liable to have inexplicable screaming attacks, resulting in something that looks very much like a fit, in which he will become rigid. This not only adds to his mother's certainty of his delicacy and oversensitivity, but has the secondary desired effect of driving away less vulnerable nurses or servants, unless they too are spoilers.

He is adept, too, at causing grown-ups to quarrel, even his

father and mother, and will manage to break up any conversation between them which is not about himself. Thus again and again a little child will be as good as gold when alone with father or mother or nurse, but a fiend incarnate when they are three together.

I have known a boy of ten who was able to put his own knee out of joint, and invariably did so, if his mother accompanied him and his adoring father for their Sunday walk; and a much younger child who choked, with great success, at every meal attended by her really devoted stepfather!

As for tears—what a power they are, and who has not known the grown woman who rules her perpetually distressed household by the tyranny of tears!

The spoilt child does not usually stop at tricks (and of course these tricks very soon become unconsciously motivated, so spontaneous that he no longer knows he is playing tricks); he frequently goes on to aggression, and it is always, and necessarily, the spoiler who is the victim of his hostility.

To understand why I say *necessarily*, it requires only to look at the whole process of spoiling. The child is made helpless, he is obsessed by fears of not being able to get what he needs, of being unable to forgo, to restrain, or to satisfy a wish by his own efforts; of not being loved to the exclusion of competitors, and of being deeply if blindly aware that he is unable to win or keep love himself by legitimate means. He becomes, as he must, humiliated, and the humiliation rankles and festers in him, turning to aggression against the one who has caused it.

Unhappily it does not end there, for everyone whose love he wants in adult life will be identified with his mother, or whoever it is who spoiled him, and aggression, varying from childish sulkiness to real cruelty, is always ready to overwhelm him, and to enter into and probably break down all his human relationships.

His victim will be whoever loves him, because the fact that people do love him gives him the power to hurt them; in this way they are weaker than he is, and he can forget his humiliation by exerting the only power he has. In the nursery the humiliated child is likely to pull the wings off flies; in the world those who love him will take the place of the flies: those who do not love him, of course, would not tolerate his exactions for an instant.

I do not think this indicates any disproportionate urge for power in human nature, but only a natural wish to be independent and to be able to use the will normally. People who have not been frustrated seldom become violent or insanely ambitious; it is the humiliated who lose all sense of proportion, seek out the defenceless and weak and abuse the power they have over them.

When he lives on in the adult, the spoilt child will usually exert his power in the old way, by causing anxiety, by making excessive demands; he will use his weakness as a weapon, domineer by illness, by helplessness, and hurt others by coldness, ingratitude, and outbursts of frightened and wounding jealousy.

Crushing by over-severity also produces a humiliated, because helpless, child. The child who is made to fear those whom he should be able to love, whose every act, even every thought, is to be motivated by his parents' relentless authority, can no more develop self-respect and initiative than the spoilt one.

He will certainly have an attitude of aggression and probably resort to violence. He will secretly feel that everyone is his natural enemy, and that they are stronger than he is. Supposing everyone to be down on him, ready to deny his right to live, he will think that any open expression of his own wishes will rouse hostility. He is always on the defensive because he sees a dangerous enemy in everyone. Sometimes he will try to get his own way by cunning, sometimes by violence. In extreme and tragic cases he will simply seek for victims who are little and weak through whom he may ease his humiliation. In this there is a key to the reason why people capable of the most appalling crimes often seem excessively meek and gentle. Indeed one should beware of those who always flatter, and who cannot say "no" to an invitation or to anyone who wishes to sell them something.

In his confession, the Düsseldorf murderer, who was outwardly the gentlest of men, but roamed the darkness looking for little children to murder, stated that he had been crushed and bullied unmercifully by his father, and had begun to murder smaller children than himself at the age of nine, with feelings of exaltation.

Less terrible, but tragic enough, alcoholism is often the result of oppressing a child.

The cynical child, who becomes actually hostile to God and to all authority and order, is usually the child whose parents have betrayed him, the child of the broken home, the faithless marriage.

Instinctively a little child accepts without doubting the certainty and permanence of his home. He believes that he comes first in his parents' love, without question, and with the innocent egoism of babyhood he accepts his kingship as his right. For all practical and psychological purposes he expects of his parents all that he actually has from God; they *are* God to him. If they betray him, they destroy his innate faith, and strike at God and all that is in any way representative of God. The betrayed child will grow up with a grudge against life; his attitude will be one of mistrust. His natural enemy (as he will think) is authority. He will wish to revenge himself on God. From his ranks most delinquents come.

Do not imagine that most delinquents are those who find their way into the children's courts. There are as many or more among the so-called "privileged classes", hidden away behind the doors of the private consulting-rooms of the psychiatrists or under the wide skirts of wealthy relations. But they do not always go on enjoying such comfortable and such private hiding-places. Evil is too strong and too dark a current to be held back for long by unaided human hands. It breaks down the banks of the most self-sacrificing and protective natural love and sweeps away the pitiful attempts that men and women make to dam it up.

Go to the prisons, go to the mental hospitals; there you will find the twisted child in man, the spoilt, the frustrated, the betrayed child, the child who for a time was denied, locked up and hidden, but who has broken through the adult's defences and taken control.

You will not find the sweetness, the winning and endearing qualities, that sentimentalists associate with childhood, but on the contrary much that is cruel and aggressive and overbearing, even much that is murderous—the appalling mixture of naked evil and innocence which in the actual child is, because of his physical littleness, impotent, but in the criminal or the insane person is terrible with the ruthlessness of the child who has not yet the use of his reason or the control of his will, but has the grown man's physical strength and power to destroy.

Because original sin is not a pious fancy but a terrible fact, human nature, even before the dawn of reason, is awry. Because of it, tiny children who cannot sin *can* suffer pain and terror and grief and death; they can be crippled or misshapen. In the orthopaedic hospital they lie stretched out on splints, minute crucified Christs.

The pattern of evil can also be stamped on them psychologically, there together with the image of God, baffling everything in us but faith. A tiny child, who because he is baptized but not yet capable of sin must if he dies go straight to heaven, can nevertheless show us a map of evil.

In most insanity there is some regression—that is, a return, usually a sudden return, to some stage of the patient's early childhood. Usually the occasion of this is an intolerable situation which the adult cannot face, but which because of conflict in himself he forces himself to try to face. Thus a soldier who feels very intensely that it is wrong to kill, and equally that it is wrong not to go into battle to defend his country, will often escape the situation by what used to be called shell-shock, and usually is simply a flight backwards to the merciful irresponsibility and helplessness of childhood. There are heroes of the last two wars who are crawling on all fours, playing with toys, learning to eat with a spoon, trying, less successfully than real babies, to learn to talk.

There are countless other cases of regression even more tragic, because the sufferer is frightened, and in proportion to his fright he is violent. The child in him, who has taken control, to whom he has surrendered his whole personality, his whole will, is a frightened child, and a frightened child is an aggressive one. He wants and tries to use violent means to assert his will; because he is little and powerless he will do all that he can to force his wishes upon those who can grant them.

G   M

Witness an infant kept waiting for his feed; he will not croon softly and smile for it, he will open his mouth and scream, he will go red in the face and beat the air with his fists; he would like to beat something more vulnerable than the air. It is because he feels powerless that he uses violence, and only because he is little that his violence is powerless.

Angry little children shout out "I will kill you!", and so they might if they were able to, for they mean what they say. They have not learnt to overcome obstacles by reason or skill, they have not the least idea of the value of human life, they do not realize that, having killed you once, they will not have the satisfaction of doing it again. The fairy-stories given to the dear little child by his gentle maiden aunt really tell us what is in his own heart, for that is their real birthplace, and there they would be conceived and told and retold if they were not put into his hands. They give him ample opportunity of identifying himself with the killer, who is always the hero of the story, always the most loved character in it, and who always kills someone enormously bigger and more powerful than himself, a giant or a dragon; and mark this, the giant or the dragon usually has not one head to be cut off but several, and so can be killed several times.

In the regressed adult, frightened by the many-headed monster of civilization, or his own environment, or whatever it may be, you have the most dangerous person imaginable: the unreasoning child who stamps and screams in the nursery "I will kill you!" is not now helpless, though his feeling of helplessness is still the aggravating factor, but with a man's strength, the adult body, the heavy fist which can in fact kill.

However, in spite of the increasing neurosis and crime and insanity in our days, it is not the deeply humiliated child or the cynical child who prevails in our society, but the *negative* child.

At first sight it seems that this child, who is the child of the vast majority of colourless mediocre parents, is less tragic than the others, but I think the truth is that he is only less spectacular. The others are helped by society, even if it is only in order that society be protected from them, but the negative child will have no help at all unless he helps himself; he has no escape from a dilemma which he feels, and *is*, inadequate to face; and to a very large extent his existence in such huge numbers is a cause of the other tragic children's existence.

The negative child is the one in whom childhood remains buried, so that it never becomes a power in his life. His emotional education has been colourless, and so limited as to be almost negligible. Heaven forbid that anyone suppose that in speaking of emotional education, I am advancing the idea of parents "forming" their child's character, of "making" him as they wish him to be. This seems to me presumption. It should at least presuppose the parents themselves to be perfect and to have conceived an idea of their child which is exactly identical with God's!

Parents have very seldom formed themselves, and they are very often incapable of doing so; moreover, when they are materialists they are absolutely incapable of having any conception at all of God's conception of a child, and this no matter what religion they profess.

The only really effective way in which anyone can educate a child is by educating himself. The only really effective way in which anyone can "form" a child is by forming himself. If a man is whole, his wholeness can be his gift to his child. If he has integrity, he can give that to his child. An integrated person is one who has become whole, and wholly himself, through oneness with Christ, and through Christ's response to the Father. He, and we have it on Christ's word, is a light, "the light of the world". It is in the light of God radiating from his parents that a little child can develop the perfection and power of childhood. This is on the natural plane; I am not speaking in terms of mysticism or miracles, but in terms of nature, of the natural, and normally inevitable, psychological process in human nature.

For very much longer than most people realize, the child is one with his mother, for long after birth has severed the physical union the child's psyche (which means all the invisible parts of his nature) is united to his mother's soul. The mother's soul is the natural environment of the little child's psyche, in which, given the right conditions, the loveliness of essential childhood can unfold from the seed and grow towards its flowering.

From time immemorial, humanity has known the earth to be the symbol of motherhood. Not only the mother's body, but her soul too, is like the earth. In it the child's psyche can grow. But only if the mother's soul, like the earth, is penetrated by light, and saturated by the living water of life. She has no direct power to *give* life. It is the man, the husband, who can give natural life; the man, the priest, who through the sacraments can give supernatural life. In the supernatural order, the priest, through the power of his priesthood, is the giver of Christ's life. It is he who can change bread and wine to the living Christ, to be the life-giving food of mankind, he who can give the life of Christ in Baptism, and who can even give back life to the soul that is dead by the words of absolution.

In the physical union of man and woman in the natural plane, it is the man who gives the seed of life, the woman who is fertilized by it. He is the seed, she is the earth. But it is in the woman that the life that is given grows, and we learn from the earth that rest and darkness and secrecy are essential for the growth of life.

Christ made no exception of himself. Indeed nature itself is only an imitation of him. He gave the whole world life, by plunging his own light into the darkness of his Mother's womb.

The man may be compared to the sun. If he is one with Christ, he will radiate, not his own light, but the light of God from his soul. Here we touch upon the glory of marriage. It is not only the giving of natural life, but also of supernatural life. The husband's love, which has become sacramental, shines down into the darkness and secrecy of the woman's soul, penetrates it with a ray of God, making it a soil in which even the psychological life of the new-born child can unfold.

A flower is a wonder of loveliness, tethered by a green thread to the soil that has nourished it. It is lifted between earth and heaven; it is living water given form and colour by the sun, the blossoming of water and light. It is a true image of the little child whose environment in his mother's soul is the environment of God. Informed by the mystery of the baptismal water, rooted in earth, he too stands between earth and heaven shaped and coloured through and through by the uncreated light.

But when the light of God is not in the mother, then we have a psychological environment in which children cannot grow naturally. No one else can wholly take the place of the mother, because she has the sacramental love of her marriage. The child of a mother in whom the light is darkness is more truly an orphan than the naturally orphaned child whose mother's soul may still surround it from eternity.

The tragic, negative child is the child of materialists. His mother must be compared not to the earth, but to an underground cellar. She has built a wall between herself and nature. (Remember, it is part of human nature to be irradiated by supernatural love.) She has put a stone floor between her consciousness and the earth that is part of herself and a stone ceiling between herself and the blue sky of heaven. She has built four walls around her against the light. The result is very like a tomb.

If a plant is put to grow in a cellar, it will be weak and colourless and twisted; it will not grow upright, but to one side, in one direction, twisting and straining towards any little chink that lets in even a pinpoint of light. To this plant the materialist's child may be compared.

The materialist lives in a world of things. Not those living substances, capable of carrying supernatural and natural life, of being living symbols of love, capable even of transubstantiation. He lives in a world of lifeless, soulless things. His treasures are things in which there is no potentiality of life, and yet he clings to them as fearfully and pitifully as if they were his *only guarantee* of life.

It is a matter of awareness. He is unaware of the invisible world. To him, only the most perishable things are security, because only the most perishable things are reality.

Even on the superficial plane, the child whose environment is materialism is liable to grow up a colourless, visionless human being. He is likely to bring an attitude of anxiety and fear to life.

A child's natural inheritance is of the invisible world; his right and his necessity is wonder and mystery. In everyone's "unconscious" there are, besides the terrible shadow of evil, depths upon depths of mystery, of knowledge, and of the accumulated beauty of the ages of mankind.

In overcivilized men, materialists above all, the whole of that force of spiritual life is inhibited; they have repudiated it completely. But in primitive people and children it is much closer to consciousness, it is the unguessed motivating power of much that they do, the secret of many of their incommunicable joys and sorrows.

Every child born into the world inherits original sin from his parents with all its resulting conflict and darkness, the guilt and potential suffering which Jung has named "the shadow". But he also inherits the structure of his brain that has been formed by the experience, not only of darkness, but of light, of generation after generation of human beings; the experience of humanity of which Christ is the pattern, and which has been inlived by Christ in individual after individual.

Man does not inherit his Christ-consciousness; that comes to each individual from his own personal response to Christ's action upon him; but he inherits a humanity which can be compared to the bed of a great river, shaped as it is by the continual flowing of the water through it, so that only a reversal of nature could prevent it from flowing on in the same channels. This river is a symbol of the great stream of memory, tradition, emotion, desire and fear that has motivated mankind through the ages, flowing through the individual heart of every man, shining from the touch of Christ, but muddy from the touch of man. Like the flowing river, it sometimes moves underground in darkness, sometimes on the surface; sometimes it flows freely and sweetly, sometimes it is dammed up and bursts its banks.

Thus the forces that have returned to the world again and again in individual after individual through the ages act upon each one's human nature, moving through the deep grooves of the "unconscious" and the conscious mind. Jung, borrowing from St Augustine, names these forces "archetypes". They are usually in the unconscious, but sometimes they break through into consciousness in the forms of symbols, dreams, and fantasy, in art or poetry, and in the myths and fairy stories of the world.

To many people the "unconscious" simply means some part of the mind, like a dungeon, where a man's "repressions" are locked away out of sight. There is nothing in this dungeon, they imagine, but what man has thrust into it himself, those things in himself which he refuses to accept because he thinks them too disreputable or too violent or brazen to be tolerated by the pseudo-self which he has built up to save his face.

The unconscious is very far from being a dungeon. It contains very much more than our inhibitions or repressions. Just beyond the ordinary reach of awareness, in that mysterious part of our being, is our childhood and our infancy. Our first fears are there certainly, but so is our first reassurance. All our memories are there, every experience we have known in any way, those that were always out of reach of thought as well as those which thought has reflected, the experiences of feeling and the senses and apprehensions of every kind that are still undefined.

Look at an old peasant woman in her wooden rocking-chair by the fireside, rocking happily to and fro as she dozes in the warmth of the flames; she is still being rocked to sleep in her wooden cradle by the young mother whose tender face is a memory. They know little of human nature who say that a new-born infant is only a little animal needing no reassurance and no spiritual environment, because he has no memory of his first days and weeks of life. That earliest reassurance will still be the reassurance of his soul when he comes to die. All through his life, if in the beginning he was loved intelligently, from the depths of his unconsciousness reassurance will come to him in his need, and he will know in secret the security of the strong arms that first encircled him and of the first love that fostered his life.

How often flickers of beauty drift into our consciousness, un-recognized as memories, and not only in dreams. We do not know where they come from, or why—seeming such trifling things, and so evasive that we can never quite lay hold of them—they yet stir us so profoundly. Indeed in a mysterious moment, that seems no more than a moment of nostalgia for an already half-forgotten dream, the whole course of our life may be changed. We may hardly know what it is, what memory came to us hidden in the flicker of flames on the wall, in the sound of bells ringing across the fields, or the glimpse of the tea-table through the window of a lamp-lit room; yet it has restored us to the simplicity which we had supposed our complex maturity had lost for ever.

What gives these fragmentary and subtle experiences their extraordinary effectiveness? Surely the fact that they are for-gotten memories, the earliest tenderness, the earliest delight opening their secret flowers again in the secret places of our soul.

We go through life with dark forces within us and around us, haunted by the ghosts of repudiated terrors and embarrassments, assailed by devils, but we are also continually guided by invisible hands; our darkness is lit by many little flames, from night-lights to the stars. Those who are afraid to look into their own hearts know nothing of the light that shines in the darkness.

God's dealings with man have had their effect on the unconscious, the story of Creation, of course, and the eternal Christ. Naturally evil is there too, since man has brought Satan into the story, but as well as evil, there are aeons of light. The child of materialists is taught to inhibit all this mystery and beauty at an early age, and at the same time to blind himself to the evil in himself. Neither is he taught *about* God, for the parents cannot teach what they do not know. It is hardly surprising that he grows up a spiritually feeble, colourless man, lacking the qualities that are in the vital child, who knows God —a certain divine recklessness, a delight in the freely given loveliness of the world, and trust that overcomes fear.

One in whom childhood has been nipped in the bud, so that the essential childhood has never come to its full flower in him; who has learnt early through the materialism of his environment and the spiritual blindness of his parents to frustrate the supernatural in himself, or at least his own consciousness of it— such a one grows up not knowing himself, having missed the loveliest experiences of his natural childhood, and having been crippled for his adult life.

He knows very little of himself, and though he is vaguely unhappy, he often has a tragic resignation to the aimlessness and mediocrity of his life. It is the men and women in whom real childhood is not developed at all who fill up the ranks of the great unfulfilled. It is impossible to contemplate them, this great multitude of nerveless, defeated, unchilded children, and not to echo St Teresa of Avila, speaking from the passionate heart in which love had defeated compromise: "I think I should like to cry aloud and tell everyone how important it is for them not to be contented with just a little."

XVI

THE CHILD IN GOD

*One secret at least had been revealed to her, that beneath the
thick crust of our actions the heart of the child remains unchanged,
for the heart is not subject to the effects of time.*

FRANÇOIS MAURIAC, *Thérèse*

W E LIVE in a world of disenchantment, but there can
be few who have not at some time or other experienced that sudden poignant sharpening of awareness which reveals the sheer loveliness of our environment, a
loveliness we had been blind to before.

Sometimes there is an obvious cause: we are looking at our
childhood's home for the last time; or our little street has been
threatened with destruction, and now, after last night's bomb-
ing, it is still there, but seen for the first time; or we ourselves are
threatened, by parting or by death: we shall not see this familiar
street many more times.

But more often there is no explanation at all. We got up in
the morning as blind and insensitive as before, and suddenly,
like the unpredictable breath of the Spirit, the wonder of the
world we live in is upon us. We see. We see the dearness of the
little drab houses, the pathos of the two crooked chimneys that
lean together, the purity of the flowering weed growing on the
ash heap, the blue of the sky above the chimneys. It is as if we
have dimly experienced something like Tabor; we have seen the
invisible in the visible, touched the intangible in the tangible,
felt the inexpressible loveliness of the supernatural world within
the natural one.

To a child this is not a passing experience, but the commonplace of every day. If he is a real child, in whom the essential
qualities of childhood are alive and vibrant, he walks every day
in a world of mystery and wonder, and receives the loveliness of
it into his soul and into his senses. If he runs on the sea-shore,
the cool breeze, the light movement of the little waves, and even

the drift of the white clouds overhead, are in his blood. He feels the multitudinous golden grains of soft sand through his thin sandals; he is like the sea-shell he lifts to his ear to listen to the singing of the oceans—a tiny, fragile creature into which the beauty of the world is poured.

To him the world is more like a person than a dead thing, a person capable of magic, one who at will can suddenly scatter the shore with sea jewels or the woods with primroses or the dusk with stars. A person whose love is round him in the milky softness of the spring sun, in the coolness of the early morning and the drowsy heat of noon, and folds him in the silence of darkness.

A child, not vitiated by grown-up people's materialism, is aware of the mystery of love in all creation; his environment is an inexhaustible source of delight to him. Wherever he turns, he finds treasure.

Water is his comrade; he can float and swim in it; it supports him and touches him with the touch of ecstasy. Fire is his friend; he walks through the dry leaves of autumn woods and kindles it in the clearing to cook himself a little meal, or for the joy of the flickering and dancing flames; and the flames leap and blaze for him until their gold and coral light shines from his own face. The rain is his friend, and the sunlight, and the snow. The stars belong to him.

A world of animals and birds and fishes is given to him, not only out in the open country, but in the cities, for he has his heritage wherever he is. Animals, strange and beautiful, grotesque and lovable, are his; dogs and cats and squirrels and rabbits, sparrows and wild birds, speckled fishes and silver minnows.

He is in fact like Adam, a new man, for whom the whole world is made, because he himself is new.

But the child inhabits more worlds than one; he lives not only in the world of nature with all its mystery, but in the world of myth and fairy-story.

Adults for the most part imagine that it is only from the brightly illustrated books that children learn fairy-stories; but they are wrong; they are already present to him in his unconsciousness, which is not only his own unconsciousness but that of all children of all races and all time; and among children I include primitive peoples of any age who keep the quality of childhood and are influenced, as children are, by the symbols of mythology and, as children do, see personality and individuality in everything, in wind and water and trees and all else.

Many adults, especially those who are materialists, try to deny their children experiences of sorrow or fear, and the knowledge of evil. They sometimes realize the terrible character and terrifying themes of many traditional fairy-stories, though more often they have forgotten them and innocently hand the books to their children, who having been kept in ignorance of the fact of death, turn over the pages until they come to the Babes in the Wood lying dead in each other's arms, while the birds cover them with leaves; or Snow White in her crystal coffin surrounded by the little gnomes in their peaked red caps and patched breeches, red-nosed and red-eyed from weeping. Or while the parents congratulate themselves on the child's quietness, he is in the corner relishing every word of the horrible story of Blue Beard!

But even if the child is denied the book, the fairy-stories will invade his secret soul and give him those tremendous experiences to which he has a right and which he inherits from all childhood. He must walk into the tangled and enchanted woods and there, lost among the shadows and mists under the tall trees, encounter witches and wolves, magicians and gnomes. He must be led by a compelling spirit of adventure out on to the invisible plains and wildernesses, where he will meet the dragons that breathe fire and have seven lives: and climb the steep cliff to the enchanted castles where the giants await his challenge, and smelling his human blood from far off, lick their lips and mutter with muttering that comes to him like the rumbling of thunder.

Moreover, he must find the tiny things of magic, the little ones under a spell: the Frog Prince with his whole polished green body quaking in the beating of his heart, and his golden crown on his little flat head. He must enter the enchanted garden where Beauty comforts the poor shaggy Beast, whose tears make dark rivulets on his furry face; and he must go up the winding stairs, through the great curtains of hanging cobwebs, to the tower where the Sleeping Beauty lies awaiting the kiss of love.

All this the child is led to because he has the right to experience fear and compassion and love. If these things are kept
from him in the conscious world, he will be led to encounter
them in the inner world where he inherits, not merely fantasies,
but childhood itself.

In his inner world of fairy-story there is a central figure, a
redeeming and saving figure, and with him the child will identify
himself. This is the figure of the Hero.

The Hero stands radiant at the heart of every fairy-story.
Either he is the King's son, or else he is a poor woman's child
who in the end wins the Princess and the kingdom by defeating
evil. Sometimes, as in Jack and the Beanstalk, he is given some
magic seed that he must bury in the earth; or, like Aladdin, a
lamp which seems no more than a little light to set up in the
home, but in fact has magical power.

When he is the King's son, it usually happens that the Prince
falls in love with a maiden of low estate, a beggar-maid, a
shepherdess or some such; and to win her he too puts on the
clothes of a beggar and comes to woo her as a poor and ragged
boy, needing the poor girl's pity and kindness.

The Hero, whether he is in crimson and gold or the peasant
clothes of a working woman's son, is always both saviour and
lover. He goes out to meet the terror, faces the evil thing threatening the kingdom; alone with his sword he strikes off the seven
heads of the dragon, and returning with his wounds upon him
like jewels, he claims the bride his humility and his valour have
won.

Observe in what detail the Hero, with whom the child inevitably identifies himself, or rather with whom he is already identified by his destiny, parallels the story of Christ.

The fairy-stories, like the myths, get twisted and confused as
they pass in their great procession from human heart to human
heart, from generation to generation; but the deepest meaning
of them always reappears, always emerges from the darkness of
the unconsciousness; they always adumbrate the story of Christ.

It is the story of Christ clothed in the fantasy and symbol that
the child's heart creates for it, but the deepest meaning and purpose of it is more than fantasy and symbol. It is reality; and it
comes, without any beginning, from Christ in eternity.

Now we see why all the fantasies and symbols, the fairy lore of all children in all ages, are so alike as to be practically identical. The story of Christ told in the symbols of the human mind is in the heart of every child, because every child is made in the image of the child Christ. Just as it is man's destiny to be a Christ, so it is the child's destiny to be a child-Christ, and Christ is, from his first human breath to his last, the lover.

It is he who is the Prince who comes clothed like a beggar to the wretched and lowly human heart, to sue for love; he who goes out in his youth on the great impulse of the Spirit to meet and overcome evil; he who destroys the dragon whose seven heads are all the sins, and comes wearing his wounds like jewels to make the poor, suffering, needy and ignoble human race his bride.

The child, because he is made in the image of the child Christ, has his inward experience of fear and sacrifice, compassion and love, by right. No one can take it from him altogether. If people succeed partially in doing so, they will succeed in the most terrible act possible to a father or mother: they will crucify the Christ-child in their child, twisting the instincts of divine love into that other pattern also innate in a human child, the pattern of evil.

The child who is taught that there is no evil will still have the instinct to destroy something, to kill something; and somehow sooner or later, he will do it. That which is true of man is equally true of the child; he is only safe when he is consciously fighting the evil within himself. He must know it exists, recognize it, and face it; he must go out to meet it. In him as in man, the Kingdom of Heaven must suffer violence.

So the real child is aware of more worlds than one. He is aware of the natural world and of the supernatural love pervading it; he is aware of the secret world of all childhood, the world of myth and symbol and dream. But what is the function of this extraordinarily aware and beautiful and brave thing, childhood, in the integration of the whole man?

First, to make man carefree. We have been speaking about fear: the average man or woman enters adult life afraid of fear, certainly not equipped to face it, not aware that it is an essential experience of his likeness to Christ. He is not aware, because he did not come to the full flower of childhood in which he could have learnt the secret of the Prince: so that the child is now going into the world only half developed.

But there is something worse than fear that puts the man back. This is anxiety. Fear is a rather rare, if essential, experience; anxiety is constant. Fear musters all one's forces and braces one to meet it. Anxiety fritters and drains away all one's courage and all one's trust. Fear is reasonable and can be met by reason. Anxiety is unreasonable and reason does not touch it. The difference between fear and anxiety is that a man or woman experiencing fear is afraid of some real danger, but a person who is anxious is afraid of an imaginary or potential danger. Fear is in proportion to the cause: anxiety is out of proportion. A woman whose child is lying ill with meningitis has every reason to be afraid, but a woman who falls into a state of fear because her child might possibly catch a cold, is definitely the victim of anxiety neurosis.

Anxiety is the undercurrent of many people's attitude to life; it produces hesitation and indecision about everything. The job a young man is offered may not suit him; he may lose it; he hesitates to take a room of his own—he may not be able to pay the rent; he is anxious about the impression he may, or may not, make on other people: secretly obsessed by guilt, he is anxious about his health, his moral and physical stamina in the world, the moral and material consequences of falling in love, and a multitude of other things. If one anxiety is relieved, another takes its place immediately.

He soon realizes, if he makes any attempt to overcome his anxiety, that a direct attack is doomed to failure. Friends tell him to "pull himself together" and to "use his will"; but as the only method he knows of for using his will consists of an act of violence to himself which he has not the spiritual force to sustain, the result is destructive. The fact is that no one can depend upon himself; and equally, no one can depend permanently on another human being.

Everyone needs to depend on someone who has qualities which are not to be found in any human being. He must have absolute power—power over life and death. He must be always and everywhere present and accessible. He must have illimitable love for oneself, and for those whom one loves. Short of any of these assets he is useless. A friend may indeed be a rock of strength and ready to go down into the depths with us, but he is actually as powerless as we are in the face of the immensities of fate. A father may have the most devoted love, but he too is powerless before life and death; he can only be in one place at a time, and he is not immortal.

In fact if we are anxious, all those we love aggravate our anxiety instead of easing it, for we centre all our exaggerated fears upon them.

> A pity beyond all telling
> Is hid in the heart of love:
> The folk who are buying and selling
> The clouds on their journey above
> The cold wet winds ever blowing
> And the shadowy hazel grove
> Where mouse-grey waters are flowing
> Threaten the head that I love.*

Anxiety makes every circumstance intolerable and every affection a torture. It is equally destructive of supernatural life; its victims even approach the sacraments in fear of an endless variety of trifling possibilities which may turn their sacrament to sacrilege.

Now we see the function of the child in man. It is to trust the Father, God. If the Christ-child is developed in the natural child, he will trust the Father unquestioningly, and his trust will be something far more than merely taking it for granted that God will supply him with his material needs. He will take that for granted, but he will know that whatever God allows to happen is allowed only because of his infinite love. God loves him too much to allow him to suffer anything that is not essential for his ultimate happiness. Whatever God can possibly spare his child, he will spare him. This kind of trust can only be come by through direct knowledge of God the Father; and only the child in man can have this knowledge. It comes, as we have already said, by realizing God's power through our nothingness; knowing his love through our need.

* W. B. Yeats, "The Pity of Love".

The child concentrates not upon the dangers around him: he knows the Father in the whole awareness of childhood, in the love that is almost audible, almost visible to him: in loveliness: in the gifts given with such extravagance of joy in giving: in the impulse that has overcome evil and possessed the Kingdom through all the ages of Christ-childhood.

The only way in which anyone can learn to trust is by knowing the Father, and the only way to know the Father is to foster the Christ-child in us, since only he knows the Father's love through the direct experience of his own littleness.

It is not enough to wait for the crisis and then make verbal acts of faith in God. Such acts are again only acts of violence to the human will. It is absolutely necessary to learn to know the Father, as only the child can—every day, always, as the background and sustenance of our whole life.

There is a second function of the child in man which is a necessity for man's happiness. It is to make new. At the root of at least half of man's discouragement is his staleness and his inability to rid himself of the old sores and miseries of his old sins and sorrows.

Everyone longs to be made new, to be young, to be born again—not merely to be patched up, or made to look young. Even wounds drag at our vitality less when they are new than when they are old: the ache of an old wound wearies, it has a long, long accumulation of fatigue behind it. The anguish of an old sorrow corrodes, it sinks deeper and deeper in, and gradually saturates more and more of our thought and saps more and more of our vitality: and old sins are unimaginably destructive. People have the curious delusion that the guilt of a sin committed long ago and unconfessed, grows less with time; but the truth is it acts in the soul as a slow poison does in the body, spreading a more and more misplaced and dissipated guilt feeling all over the personality, until every pleasure is overshadowed by vague anxiety or fear. Sometimes the end is despair and insanity.

The child is always new, childhood is new, and to the child the world is new every day. He has no past, except the ever present past of all childhood; he has no apprehension about the

TERESA MARTIN

future: he lives in the eternal—now. Old sin does not remain in
a child; he has the humility that confesses and knows the immediate joy of the Father. By his very nature he is new. The
Christ-child in man is the continual renewal of life, of joy, of the
capacity for joy, of trust.

Because the world is always new to a child, and every lovely
thing in it, every pleasure, every experience of love, is new to
him, he is never bored or blasé or dependent on material things
for his delight. He cannot help retaining the sense of wonder, he
cannot help keeping the poet alive in the man whom he inhabits. He is the echo through all time of the cry of the young
Christ, of birth and resurrection: "Lo! I make all things new."

It is not only at the beginning of adult life that the child is
necessary for man's integrity. In the beginning, the child gives
him the trust in the Father which in turn gives him the courage
to face the world, to overcome obstacles and to wrestle with evil,
to dare to live and to dare to love.

In mature life—with more responsibilities and with the inevitable loss of many on whom he tried to depend; with more
puzzling sorrows; with many seeming injustices to accept, and
with the early natural sense of wonder wearing out—the child
is again his renewal and trust and the secret of maintaining his
joy and zest in living.

In old age, when even on the natural plane he must in so
many ways become like a little child again, the humility of the
child sweetens his humiliation in growing old, and the child's
love of the Father brings him ultimate comfort and peace.

The secret of childhood is knowing the Father, and knowing
the Father is the secret of trust, the remedy for anxiety, the overcoming of evil. And this is because to know the Father is to
know ourselves loved and possessed by the power of the Trinity.

Once again, it will not be through any superhuman effort, any
violence of the will, that we shall bring the child in us to its full
flower. It will not be through going against nature, through
achieving some kind of austerity that can make poverty and
want attractive to us. On the contrary, it will be through not
frustrating the child who is already in us, and always because of
the unconquerable strength of nature, ready to wax strong in us
—ready even if it has already been frustrated. If only by the

G   N simple process of responding to the Father's love, we will restore the frustrated little child to his kingdom.

The response to the Father's love will not demand any mystical flight from us; it will come naturally to us if we look for it in everything around us. That in itself will restore the child in us, for it will be the beginning of continual awareness of the beauty of the world, of the visible in the invisible, of the realization of the gifts that are strewn under our feet. Following on this new awareness, and all the right values which inevitably go with it, we will be able to make spontaneous acts of faith in the Father's love in all our circumstances, and even in all his dealings with those we love.

There is a certain strange detachment peculiar to children which is always baffling and sometimes shocking to adults; but it is grounded in the child's consciousness of the eternal world and his certainty of the Father's love. He does not analyze it, he could not explain it, but there it is. He is not upset by poverty or concerned about the next meal or what he will wear; he is confident that somehow all he needs will be given, and pathetically content with whatever it is when it comes. He is curiously indifferent even about the deaths of people he knows and is fond of; death itself has no finality for him. Eternal life, the unfailing love of the eternal Father, the new world of loveliness that it gives to him daily, these things are real to him.

The child in the adult will not make the adult callous and foolhardy, but it will give him just that strange crystalline hardness that makes him able to suffer even cruel circumstances without being made incapable of recovery and new joy. It will make him able to enjoy life in poverty if need be, and to accept bereavement without being completely broken by it. As the child is restored in him, he will cease to be overcome by anxiety, and even as he grows daily to love the world more and to delight in it more, he will also become consciously less dependent on it and more dependent on the Father, who made it for him. He will say: "And elsewhere, Lord, thou hast laid the foundations of the earth at its beginning, and the Heavens are the works of thy hands. They will perish, but thou wilt remain, they will be like a cloak that grows threadbare, and thou wilt lay them aside, like a garment, and exchange them for new."

XVII

THE SON

The hearty man is inclined, shrugging his shoulders and rather dis-dainfully, to gloss over how intensely the sensitive man looks for confirmation of himself and of his innermost being, for faith and acceptance, to his own family; and breaks down when he feels that he isn't understood in his own home.

MAX BROD, *Franz Kafka: A Biography**

THE VERY YOUNG CHILD suffers from the materialism of his parents without wholly realizing it, but when the child has grown to adolescence, the suffering becomes only too well realized, and takes the form largely of anxiety and fear, the worst possible preparations for adult life. Not only does his parents' own attitude foster this by its very existence in them, but they frequently drive it deeper and deeper into him by a stream of suggestion intended by them to have the opposite result.

They continually repeat to him that it is by no means easy to earn money, and that this must be the main preoccupation of his life, on which everything else will depend; on what he has, not what he is, will the world's esteem depend. He will certainly be made to feel guilty if his inclinations are towards a life which, if it is lived honourably, must in our days almost certainly mean poverty, such as the life of a poet or an artist. They impress upon his shrinking mind the fact that their own lives have been one unremitting struggle endured for the single object of fitting him for a life equally drab and formidable, and if he sits over his homework biting his pencil, ruffling his hair with a vacant look in his eyes, they remind him that he will not always have them to fall back on, and therefore he must matriculate or perish.

There is a type of parent, who has struggled out of real poverty by hard work, and who in his own boyhood suffered great hardship, who seems to feel that he owes his own children as well as young people generally a grudge for what he had to

* Secker and Warburg (London, 1947).

endure. He never ceases to relate stories of his hard lot and his own fortitude, and seems to resent it if his children enjoy the comparative ease and comfort that is the fruit of his toil!

Some materialists go further than that; they demand that their children shall either educate themselves by scholarships, or pay them back for what has been spent on their education when they begin to earn money. In these circumstances the boy is a ready prey to feelings of humiliation, which in extreme cases lead to neurosis.

If he has never been taught the difference between good and evil, if, as is very frequent, his conscience has not been educated at all, he will have an "unresolved guilt conflict"—that is to say, he will have a shallowly buried sense of guilt, for which there is no obvious cause, and which is ready to fasten on to any suggestion made to him. The suggestion made to him countless times a day by the materialism of his parents will be that all his finer feelings are guilty—above all, unworldliness is guilty— that the only way he can prove himself is by succeeding in the competition which begins even at school.

How often we read in the newspapers of the tragedy of boys and university students committing suicide because—so the coroners imagine, or say they do—their minds became temporarily unbalanced by the strain of overwork for an examination. The strain here does not begin in overwork; it begins in the fearful importance with which the parents, as well as the school teachers, charge the result of the examination. It is emotionally charged out of all reason; on it depends, in the parents' eyes, not what the boy knows, but what he is. His failure will be, not so much his own disappointment, as a shattering grief for the already martyred father and mother, a new and unbearable source of guilt for the boy. Consequently, many brilliant but sensitive boys fail, and many less intelligent but insensitive ones pass with honours. Examinations are not a test of knowledge or intelligence, of character or intellect or ability, but simply of nerve; and the whole life of the schoolboy and the undergraduate is measured out by a series of these nervous crises.

All this nervous tension is bound up with the boy's relationship to his parents, and in particular with his relationship to his father, which is perhaps the most vital thing in his life.

It is not surprising that those who are sensitive shrink from entering into the unequal competition that commerce offers them, that anxiety is the undercurrent of their daily life, that they feel that the essential, holy things are for ever out of their reach, and so they compromise at every turn.

Instead of adventure they accept security, instead of joy of the artist in work, the boredom of the wage slave, instead of passion and love, the mockery of a cautious, self-centred, unnatural and childless marriage, an unwilling, festering celibacy, or the life of petty immorality that frustrates human nature.

The young man who has been given no conception of God the Father, and who has been compelled by the fact that he is made according to the pattern of the Son of God, to seek for God, however blindly, in his earthly father, and to look to this earthly father for the confirmation of his own Christhood, can hardly escape the fate of deep inward humiliation and shame, of a sense of his own inadequacy for life, and of being a failure from the beginning, through compromising on both sides, trying to serve God and Mammon.

"Blessed are the poor in spirit, for theirs is the Kingdom of Heaven" was never more true than it is today, when everything that is essential to the peace and joy of living, to happiness in work and love and home, depends entirely upon having Christ's values, and Christ's trust in the eternal Father.

To nearly every normal small boy his father is unique among men. In fact, he is God. The boy worships him in secret, perhaps even secretly from himself. In a way, he is sorry for all other boys, and feels superior to them because his father is thus and thus, and he identifies himself with him. In that identification is all his pride, all his self-esteem. There is nothing about his father that is ordinary, he is different to all other fathers; even his movements, the way in which he swings his hand round to look at his wrist watch, his manner of walking and sitting, and the way he draws his breath in when he is smoking his pipe, are uniquely his own. The smell of him is magnificent too, the particular tobacco he smokes and the tweed of the old coat that he wears when he is at home. He is the essence of manhood, and he is God.

It is necessary for the child's self-confidence that the father should be perfect, and necessary for his self-esteem that the father should love him and approve of him, and that he himself should be like his father.

But the time will come when he will know that his Father is not God. Parents seldom know when the child is disillusioned, for children are passionately reserved about that which afflicts them. One, who was quite inarticulate at the time, told me years afterwards when he was a grown man, how one morning he went into his father's dressing-room and saw the smeary tooth glass on the washstand, and knew that his father was just like other men and other fathers. He could not have spoken to any-one of the sense of personal humiliation that he experienced. No child can speak of or understand his own bewildering shame that comes with the discovery that his father is as ordinary, as sordid and embarrassing as all other fathers.

But from the time of this discovery, conflict begins in the boy's emotions, because it is not simply a matter of vanity to him to want a Father whom he can worship; it is an instinct at the root of his being; the fall of his idol threatens his own being. In some hidden way, to him inexplicable, the development of everything positive and vital in himself seems to depend upon his response to the perfect father whom he himself has created out of his inner necessity—his own manhood that is shut in the small hard bud of his childhood needs the sun of his father's glory to open it. In the negative mood that follows disillusionment, it begins to shrivel in bud.

He does not, of course, analyse his emotions and formulate ideas about them while he is a child; he simply suffers, without defence, from the dull depression and emptiness that follows dis-enchantment. The world of his inner life is clouded and its colours are made dimmer. Sometimes he becomes openly moody, sulky or aggressive. Without his having the least idea why, his father's company, which was formerly his delight, is embarrassing to him. This is liable, of course, to rouse his father's anger: and for some boys the mother's gentle remon-strance will aggravate the situation, for it will only stress the father's limitations that he must be bolstered up by a woman, that after all he can be easily hurt or provoked, and instead of being someone who can be worshipped, he may be someone who must be pitied. Out of such seemingly trifling conditions hostility can grow, and with it the boy's sense of guilt. Indeed the extraordinary and complex effects of whatever his father's attitude to him is are knotted into his ready predisposition to the feeling of guilt; nothing stirs this more profoundly than an unhappy relationship between father and son.

But the strange thing is, that even if the son discovers as time goes on, and long after the childhood disenchantment is almost forgotten, that the father is not only ungodlike, but is the opposite to all that he himself admires and could wish to be, he still feels inferior to him, he still secretly despises himself for being unlike him, and he will still be discouraged to the point of frustration by his father's disapproval.

This attitude becomes completely crippling when the father is the hearty, insensitive type, in whom a coarse physique and a certain kind of boisterous egoism are positive elements in his worldly success; for then the man's self-confidence will seem to the boy, and afterwards the young man, to be a reproach to himself. He will doubt himself and come to feel that his sensitivity, possibly his frailer body, and his deeper interests and desires reveal an inadequacy for living. With his father's ideal of manhood unreasonably but persistently obsessing him and colouring his own, he will be overwhelmed by the feeling of being unable to face the world and to win his own rights as a man, because of his lack of his father's overbearingly masculine qualities.

Such a situation is very common, and it is among the major causes of the inward humiliation that leads to the ego-neurosis already discussed, with its pitiful withdrawal from maturity on its very threshold.

Literature, and especially modern literature, is obsessed by this theme; it is expressed in writing, as it is in life, diversely, and through the contradictions that arise out of something which is innate in man and to which he cannot adjust himself. Sometimes it is shown as consciousness of insignificance and defencelessness, sometimes a hostility to all authority, even to divine authority, but it requires no skill to see the child's tortured obsession about his father in it all.

That this is particularly a characteristic of modern literature points to the fact that there is an increase of this father-son complex in our own days. And that it is the theme that has haunted writers of genius points to the fact that it is closely related to something that is universal to the human race. For it is the distinguishing sign of the work of genius that it expresses the *universal* experience of all mankind.

The artist no less than the saint is destined to be the vessel through which all the suffering, joy and love of the whole of humanity are poured. And this destiny is a doom to those who resist the Christ-life in themselves, since only the power of Christ can enable a human creature to surrender to so overwhelming a destiny and not be broken by it. This is the key to the tragic frequency with which genius meets disaster, as well as to the threat of insanity that haunts it. Again and again the genius cannot carry the stress, and he breaks down into neurosis, seeks relief in drugs and alcohol, or succumbs to the exhaustion that follows the attempt to pit his own individual little emotions against the torrent of the agelong passions and dreams of the whole human race.

On the one hand we have the swarm of pseudo-artists who are absorbed in continually refining and polishing a technique, through which they express only their own peculiarities; they tend to exclude everyone from their consciousness but a small clique of admirers, and have no real communion with mankind. Consequently their art is an ineffective form of neurosis.

On the other hand there is the artist whose voice is the voice of the whole world, who sheds the tears and burns with the desires of all humanity. This is the man of genius; the myths and dreams of the centuries awaken in his soul, and his works crystallize the joys and sorrow of all mankind. It is significant that the writing of genius has for some time become more and more concerned with the father-son situation, and this has also filtered into the works of writers on the borderline of genius.

There is scarcely a word written by Samuel Butler on any subject that is not really an expression of the same tortured mixture of hostility to, and identification with, his father which he revealed in *The Way of All Flesh*. It seeps into the novels of D. H. Lawrence, and snarls out of much of his poetry, where it is confused with class-consciousness.

It is present in the fiction of contemporary Catholic writers in the critical attitude they often reveal to the priests, who represent the parent Church which they belong to and love. How often a priest in a Catholic book is drawn as a mental fumbler, or almost ludicrous in his purely natural humanness—in fact, the father who represents God and who disappoints the son.

It would be difficult to invent quite so stupid a priest, even for so stupid a penitent, as Graham Greene's Father Rank in *The Heart of the Matter*, without the pressure of that disappointment, and it would be impossible to create Pinkie in *Brighton Rock*, with the agonized twist that makes the juvenile delinquent the pitiful rebel against authority that he is, without having quivered oneself with the universal suffering of the boy's disillusionment.

In Jean de Mirbel, the "difficult" boy in Mauriac's *Woman of the Pharisees*, every fine shade of disenchantment, and its pathos both from the point of view of the child and the parents, is experienced. It is lived through from beginning to end of the book, in the boy's relationship to his uncle, to his mother, and with culminating beauty in the mutual failure of his relationship with the, this time wonderful, human *and* saintly old priest, the Abbé Calou.

Many other writers could be mentioned, but in one, Franz Kafka, we have not only a genius whose writing is saturated with this problem, but one whose personal life was dominated by it, and who is the mouthpiece of all the inarticulate children in the world. In his life of Kafka, Max Brod writes: "The child trusts his parents and wants his parents to trust him too. This is the point out of which arises one of the first great conflicts to which the soul of man is exposed."

The inclination of the boy to make his father a god, and to cling to the idea that on his father's approval his own manhood depends, is much more than a delusion; it is an instinct with a hidden purpose, which is necessary for the defence of his personality.

It is an innate instinct which makes the child seek perfection in his father, and build his own father-idol in his heart. Even the child who does not know his father or who is orphaned creates an ideal father in his own mind, for he is driven by the same necessity, and his fantasy father is a reality to him that has a profound influence on his development. Again, some children who have had brutal fathers, or who have lost their natural fathers through death, seek for a father-substitute in some other man. This applies to girls as well as to boys, and again and again we find women who have literally idolized an old father, and who when he dies, or soon after, marry an old man—who is really a father-substitute.

Dr Douglas Hubble in an analytical study of James Boswell* attributes Boswell's biography of Samuel Johnson to his search for a father-substitute. He says of Boswell and his father: "Whenever James was in the company of Auchinleck [his father] the image of himself dwindled until it was no larger than a small boy, beloved and indulged by his mother, but intimidated by the stern and sarcastic tongue of Alexander Boswell." And he adds that the effect of this was that Boswell sought and found a great and good father-substitute in Johnson.

The son wants the father's influence to foster and develop what is best in himself. But it happens only too often that to fulfil his father's ideal for him would be a degradation for the son.

The boy secretly wants the father to approve his own idealism, to take pride in that, and not only in his successes in examinations and sport. Above all he wants some deep assurance that his own most intimate spiritual aspirations echo down to him from his father's own soul, and are an essential element in his identification with the father. If the father is irritated or amused by the sensitivity of the boy's spirit, he may, so illogical is the guilt feeling, become ashamed of what is holiest in himself. It is only when the father loves the best that the son is capable of becoming, that his love is creative in his son's life.

What the child wants is a father whom he can adore with illimitable confidence, and with whom he is one. This desire is put into the child by God, and it is given to him to enable him to respond to the divine Father of whom the earthly one is only an image.

In the beginning, it is true, the human father takes the place of God in the child's life, and his human love for his son *is* God's love, but unless the child is told that he has in fact a Father

* In *The New Statesman*, December 28th, 1946.

who is God, of whom his earthly father is only an image, the disillusionment and disappointment must come. If, however, he is told the truth about God's fatherhood, and that his earthly father is fallible and human and yet reflects God's love in his, all the longing in the boy's soul will be filled and overflowing.

He will realize that he *has* a Father who is God, and whose gaze does penetrate to the innermost secrets of his soul, and who desires of him only the best that he is capable of. But though he wants the finest that the boy desires for himself, this Father has pity on his weakness and will not forsake him or cease to love him when he fails him, but on the contrary will restore him to oneness with himself and lift him up again into his own glory.

In the light of that glory, the hard bud of manhood in the boy's heart can open and flower and bear fruit.

The father's approval is the one reassurance that is necessary to the individual for his initiation into adult life. The child who knows God and knows that he is himself inlived by Christ, so that the eternal Father sees him as his beloved Son, and desires of him that he will be a Christ in the world, will have this assurance, even if his earthly father fails him, even if he despises him.

It is because the pattern in which every man is created is inescapably the pattern of Christ, the eternal Son, that the *son* in him clamours persistently for its fulfilment and joy in filial love and honour. He has come into the world first of all to be a Christ; to the world, after that condition is assured, he can, if it is consistent with his own individual Christhood, be a labourer, a clerk, an artist, a schoolmaster, or enter any other trade or profession that he is fitted for. He has been sent into the world by his eternal Father, as Christ was sent into the world, because the Father "so loved the world that he gave up his only Son to save the world."

It is this relationship that should be reflected in that of the earthly father and son; when it is, the boy who is facing the adult world has every chance of overcoming the difficulties that often defeat those who are already humiliated and intimidated by their father's materialism and his disapproval of their unworldliness.

If he approaches his manhood with the mind of Christ, led as Christ was by the Holy Spirit, his values will be those of Christ too. The work he chooses will be his own choice, not something forced on him, and it will not be chosen as the one most likely to get him a good social standing or the most money; it will be one which will enable him to serve God best, and which will be in itself, as work should be, a means of contemplation.

It is untrue to think, as many people do, that work is a punishment for sin. Before Adam sinned, he was given work to do in Eden. He was put into the garden of Eden "to dress and to trim it". In Eden there was only joy, and all the joy was in contemplating God—work, therefore, could only have been one way of comtemplating God. Adam was given the work of a gardener. Something of his Creator's joy when he looked upon the world that he had created and found it was good, must have quickened in Adam's heart, when it seemed to him that the first spring flowed from his finger tips: when those trees and flowers that he had dressed and trimmed suddenly broke into profusion of young green life, an increase of loveliness beautiful to look at, to touch, to smell and to taste, beautiful to listen to.

Only when Adam sinned was hardship and painful effort added to work; then indeed he was to earn his bread, not easily and delightfully, but by the sweat of his brow. Even so, work today is restored to its dignity and its beauty and can be prayer again. For Christ restored it to its primal beauty, working in the sweat of his brow at a carpenter's trade in Nazareth. Now, work can be a contemplation, an experience within the worker's own heart and mind, both of the Creator's joy, and of the joy of the Son who has given the zest of his love to the very effort itself.

One of the greatest justifications for the lives of artists today is that they show men the joy that can be known simply in doing work that is good in itself: in order to be free to make beautiful things rejoicing, they often choose to be poor, as poor as apostles should be, having only one coat—and that usually not an overcoat—and no money in their purses!

It is fairly certain that at all events in the beginning of life and perhaps all through it, the young man who has not succumbed to materialism will have to be poor if he is to work and live as a Christ in the world; he will probably have to be content with a humble place in his profession, and from the world's point of view he will unquestionably be "a fool for Christ's sake".

This is not because there is anything opposed to the Christ-life in success in itself—Christ knew his moments of triumph; the moments when the people threw down their garments under the feet of the exultant little donkey that carried him into Jerusalem; the moments when the whole world went after him, when the sick became well and the blind saw, and devils went out of men, and the dead became alive at his touch. And all these experiences glorified his Father—the crowds thronging to hear him preach were given his Father's message, they were shown how the Father could be glorified even in their own dark hearts. The multitudes who followed the widow with her dead son, the mourners for the little daughter of Jairus and at the sealed tomb of Lazarus, all were shown the pity and the power and the glory of the Father.

So there is a Christ-life in successful life, and one that glorifies the Father, for men today; but it is one that, as in his own life, entails relentless effort and a purity of heart and purpose that few men are capable of. The challenge to the average young man facing "the kingdoms of the world and the glory of them," and wishing to live a life of natural happiness, to fall in love, to marry, to make his own home and to bring up his own children, is to enter into competition with greed, avarice, dishonesty, trickery, with hordes of relentlessly selfish, self-seeking men and women, who will ride rough-shod over all fine feeling, who will have nothing but contempt for idealism, or even honesty, and will consider it fair game to exploit it. The earthly father who loves and approves the Christ in his son, will give that son the greatest help to being a success as a human being, even if he does not give him much help to being a success as men ordinarily estimate success.

He will help him towards psychological happiness, and the courage which does not shrink from growing up, because whatever hazards await him, whatever the price of joy in effort and self-denial and fortitude, he will be certain that always, at all times, in every circumstance, "under him are the eternal arms".

If every earthly father gave to his son the love of which he is trustee, the eternal Father's love, every son should be able to go from his boyhood to his maturity as Christ did, with his father's spirit resting upon him and his father's voice, telling his joy in him, ringing in his ears—with his own pride and glory in his identification with his father.

Christ's entry into his public life takes one's breath away by its sheer beauty:

"So Jesus was baptized, and as he came straight up out of the water, suddenly heaven was opened, and he saw the Spirit of God coming down like a dove and resting upon him. And with that, a voice came from heaven, which said, This is my beloved Son, in whom I am well pleased" (Matt. 3.16-17).

The child who knows the eternal Father will be the man who is able to overcome the inward humiliation that crushes those who do not, and to face the labours and the loves of a mature life, knowing himself, just as the early intuition of his childhood told him, dependent for his being on his heavenly Father's love; without that, nothing. And because his father is God, and he is destined to live in the life of God's only begotten Son: "... a son, who is the radiance of his Father's splendour, and the full expression of his being ..." (Heb. 1.3).

XVIII

THE MEASURE OF JOY

Fain would I be saved: And fain would I save.
Fain would I be released: And fain would I release.
Fain would I be pierced: And fain would I pierce.
Fain would I be born: And fain would I bear.
Fain would I eat: And fain would I be eaten.
Fain would I hearken: And fain would I be heard.
Fain would I be cleansed: Fain would I cleanse.
I am mind of All,
Fain would I be known.
Divine Grace is dancing: Fain would I pipe for you.
Dance ye all!
Fain would I lament. Mourn ye all!

Fain would I be ordered: And fain would I set in order.
Fain would I be enfolded: Fain would I enfold.
I have no home: In all I am dwelling.
I have no resting place: I have the earth.
I have no temple: And I have Heav'n.
To you who gaze, a lamp am I, to you that know, a mirror,
To you who knock, a door am I, to you who fare, the way.

Ye could not know at all what thing ye endure,
Had not the Father sent me to you as a word.
Beholding what I suffer, ye know me as the sufferer.
And when ye had beheld it, ye were not unmoved.
But rather, were whirled along. Ye were kindled to be wise.
Had ye known how to suffer, ye would know how to suffer no more.
Learn how to suffer and ye shall overcome.

Know in me the words of wisdom!
And with me cry again—
Glory to Thee, Father!
Glory to Thee, Word!
Glory to thee, Holy Spirit! Amen.

From HOLST's "The Hymn of Jesus",
trans. from the *Apocryphal Acts of St. John.*

WE TURN at last from the pitiful figure of man broken
and twisted by guilt, and by his futile efforts to
escape from the suffering of guilt, to man restored
to the image of God in which he was created—the miracle of
man inlived by Christ and given the power of his love. In his

presence we no longer sigh after the lost image of God, but stand amazed before the splendour of the redeemed man in whom the risen Christ lives on. To become whole, to live fully, to be in harmony with himself, each individual must turn his face to God. He must live consciously in the life of divine love, he must know himself to be in the Being of God.

But now, God takes him and quietly turns his face back to the earth: very lovingly he reminds man that he cannot love God without loving his fellow men. Neither is God content that his little creature, whom he put into the world that was made to be the cradle of his Son, should despise anything in that world.

He is to remember that his body and the bodies of those he loves are made from its dust, and he is to delight in the loveliness of life that flowers in them from that dust. His senses are meant to delight him in the life of flesh and blood, blossoming into the softly coloured skin of men and women and children to the warmth of ivory, of gold and brown, of rose and ebony. He is to put his hand on the pulse of the human heart and marvel at the miracle of its beating, he is to realize the beauty and the mechanism of the lovely filigree of bones, of the unfathomable mystery of the human brain and of physical life itself.

But God has made the dust not only lovely, but holy, for God has made himself in dust. He has made himself in the substance of human nature, and he abides in man.

Through the ages Christ lives on in man, and because Christ is love itself, mature man is a lover, his maturity is love. The meaning of man's life on earth is to transmit life through love. He lives fully only when his living is a giving and interchange of life; and this, in God's plan, is not to be done in a vague insubstantial way, but through visible, tangible things, through the profound simplicity of the sanctity of natural love.

In order that we may never forget this, God has locked man's salvation in the commonest materials, water, bread, wine and oil.

To give life is the meaning of love, and the deepest compulsion of love is for the lover to give not just life, but his own life, his own body and blood, his own heartbeat; his giving of life to the beloved must be his giving of self. This compulsion is from

Christ, and only the man in whom Christ has risen from death and lives can know the completeness of love that comes from this self-giving.

To enable man to achieve this—and yet more wonderful, to achieve it himself as man—Christ by his Incarnation, by his touch upon the world, has made human nature sacramental nature. For this purpose the Father created the pure and selfless substances of the world: for this the Spirit breathed upon the water, and the Son laid his blameless hands upon the bread.

The life which men are to give to one another on earth is the risen life of Christ. It is the life which has overcome death, the life in which self-love has died, and to which the lover has been born again, made new.

Christ has overcome the world in the heart of this new man, and he comes from the dark night to the morning of his resurrection awakened; he sees a new heaven and a new earth with newly opened eyes. He touches the material things of life with awakened hands, hands that bear Christ's wounds and have his power, and restored as he is through Christ to the primal beauty of his likeness to his Creator, his experience becomes no less than an inward experience of God within himself—his life, and the life his living transmits, is his Creator's joy in the goodness of his creation.

The years before him will consist of gradual experience of the wonder which is at once too simple and too mysterious for him to understand—or to grasp at all, except by faith—namely that his daily life is a life of miracles, that whatever he makes, whatever he touches, becomes radiant with his Christ-life as the world is radiant with its Maker's life; and that his *natural* love, that which is irresistibly sweet to him, which rises in his blood as the spring rises in the sap of the trees, *is* actually that love in which he can attain to the fulness of life, the wholeness of joy, the completeness of human destiny.

That is the miracle of heaven on earth, that the love of God men give to one another is hidden—but hardly hidden—in ordinary, common things. It is the bread on the table, the touch of water, the smell of the newly cut lemon, the grain in the wood, the taste of wine and food: the flowers in the garden, the flame in the lamp, the roof and the walls of the home. And it is in fact, invisibly as well as visibly, sustenance, purification, beauty, and security.

And men give this love to one another through their ordinary human relationships and the ordinary means by which everyone communicates what is in his mind or his heart to another, by his words and his silences, by his labours and his rest, by his caresses or the withholding of his caresses, by his sympathy and by his delight in the one he loves.

He gives himself, and in himself Christ, to others, quite literally with his own hands, just as Christ did on earth himself, when he took the bread into his holy hands and gave his Body and Blood in it, to be the life of men.

And the worker becomes the maker, whether he makes something concrete with his hands, or something abstract with his thought, or if he simply makes his home from what he earns in his office. When the maker lives in man, all that he makes is beautiful with his life, and ultimately the cities that he builds are beautiful, because they are no longer labyrinths or tombs, prisons and factories in which men are machines and slaves, but instead they are the expression of what is in the human heart.

In the mystery of man's thought, his likeness to God is manifest, and man the thinker is inseparable from man the maker; what he makes is the thought that is in him, it is the word of his love, "the Word made flesh".

Man thinks of the woman he loves and his thought becomes the things that are in his home: the tables and chairs, the bed, the wooden porringer for the child, the thick thatch and the mown lawn—into the making of these things the life of the maker flows.

The woman sews a dress for her child, or mends the man's shirt, she kneads and bakes the bread for the family, and her own life goes into the old patched garment, the little dress and the loaf.

Man thinks of God, and the Cathedral of Chartres grows up from under the ground and ascends to heaven.

The law of natural life is a musical law; the natural environment in which man lives, the universe, the stars that encircle him, his own world, move perpetually in rhythmic cycles of life, birth, death and resurrection, to the beat of a hymn that has no sound. The pure majesty of that hymn swells in his own heart, it is in the beat of his pulses and the ebb and flow of his blood. Even his spirit must move on this rhythm if he is to be a whole man.

This natural law is a symbol of God's law, and man needs to give expression to it in his earthly life, and in that expression to become continually conscious of the oneness of his soul and body, by setting the pace of his own tiny living to the measure of the Life that is the source of all living.

His need is answered in the liturgy and ritual of the Church.

Man cannot live only in spiritual terms, for he is matter too. If the realities of invisible order, and the movement of the power of divine love, are to be brought into his consciousness and made to take hold of him, as they must be for his integrity, they must be expressed consciously in the whole of his nature.

The movement of the universe must be seen in his movements, he must clothe himself in the colours of light, he must hear the soundless hymn in his own voice. He must give a voice and a will to the world of animals and inanimate nature. He must give a voice to all that is dumb and inarticulate in the heart of man.

He must make a pageant of the life of Christ, which under all the ugliness of sin is the procession that is moving through his life, and show its hidden beauty in symbols; he must bring in lights and flowers to his altars, to show visibly the light that shines in the darkness of his soul and the life that is ready to break into flower under his hard crust.

Therefore God has given him the Church and its ritual, that the invisible world may be visible to him, the intangible tangible, the soundless music audible.

The prayers of the Church are the agelong poetry of mankind, lifted above the perfection of poetry, for they are the prayer of Christ on earth. That is what the ritual means, with its ordered movements, its wide encircling gestures of love, its kiss of peace, its extended arms of sacrifice.

Every step in the sanctuary is counted, every pace measured. The vestments clothe man's emotions in the colours of mourning and of joy, of the blood of the Lamb, and the snow of Tabor.

The liturgical year moves through seasons of Christ-life as the natural year moves through seasons of natural life. It imposes a sweetness of order upon the human heart, measuring its sorrow and its joy, its waking and its sleep. It prevents man from being swamped and carried away by the excess of his emotions, and yet it carries him forward into an immensity of energy infinitely greater than his own.

It has its winter, its season of Advent, when the seed sleeps in the virgin Mother, and man knows by faith that he too holds the seed hidden within him, but without any sign or hint of the coming sweetness of spring.

Christmas comes. This is the time of newness, and if man has grown jaded, or if his first awareness of the sheer loveliness of life has become blunted, now is the time when he will be made new.

The cycle moves on to Lent. Man must go into the wilderness now and come face to face with the shadow. The time of austerity and fasting has come, the time for the lover to turn his face steadfastly towards Jerusalem, to know love, not only as the fire of spring and the music of flutes, but as the strength of the rock below the grass and the silence in the tomb hewn out of the rock.

We come now to the season of the Passion and the Crucifixion, and in it the pattern of love in which man's completeness is realized is spread out before us. Christ's love is shown to us in its naked realism.

On Calvary we are offered the seamless garment shaped to Christ's humanity, and warm with his body. But before we can put it on we must be stripped, we must be stripped of our delusions, of our fancy dress, of our wishful fantasies. We must be stripped naked as Christ is on the cross.

In all his loves man longs for union with what he loves, and above all in the love which is his commonest natural sanctification, the love between man and woman. But it is this expression of love which has been made most difficult of all by guilt; it has been split, and sex has literally become schizophrenic. Now it contains elements of conflict, hostility, sometimes even hatred. Many people declare quite casually that it *is* nothing more than a tension brought about by a conflict of sadism and masochism; and a frequent type of murder, which often happens where love is said to be present, is officially known as "sex murder".

Even among married people, in the measure in which self-love dominates one or both, they will be swamped by violence or lust, or frustrated by impotence, and their physical unity will sever their souls. Complicated by conflicting emotions, which after all are inseparable from disintegrated individuals, the very act of union in love has come to demand a life-giving, that is also an emptying of life, a spending of self that is a little death. It has an inescapable element of sacrifice. But to this the love of Christ on the cross is the glorious answer. For Christ-love *is* inseparable from sacrifice, inseparable from the consummation of death and from resurrection.

Just as the condition of natural life is the balance of light and darkness, of movement and rest, of winter and summer, of birth and death, death and resurrection, the condition of psychological life is the reconciliation of opposites. Guilt must be reconciled with innocence, the shadow with the light. Since sin has made suffering part of all human experience, and man was created for happiness, joy must be reconciled with grief in him, and pain with pleasure.

The only principle which can bring about this reconciliation in human love is redemption. The unifying principle of redemption is nothing else but Christ's love. In Christ on the cross the opposites meet and are reconciled. Guilt becomes inseparable from innocence, suffering from joy. It is necessary to find a new name for these two fused into one, and the only descriptive name is redeeming love. Even life and death became one, when the Lord of life bowed his head and died, when the seed of his blood was sown in the dust and the whole world was pregnant with God. In the consummation of Christ's love on the cross, all love was consummated. The loves of all men in all time converged, flowing backwards and forward to that single timeless point of consummation.

Because all love is consummated in him, no one who lives in him can love and not be fulfilled by loving. There are passionate loves which it seems must be torn out of the human heart, there are loves which seem to be barren and empty, there are those which seem to be fruitful only in sorrow; but all this is only seeming, for no one can love with Christ's love without consummation. Christ has consummated all our loves.

In the passion of gentleness of the arms nailed back on the
cross was all the restraint, all the tenderness and forbearance, of
all the love of the ages of mankind. In every human love the
drama of the Crucifixion is repeated, every surrender to love is a
dying to self, every dying to self is a resurrection. The same
pattern of love, the death and resurrection of Christ, is evident
in all manifestations of human love. Love between man and
woman is a little mystical death, and man awakes from the deep
sleep of that death a new man: his awareness of the morning is
the awareness of first love.

When a man has joined his own will with Christ's and surrendered it to the Father's will, his life is no longer frustrated by
his withdrawal from suffering, he has accepted all human suffering; he is no longer crippled by anxiety, for the labours he
must undertake, the sorrows he must accept are all means by
which he will transmit life; the suffering of the world is integrated into his joy, he lives now in the life of love that has overcome death, and in communion with the whole world.

> Jesus said, wouldst thou love one who never died
> For thee, or ever die for one who had not died for thee?
> And if God dieth not for man and giveth not himself
> Eternally for man, man could not exist, for man is love
> As God is love: every kindness to another is a little death
> In the Divine Image, nor can men exist except by
> brotherhood.*

Man's risen life in Christ is the season of the ripe fruit, the
time of the breaking of bread and the oneness of all men in the
bread that is broken, the time too of Christ's joy in his Father,
of his Ascension into Heaven and the descent of the Holy
Ghost. Should man forget this, the season of Pentecost in the
Church will bring it to his mind, and with it yet more realization
of the fulness of the life in which he himself is resurrection.

The risen life is a sacramental life, and it is part of the design
of God's love, that through the sacramental life men shall know
their communion with one another not only as they do know it
invisibly by faith, but in action. Some men, cutting themselves
off from the blessedness of the sacramental life, say they go

* William Blake.

"straight to God", but God comes to man in man's hands, at man's bidding, and in the sacraments as well as in the transmitting of sacramental life through human love, he ordains that men shall give him to one another and shall come closer to one another in compassion in the giving. Thus no man is meant to be wholly alone in any crisis of his life, no man however outcast to die without another man seeking him out and coming to him with Christ in his hands.

In our sacramental life with God, we are to give one another our voices, to carry one another in our arms, to take one another's place before God, to give Christ to one another and to be Christ for one another.

The sinner hears God's forgiveness in a man's voice, the helpless infant does not have to wait for Christ's life in his soul until he can go "straight to God" by his own intellectual act, or even on his own feet; he is carried to the living water in his godparents' arms, and they stand before God holding the flame of his faith in their own souls for him, giving him their voice for his first demand for life, while the priest pours the water over his head. Wherever man goes, the priest follows him with the living bread: he follows him to the battlefield, to the depths of the sea, to the hospitals and the workhouses and the prisons; there is no outcast who is not followed by the man who carries Christ in his hands; that man walks in the footsteps of the outcast even to the condemned cell, even to the scaffold. And when man is as helpless to help himself in death as he was in infancy, once more another man's voice speaks for him, another man kneels for him before God and makes his last act of contrition.

Thus through the sacraments God brings the communion of men and the interchange of his life down to the simplest elementary terms of realism, which is to be the pattern of all our human relationships, and in giving himself to us, he gives us to one another.

Christ first gave himself to us in the hands of his virgin Mother, and so gave *her* to *us*, the one being who is the shadowless radiance of God, but wholly and only human, to be with us in every joy and sorrow of our lives, the comfort and human tenderness that our weakness needs.

In his Christhood, restored to God, man's love integrates him through an ever-growing mystery of joy—the joy of knowing his own life to be the experience of the joy of God.

Looking upon the face of his child, feeding and clothing it, laying it down to sleep, waking it in the morning, man knows the eternal Fatherhood of God for his children; he knows it in his own heart.

Making the things that are conceived in his mind, out of wood or stone, or words or sounds, man knows the delight of the Creator of the world, who is the maker of all things; he knows it in his own mind.

But the joy of the saint transcends that of all other men. Inevitably, he is as his divine Lord was, a man of sorrows. But the joy of all other men, and the glory of all other loves, is as pale as the flame of a candle in the sunlight, beside the joy of the saint on earth. For his life is the experience in his own soul of the unutterable bliss of the Father and the Son and the Holy Spirit in their knowing and loving one another.

When Christ bowed his head and slept the sleep of consummated love, deep in the black bowl of the darkest night arose the morning star. And when he came forth out of the tomb to the splendour of his risen life, Christ came forth to ascend to his Father; the dawn of everlasting day had come silently upon earth, the spring of immortal life had put forth its flower unnoticed. The shame and sorrow of Christ with the guilt of the whole world upon him had been seen by the eyes of the world, but the exquisite secret of the first breath of his risen life was kept. He went up to his Father and sent the Paraclete to flood the heart of man with his risen life.

When the saint wakens from that dark night of love in which self has died, he too comes forth, he too knows the wonder of the Trinity in himself. Christ has risen in him, Christ is formed in him, the Holy Spirit descends upon him and his life is the breath of the Spirit of love.

Sanctity is man's integrity, the fulness and the wholeness of his humanity; in it suffering and joy are one thing, love; and love is Christ.

The four great arms of the cross do not only reach outwards, pointing to the four corners of the universe; they do not only reach up beyond the stars into heaven, and down into the tangled roots under the earth, they do not only fling wide the great arms that embrace the width of the world; they also point inwards, lead inwards, meet, converge and become one at the centre of the eternal mystery of consummated love, the heart of Jesus Christ.

PART FOUR

ILLUSTRATIONS

IRMA GRESE

IRMA GRESE was just twenty-one years old when she was put to death for murder committed in concentration camps where she acted as a supervisor. She is an illustration of the effect that group membership can have—and, as we have seen all too often in late years, frequently does have—on those who have not faced the brutal part of their own nature.

What is known of Irma Grese is what was told at her trial by witnesses of her cruelty, and by her sister concerning her childhood. She was, her sister said, a very gentle, timid child and adolescent, quite unable to stand up for herself or to hold her own with anyone. She was extremely afraid of her father, who was severe with his children and who forbade Irma to carry out her one great wish, namely to join a Nazi youth movement. But Irma would not give up the idea, perhaps she could not. She may have felt her insufficiency too much to preserve her rather negative individuality alone. However, it was not until she was working well away from home, and out of her father's reach, that she dared to carry out her plan.

Until that time she remained the mild, timid child described by her sister, but soon after she had joined the German girls' youth movement, she changed—or rather, did not change, but revealed the brutal side of her nature. With the moral support of numbers, the sense of power in their solidarity and the approval of what had become public opinion for her, it required only the provocation of the insurmountable problem of the appallingly overcrowded camp, where hundreds of thousands of people who were starving were put under the control of such girls as Irma, for the brute in her to possess and dominate her.

At her trial Irma Grese showed no emotion, but only the apparent rather sullen indifference that is often shown by those who set little value upon life, and have no sense of guilt. The most common characteristic of the forty-five prisoners who were tried with Irma was indifference. They seemed for the most part to have no particular desire to ill-treat their victims in the concentration camps, but not the very faintest qualm about inflicting devilish torments on them in carrying out orders.

Kramer, who was camp commandant at Belsen, and who is known as the "Beast of Belsen", was not even fanatically devoted to Hitler and the Nazi doctrine; he took a job in the concentration camp service in 1932 because he was out of work, and he was promoted to his final position because he was utterly unconcerned about anything whatever that he was ordered to do. He was perfectly willing to carry out any order however shocking, and extremely efficient in doing so, but he took no personal pleasure in the suffering he inflicted, and no interest in it. This in slightly varying degrees was the attitude of many others, though most of them were more indoctrinated with Nazism, and justified themselves by the pleas of obedience with more show of feeling for "the Party".

Irma Grese, young though she was, gentle and timid as her sister declared her to be, stood out as being one of the few prisoners at the trial who delighted in cruelty and went out of her way to add to the already insupportable agonies of her victims.

She was an overseer and, therefore, allotted duties to others; at the age of nineteen she was in charge of a compound of 18,000 women. She was in charge of despatching the camp prisoners to the gas chambers and did so, sending thousands to that ghastly death, with unmistakable relish. She also beat prisoners already dying from starvation and exhaustion, murdered some of them herself, and invented refinements of cruelty, even in the midst of such cruelty, to add to their exasperation and torment.

I quote a witness at the trial to give some idea of one of these. The witness was a Hungarian, Helena Kopper—not a Jewess, but arrested because she was suspected of anti-German sympathies, and an anti-German pamphlet was found in her possession. She described what happened in a punishment company of which Irma Grese was in charge in Auschwitz:

"I was also in the punishment company and, during the time that Grese was in charge when working outside, we were employed outside the camp in a sandpit. There were 700-800 women working in this company; some of them were detailed to dig sand and fill iron trucks with the sand, and others had to push these trucks along a narrow gauge railway. The place in which we worked was surrounded by a strand of wire about three to four feet high and we were not allowed to go outside this wire boundary. There were twelve guards placed at intervals around the wire. It was the practice of Grese to pick out certain Jewish women prisoners and order them to get something from the other side of the wire. She always worked with interpreters. When the prisoners approached the wire they were challenged by the guards, but as Grese usually picked out non-Germans, they did not understand the order and walked on and were shot. Some even of the prisoners who did understand German and knew it was death to cross the wire, did so because they were too weary and ill to bother. Occasionally a guard would not shoot but would force the prisoner to return to the working party. ... Whilst Grese was in charge of the working party she always carried a rubber truncheon. She was responsible for at least thirty deaths a day, resulting from her orders to cross the wire, but many more on occasions."

Another witness, Klara Lebowitz, a Czech, told the following story:

"S.S. woman Grese was in charge of the *Appelle* which took place twice a day. These lasted at least two hours and, more often, three or four hours. If a mistake was made in counting the internees they were made to stand until the missing one was found, this often meant all day. No time was allowed for food and people used to fall unconscious as a result of this. When the woman Grese attended these *Appelle* she often made the internees go on their knees for hours on end or hold stones in their hands high above their heads. If an internee did not stand upright, because she was weak or for any other reason, she would beat her with a rubber truncheon, sometimes until she was unconscious. She would kick persons lying on the ground, and many people were taken to hospital as the result of her treatment. The internees were not allowed to carry anything in their pockets, and the woman Grese would often stop and search internees, whom she would beat unmercifully if she found anything on them, even a handkerchief.

"I have often seen the woman Grese with Dr Mengels selecting people for the gas-chamber and for forced work in Germany. If the woman Grese saw a mother and daughter or sisters trying to get together in selections for forced work in Germany, she would beat them until they were unconscious and leave them lying on the ground."

These are only two out of many witnesses to the incredible cruelty of this girl, of whom her sister said in evidence: "In our schooldays when, as it sometimes happens, girls were quarrelling and fighting, my sister had never the courage to fight, on the contrary she ran away."

At first Irma Grese flatly denied everything that she was accused of. Afterwards she made three statements, admitting more of her crimes in each one, and admitting some share in the guilt:

"Himmler is responsible for all that has happened, but I suppose I have as much guilt as all the others above me." [She was quoting her own statement to an English officer, and went on to explain]: "I meant by this that simply by being in the S.S. and seeing the crimes committed on order from those in authority and doing nothing to protest or stop them being committed makes anybody in the S.S. as guilty as anybody else. The crimes I refer to are the gassing of persons at Auschwitz and the killing of thousands at Belsen by starvation and untended disease. I consider the crime to be murder."

In a later statement she said: "I have now confessed to all the ill-treatment of prisoners of which I was guilty, because it has been on my conscience. I have nothing else to admit."

She did, however, admit yet more cruelty in another statement made after that one.

Irma Grese received her sentence of death without showing any emotion of any kind, apparently quite unmoved.

Perhaps the most disturbing fact about her and those who were tried with her is that they were all found to be perfectly sane by the doctors and psychiatrists who examined them exhaustively; and still more disturbing, they were not exceptional people.

There were camps similar to Auschwitz and Belsen all over Germany in which the same kind of cruelty was practised and taken for granted. In Mauthausen, Natzweiler, Buchenwald, Majdanek, Dachau and Ravensbrück, and many others, it went on daily, practised not by one or two people, but literally by thousands of normal men and women who had surrendered their consciences to totalitarianism.

LEOPOLD AND LOEB

MY INTENTION in using Loeb and Leopold was to illustrate the curious type of egoism which enables certain people to stand on trial for their lives without fear or remorse, but on the contrary boasting, swaggering and enjoying the limelight—but I need not say that they illustrate many other peculiarities of the guilt complex too. In fact psychologists continually attribute new and different ones to them, and probably the reader will find yet more himself, if he studies them further.

Their childhood, heredity and background, as well as all their pathological symptoms, were described in the greatest detail at their trial, which was the first trial in the history of the American courts in which the court allowed and encouraged a searching medical examination of the prisoners' minds. This was done at the instigation of Clarence Darrow, the defending counsel, who realized that his only hope of getting the boys sentenced to life imprisonment, instead of to death, was to plead guilty but mentally ill.

Both boys were the children of very rich, and so far as money was concerned, over-indulgent parents. Both were brilliant intellectually and precocious, both brought up by governesses until they were adolescent. Loeb's governess, though devoted, was extremely severe, and to avoid being punished by her he became a confirmed liar; he also began to practise crime while still a child. He took to stealing money and shoplifting—quite unnecessarily, as he was allowed anything whatever that he wanted; very early in his youth he took to stealing liquor and cars and to firing shacks. Dr David Abrahamsen gives an interesting analysis of him in his book *Crime and the Human Mind*, in which he suggests that he had suicidal tendencies brought about by hidden feelings of guilt and was driven to crime in search of self-punishment, and that the same hidden motive caused him to commit the murder, for which he expected to be put to death. He admitted to having frequently thought of suicide, and his childhood and adolescent fantasy was that he was in jail and the greatest criminal in society.

His egoism was enormous and led him, or at least was among the things that led him, to plan what he boasted would be "the perfect crime." To be a master criminal became his ruling ambition. He was extremely callous and seemed incapable of feeling; he was aware only of himself. He was a handsome boy, with great charm of manner, and particularly he gave the impression of being honest and open, incapable of deceit—a lovable personality!

And undoubtedly Leopold, who met him when they were both around twelve or thirteen years old, did love him—in fact, fell in love with him. He became completely obsessed by him, and attributed his part in the murder to the fact that he could not refuse to do anything which Loeb wanted. Speaking of Loeb he said, "I am jealous of the food and drink that he takes because I cannot come as close to him as the food and drink."

Loeb found Leopold a perfect tool to carry out his crime dreams with, and he himself was the realization of the other boy's childhood fantasy, which was that he was a devoted slave. The two boys, now about fourteen years old, made a crime friendship pact in which it was an agreed condition that Leopold was to be completely dominated by Loeb, and when the latter used the phrase "for Robert's sake" he was to give way to his wishes, whatever they were, without any question.

Leopold had a number of physical complaints, chiefly glandular, and was undersized and unattractive; he was very conscious of this and of his unpopularity, owing mainly to his precocity. He had already been vitiated by the unnatural eroticism of one of his governesses, who during the few years she had charge of him succeeded in making normal sexual life in future extremely difficult for him. Before this incident of the governess, he had worshipped his mother, and when she died, though he was still a young child, he turned savagely against God and religion.

In May 1924, when Leopold was nineteen and Loeb was eighteen, they committed the murder which they had been dreaming of and planning for years. They enticed a much younger boy, Robert Frank, into their car and hit him over the head with a heavy instrument. At the actual moment of the murder Leopold was frightened; Loeb, on the other hand, was indifferent and amused. Later they put the boy's body into a drain and claimed ransom for him.

When the boys were arrested they at first denied the crime but afterwards confessed it, and were brought to trial. They came into court carefully and elegantly dressed and appeared to enjoy the publicity extremely. Loeb, answering a reporter who remarked on his careful tailoring and hair-cut, replied, "Of course, this is our show: the public must not be cheated."

They smiled, joked quietly and took notes, and were concerned with one thing only, the effect they were making and their publicity. They were gratified by seeing their photographs in the paper, and showed no aversion from the jail after their luxurious homes.

On one day of the trial alone did they show any emotion; then they seemed to be swayed, like the crowd in the courtroom, by the intensely emotional pleading of their counsel. After their sentence to life imprisonment was passed, they went to serve it with apparent pleasure.

The case is given in detail in *Darrow for the Defence*, by Irving Stone, who ends his description by saying: "Within a few minutes Loeb and Leopold were on their way to Joliet, Loeb to be cut to death after a few years by a fellow prisoner, Leopold to establish a brilliant educational system for incarcerated men."

JOHN GEORGE HAIGH

I T IS NOT SURPRISING that those who make a *habit* of murder need to hide their true character from themselves, as much as they need to hide it from other people. This may also explain why it is that men who murder women with almost habitual frequency usually become attached, in so far as they are capable of doing so, to one woman, who is quite safe with them. For few men can believe in their real selves without the continual flattering reassurance of one woman's love and admiration, and still less can they believe in their pseudo-selves without it.

Thus the famous Smith who murdered three wives by drowning them in the bath, and who had an astonishing record of sordid crime and fraud besides, had one woman in his life whom he did not marry, did not murder, and always came back to.

Haigh, the acid bath murderer who has so recently perished, was deeply loved by one young woman, whom he treated with respect and apparently with affection; and since she was necessary for his self-love, it is very likely that in so far as he could love, he loved her.

For her, and for everyone, and especially for himself, he adopted the fancy-dress of a gentleman, or at all events of his conception of a gentleman, which would be a dapper kind of man, with a smart car, and a certain amount of swagger— something, in fact, more like most people's conception of a bounder. Haigh combined this gentleman with the conceit of cleverness.

While awaiting his trial for murder, he boasted continually to two other men imprisoned with him, and reiterated again and again to them that he would get off because of his cleverness, but that they, who were also awaiting trial for murder, would be condemned to death, because they were not clever, as he was. But before he was tried he adopted an air of patronising benevolence to his warders, and was generous to them with offers of cigarettes, newspapers and so on.

After his trial, when he was in the condemned cell, it became more necessary than ever for him to put on disguise, the disguise of his conception of a gentleman. His conceit and his boast of cleverness could not save him now, even from self-knowledge, but his fear of self-knowledge, and the degree of shame hidden by his seeming lack of it, can be measured by the extent of his pose as a gentleman.

Of course, in prison clothes, which until the morning of his execution a condemned man must wear, and without a car or money, he was obliged to fall back on the old trick of trying to lift himself by taking others down. He adopted an attitude of superiority to his warders, treating them as if they were his servants, and making continual complaints about them, and indeed about everything else.

It is difficult to imagine a greater strain or a more unpleasant task than to be a warder guarding a man who is to die. Means, though one can hardly imagine their being adequate, are provided—such as games, cards, chess, and so on—with which the poor warder may try to distract the prisoner, but Haigh considered it beneath his status to play with the warders and refused to do so.

At his trial Haigh's "cleverness" consisted in pretending madness, a type of religious mania, linked up with the alleged excess of religion in his early upbringing. This was sheer fake. He had learnt the symptoms of the insanity he pretended to, from another prisoner, who really had been in the criminal lunatic asylum at Broadmoor, but it is not easy to learn insanity from an insane person, who will know about it only subjectively and will not know anything about the several hundred symptoms that a mental nurse will note daily. Certainly Haigh no longer had any strong religious feeling, even if he had as a boy, but during the night before his execution he wrote a letter saying that liberty of religious thought is not tolerated in England, as he was to be executed for heresy! And to this strange statement he added, "I go forward to finish my mission in another form".

He dressed himself on the morning of his death, as he was then allowed to do, in the new suit which he had bought to wear during his trial—maintaining his fancy dress to the end.

The Church of England clergyman came to do what he could to prepare him to die; he came at six o'clock, thinking that this poor man might want some comfort, but Haigh sent him away until half-past seven, and gave scant attention to his soul.

Perhaps because this, too, would have compelled him at last to take off his fancy dress and face himself.

PETER KÜRTEN

PETER KÜRTEN is one of the most baffling murderers that ever lived. My object is to use his case to illustrate that particularly dangerous type of criminal—dangerous especially to women—who seems to be almost too gentle, too eager to please, and who is capable of almost unbelievable brutality in committing crime—a type often produced by violent and brutal fathers, who, while crushing their children to a state of servility, breed in them a hatred of authority represented in their own person, which is likely to find its outlet in crimes of a violence that can be matched against the father's violence.

Power, as these wretched children have seen it, must be exerted by brutal means. They thirst to be revenged on authority, to get power over it; and they know no other way. But fear makes them outwardly gentle, eager to placate: the revenge they plan is one that must be taken in secret, under cover of darkness. The attempt to attack a man of the father's strength is not to be thought of, and the only way out is to identify self with the father and attack a child.

In some cases this identification, mixed up, as it always is, inextricably with the father-son complex, may be a hidden means of bringing the father, in the person of oneself, to the gallows. Such a motive is not out of the question in Kürten's case, for among his peculiarities was a mania for confessing; we shall see that few people ever confessed so often, in so many ways, and so willingly. Moreover, he did bring himself to the guillotine. It was he himself who persuaded his own wife to give him up to the police, and who gave her the evidence that must lead to his death. Such is the rough outline of the theory I am attempting to illustrate by Peter Kürten, but almost any other theory about crime could be illustrated by him too—or, I was going to say, about insanity, but he was found to be perfectly sane by the doctors at his trial, and he had no symptoms of insanity.

He claimed to be a sadist, and though sadism is not regarded as insanity in English Law, many people consider it to be so in fact. However, a genuine sadist would not be capable of stopping in the middle of his criminal act if he heard someone coming, but Kürten could do that, and several times he did so. Also, a maniac of any kind who commits a crime during an attack of mania has no clear remembrance of anything immediately before the crime; his mind is confused and overcharged at that time, and has either a hopelessly confused memory of it, or none at all. Kürten had vivid and detailed memories of these moments, and not only of those preceding his more recent crimes, but of those committed years ago. He was able to describe in detail the bedroom, with the furniture and how it was arranged, where he murdered a little girl many years before, although this was the only occasion on which he had ever been into that room. He described both the outward circumstance of the crimes he confessed and his own reactions and sensations: these of course could not be proved, but the others, such as the little girl's bedroom, could be verified, and in every case they were.

Not only were there these signs of sanity confirmed by medical examination, but Kürten, considering his low birth and lack of education, had educated himself and acquired considerable culture of a sort, by reading. He attributed some of his obsession with crime, and his rather fatalistic attitude to it in his own case, to his reading of Lombroso's works on the Criminal Man, and especially to his theory of moral insanity.

He certainly knew and said that he knew the difference between right and wrong, and expressed shame and contrition, sympathy for the relations of his victims, and the assurance of his prayers for them. But he also declared that he confessed his horrible crimes, many of which would not otherwise have been known, because doing so gave him a feeling of greatness.

This particular inconsistency seems to me to bear out the theory of identification with the brutal father, which would have compensated for his littleness and weakness, and so account for the feeling of being grand and great, whilst the shame and sorrow would be the reactions of the gentle, childish side of his nature.

Apart from crimes for which he had already been imprisoned

at the time of his trial—mostly theft, threats and acts of brutality—Kürten has the following crimes to his credit:

Attempted strangling: Twenty-three, between the years 1899
and 1930

> November 1899—An unknown girl of eighteen
> 1913 Margaret Schäfer
>   An unknown woman
>   Gertrude Franken
> 1921 A war widow
> 1925 Tiedmann (young woman)
>   Mech (young woman)
>   Kiefer (young woman)
> 1926 Wack (young woman)
> 1927 "Anni" (young girl)
> 1929 Edith Boukorn
>   Maria Witt
>   Maria Mass
>   Unknown girl
>   Christine Heerstrasse (also thrown in river)
>   Maria Rad
> 1930 Hilda
>   Maria
>   Irma
>   Sibilla
>   Unknown girl
>   Hau (young woman)
>   Maria Büdlick

Strangling: Between the same years—eight

> 1913 Christine Klein (her throat was also cut)
> 1929 Rose Ohliger (a child, also stabbed after death)
>   Maria Hahn (also stabbed to death)
>   Anni (also drowned)
>   Gertrude Hamacher (child, also throat cut)
>   Luise Lenzen (child, also stabbed)
>   Gertrude Schulte (also stabbed)
>   Gertrude Albermann (also stabbed with scissors)

Stabbing: Between 1929 and 1930—five

> Rudolf Scheer (man)
> Anna Goldhausen
> Frau Mantel
> Gustav Kornblum (man)
> Gertrude Schulte (young woman)

Attacks with axe, hammer or scissors: Approximately twelve

1913	Unknown man (axe)
	Unknown woman (axe)
1929	Frau Kühn (scissors)
	Sofie Rückl (blow with a tool)
	Frau Meurer (hammer)
	Frau Wanders (hammer)
1930	Several girls
	Charlotte Ulrich
	Gertrude Bell

Killed with hammer blows in 1929

> Ida Reuter (young woman)
> Elizabeth Dörrier (young woman)

These figures add up roughly to thirty-five attempted murders, and ten murders. Beside these there were forty cases of arson.

All these are crimes to which Kürten confessed voluntarily. At his trial the cases of arson were omitted and he was charged with nine murders.

At his trial he confessed all these murders and his attempted murders in great detail. He had already confessed them to the doctors who examined him before the trial, and before that he had twice confessed to his wife all the murders that he committed in Düsseldorf, begging her, the second time, to give him up to the police. But not content with this, he also confessed to two murders of which he was innocent. These murders were committed by a man named Brink in Altenburg.

Further details about Kürten's confessions to his wife can best be told in the place in which they occur in his own account of his life. For in his confessions and statements in court and in those made to his doctors in prison, Kürten left a more detailed, clear and remarkable autobiography of a murderer than any that has ever been recorded in the history of crime.

I shall attempt to put his confessions, and some proved statements, together in such a way as to make a consecutive picture of his life, and leave the reader to consider for himself whether he was mad or sane, a sadist or not, a megalomaniac or someone suffering from appalling inferiority: or whether he was simply a sinner who surrendered to his own evil impulses. And finally, whether or not there are any reasonable grounds for my theory of the father-son complex. But first of all a brief description of Kürten's personality as it appeared to those who knew him.

On the days following his arrest in Düsseldorf, the people of the town absolutely and unanimously refused to believe that he was "the Monster". They knew him as a respectable middle-aged man of great charm—hardworking whenever he had the opportunity to work, and devoted to his wife, though it was also common gossip that he was unfaithful to her. This, however, seemed to the gossips, especially the women, to be explained by his extraordinary charm and gentleness, which few women could resist, and by his wife's being, though a good woman, prematurely old, which would hardly be likely to hold a man to whom life offered so many temptations. It was his wife who refused to let his infidelities break up the marriage, although she resented them. She had a reason for this, apart from a really deep affection for him. In her past she had shot and killed a man who had betrayed her. For that she had served a prison sentence, but she considered it just that she should serve a life-long sentence of patience and abnegation with her husband. She worked in a restaurant on night shifts, and because, when the series of murders started to terrify Düsseldorf, she felt nervous about walking through the streets, Peter called at the restaurant to take her home in the small hours of the morning—an arrangement which fitted in very well with his other plans, though it was unnecessary, for Frau Kürten happened to be the only woman in Düsseldorf who was safe.

She was safe because she was the one woman for whom Kürten had some kind of love and respect. She was also the only one with whom he had perfectly normal sexual relations.

He said that she had no physical attraction for him, but he admired and respected her and felt deep affection for her.

There was one point about which everyone, including his wife, who knew Peter Kürten agreed; this was his attraction for children. They all loved him, and he gave the impression that he loved them. He had no adult friends, but many child friends, whom he treated tenderly.

Although to everyone else who knew him personally he was excessively gentle, he occasionally showed violence to his wife, if she crossed him in any way. But she, overshadowed by remorse for her impulsive crime, accepted this as her due, and humoured him in every way.

Now here is his own account of himself in his own words,* though I have rearranged the order of them slightly to give a consecutive picture of his life.

"I was born in Mülheim-on-the-Rhine. In my early childhood my parents moved frequently from one town to another. My father was very often drunk. There were always quarrels with other people living in the house. During my early years, I, as eldest child, suffered very much from my father's drunken brutality. When I was eight years old I ran away from home and stayed away for weeks. I slept in furniture pantechnicons and a policeman caught me in one. In 1895 we moved to Düsseldorf. We were ten children and the poverty was dreadful when my father happened to be in prison. But if he were at home it was almost worse because he drank away all his money. Even in those days I was almost an outcast, and the other children at school pointed me out to one another. I kept away from them out of my own free will.

"When we lived in Köln-Mühlheim we lived in the same lodging as the dog-catcher. There used to be one in every town. Dogs running loose were caught, and when they were not claimed they were killed and eaten. Their fat was sold as a specific cure .... Seeing these animals slaughtered often gave me pleasure. I often thought of this man later on when I was old enough to catch squirrels, martens or birds for selling in the zoological shops ....

* Quoted by Margaret Seaton Wagner in *The Monster of Düsseldorf.* Faber and Faber (London, 1932).

I still have a scar on my finger where a squirrel bit me. If you seize them by the neck they let go. When I did this as a boy it gave me pleasure.

"Through reading and discussing things of the kind I came to understand that such feelings could arise. At the time there were more pigs killed at home than today. I always enjoyed looking on. As a schoolboy I always liked to see a fire, the screams and agitation of the people were a delight to me.

"When I was a boy of nine I used to look after the washing spread out by the washerwomen on the banks of the Rhine.

"We boys played about on rafts. I committed my first murder, if you want to call it that, by pushing one of the boys into the water and under the raft. When another boy fell in when looking over the side for him, I did not help him but pushed him back into the water; both were drowned. I felt very much afraid when I saw them dead and was frightened to be alone for some time, but after a while that feeling left me.

"When I was fourteen I became an apprentice in the same factory in which my father worked. In the same year my father was sentenced to a term of three years penal servitude for incest. My sister was thirteen and a half.

"I was dependent upon the favour of other people for bread. When my father came out again I had a very bad time. He treated me brutally and even attacked me with a knife. I often ran away and stayed away for some time. My father used to threaten to cut my head off and things like that. Once something of the kind was only prevented by the screams of the other children. At last I determined to get away altogether. I took some money I was told to pay in. I was sent to prison. I had two days extra for spending the night on a bench in the Hofgarten. I was handcuffed, though a boy at the time, and taken by an enormously big policeman through the whole town till we arrived at the prison. I was dreadfully ashamed! Perhaps people thought I was a murderer already at that time. But there in the police cells at Berger Gate I met real criminals. There were hard cases newly sent up again. I got myself tattooed there for the first time.

"After my release I was homeless. A woman twice as old as I was took me into her home—for her own purposes. I became her lover. Because I wanted to come in one night against the will of the other people in the house, I got another sentence for attempted housebreaking. I was forbidden to come again, but I did so, sometimes creeping over the roofs of the houses. I was a casual labourer at the time, about 1900, and got imprisoned twice for trying to get out of paying my bill at an eating-house and for thefts in shops. Sometimes I was home in Düsseldorf, sometimes I got short-time jobs elsewhere. But in November I was sentenced to two years imprisonment for renewed thefts. When I came out again I think I was a little mad. And I did something for which even today I have no explanation. [He referred to throwing stones and firing shots into a window to frighten a family.] I got a fresh sentence for that and was in prison until 1904. I was called up as a conscript to Metz, and deserted there. I took up with a woman who thieved with me and the result was seven years penal servitude. That was too heavy a punishment in my opinion: I was too young for it. I underwent this term until May 13th, 1912, and then I was flung out upon the world again. In the autumn of 1912 I spoke to a woman in the automatic restaurant, and when the waiter came up and interrupted I fired a shot. The consequence was a new punishment for intent to do bodily harm. After this I kept stealing more or less regularly, specializing chiefly in the houses where there was a public-house below and the family lived in rooms above. In Düsseldorf when out on one of these expeditions I came into a bedroom above the 'Lösch-Ecke,' where there were several children and a young girl of about seventeen—asleep. It was then for the first time, in a sudden rush of feeling I can't explain, that I fell upon this girl and tried to strangle her. This attempt lasted some time, then I escaped unobserved. ... In one particular house I was hunting around the bedroom by the light of a pocket-lamp. In a second bedroom leading out of it I saw a girl of about nine years old in bed. I felt suddenly exactly as I had felt in the 'Lösch-Ecke'—I forgot everything else. I flung myself on this girl in a great state of agitation, and strangled her, and when she was lying there quiet, took out my sharp little pocket-knife and cut the child's throat ... first of all I had only the intention of stealing, but when I saw the child, there came over me beside the other excitement the remembrance of my

terrible sufferings and humiliation during my years of imprisonment. In those days the young prisoners were drilled and 'licked
into shape' in the same yards where they play football and other
games today. We were called names and our lives made burdens.
There were special punishments of starvation diet with full-time
work. There were the dark cells as frequent punishment. I was
put into irons for a bad breach of discipline. There were
manacles with heavy chains which were kept on night and day
and rubbed sores on the body ... well, the remembrance of these
and other brutal punishments, which in my opinion were often
unjust and served out arbitrarily by despots, combined with the
strong sexual passions I have inherited from my father, made
me absolutely crazy. The first reason is the principal factor,
though I think perhaps I would not have done it if I had not
had memories of torture I had undergone to do away with the
last inhibitions."

After this Kürten described three of his unsuccessful attempts
to murder, ending with, "All these things gave me sexual satisfaction", and questioned by the judge concerning his crimes of
arson, he went on: "In 1904 when my desire for injuring people
awoke, the love of setting fire to things awoke as well. The sight
of flames delighted me, but above all it was the excitement of the
attempts to extinguish the fire and the agitation of those who
saw their property being destroyed. I set light to barns chiefly."
He added that the thought of possible human victims of the fire
gave him pleasure.

He continued to describe murder after murder and attempted
murder after attempted murder. He said that usually he followed
up a murder by a fire. Far from the display of indifference so
frequently found in murderers of this type, Peter Kürten showed
signs of distress, and mentioned that on looking back he was
glad that his long prison sentences had prevented him from committing yet more crimes. He constantly associated his father's
brutality with that of the prison authorities; thus, following the
confession I have just quoted, more or less, he said:

"My youth was a martyrdom. We never had a Sunday because my father used to make us work. He had made a little

FRANZ KAFKA

workshop for moulding aluminium utensils in the cellar. My
mother was pure and good. [It is interesting to note here that
the reason he gave for his affection for his wife, who was some
years older than he, was that she was a good woman.] I was
witness of his brutal treatment of my sister. In prison I began to
think about revenging myself on society. I did myself a great
deal of damage through reading blood-and-thunder stories, for
instance I read the tale of 'Jack the Ripper' several times. When
I came to think over what I had read when I was in prison, I
thought what pleasure it would give me to do things of that kind
once I got out again. I see now that I ought to have resisted
putting such thoughts into practice. Setting fire to things gave
me just as much pleasure, from the fright and agitation of the
people whose property was burning, from the crackle of the
flames and the thundering of the big heavy horses who used to
draw the fire hose. I think with relief today that my long terms
of imprisonment prevented me from doing more harm. I was
only sixteen when I found out what pleasure it gave me to try
and strangle a girl I took out with me into the woods near
Grafenberg. The woman who took me up when I first came out
of prison was one whose temperament was the very opposite to
my own. She liked cruel treatment."

Kürten agreed with the suggestion made at this point by the
public prosecutor that this last fact increased his tendency to
sadism.

He mentioned again and again the pleasure he derived even
from the secondary excitation of his crimes. Referring to the day
following one of the most shocking of his child-murders, he
said, "There is a café opposite the Klein's place, and I sat there
and drank a glass of beer and read all about the murder in the
papers. People were talking about it all round me. All this
amount of indignation and horror did me good."

Referring to the two murders which he confessed but had not
really committed, he said, "The news of them made a great
impression on me but I did not do them."

He denied that he went out to search deliberately for someone
to kill: "It is not a fact that I went out in search of somebody to
kill, no matter whom. I looked for a victim in so far as I

believed that the injury and the cries of the victim would give me the satisfaction I wanted and relieve the sexual tension."

Describing how after one of his cruellest murders, that of a child, he went out to set fire to the little body, he said: "I derived no sexual satisfaction from what I did. My motives were simply to arouse excitement and indignation in the population. Through setting fire to the body I thought I could increase the rage."

Again, after the murder of a young woman whom he stabbed in the heart with a pair of scissors, he relates: "Next evening I went back to the spot and thought over where I could bury the body. I thought how nice it would be if I had something of the kind to sit by when I took a walk. I went back home and took a spade with me and dug a deep hole in a woody corner of the field. I lifted the body and laid it just as one would lay an ordinary corpse in a grave. I took the wrist-watch off her arm—I had a feeling of solemn tenderness all the time. I stroked her hair and shovelled in the first spadefuls of earth very evenly and carefully. I hid the spade in the brook and cleaned my shoes. I went to the grave many times afterwards and kept on improving it. Later on I must have been to the spot at least thirty times, and every time when I thought of what was lying there I had a feeling of satisfaction."

To his defending counsel Kürten confessed privately that at ten years old, a year after his first two murders—the two boys he pushed into the river—he murdered another two by the same method.

There was continual evidence in Kürten's own statements that he had a mania for grandeur. He said that one of the strongest urges in him to confess was that it gave him a feeling of grandeur, and moreover it was a form of re-living the crimes, like day dreaming. He did indeed seem to be one who lived in a borderland between daydreams and reality. In the confinement of his long imprisonments his vivid imagination gave him the fearful satisfaction he longed for; when he came out of prison he translated it into reality, and while awaiting trial he re-lived his crimes in his confessions.

Yet while making those confessions he showed some remorse in his manner, and repeatedly declared his sympathy for the victims.

"I must insist," he said, "that I feel deep sympathy with the victims and particularly with the poor children."

Perhaps the most baffling thing he ever said was this, spoken to his father confessor in his cell. He was speaking of little Gertrude Albermann, the child of five:

"The child was so sweet to me and put her little arms round my neck when I lifted her up and carried her, and laid her cheek against mine and was so trusting."

After he was condemned to death Kürten behaved calmly and gave no trouble at all; he went to the guillotine willingly and did not, as might have been expected of him, attempt any exhibitionism. Asked if he had any last wishes, he said "No" with no sign of emotion and no comment.

He had not been practising his religion for many years, but he made his confession in preparation for death. This time it was a sacramental confession, and after it he said that his obsessional daydreams ceased entirely and did not return. This fact as well as the others is worth pondering.

BENEDICT JOSEPH LABRE

THE STORY of Benedict Joseph Labre illustrates the way in which God sometimes uses neurosis to lead a man, whose will is surrendered to him, into a vocation which he would not even imagine for himself.

How *could* Labre have known in 1764, when he was sixteen years old, that he was to take the guilt of our own generation upon himself, and to sanctify in himself the terrible suffering which millions of men and women and even little children were going to endure in a not far distant future? How could he have chosen just those sufferings that would be the outcome of our ideologies and wars, and which in Labre's times it would hardly have been possible to imagine as the fate of millions of people?

I mean the suffering of the millions who have died in German concentration camps, after suffering starvation, filthiness, contempt, raggedness or nakedness; and, when they were not driven into the gas-chambers, death from exhaustion. And those who today are in Communist prisons and camps, hidden away, out of reach of human help; as well as the thousands known by the dreadful description "Displaced Persons", who, deprived of home and country, are wandering destitute about the world.

Poverty, austerity, and a wandering life other holy men had often chosen before him, but he went further, he was verminous, he ate scraps from garbage heaps; he was not only without a home but without a country, ever going from one shrine to another, from one city to another. His clothes were rotting off him, and in the end he died of exhaustion.

This is all too familiar a picture of human suffering now, but how did this man, so clearly a prophet of our times, know to choose it?

He did not choose it. He chose only to surrender his will to God, and even that he planned to do in quite a different way, by a life of contemplation within the tranquillity of the cloister.

Until he was sixteen years old he was able to study successfully, and there seemed to be no reason why he should not carry out his intention. But no sooner did he attempt to do so than he was defeated by mental suffering, which certainly bears out the idea that he was our prophet-saint, for he was led into the amazing life God chose for him by our most widespread suffering, neurosis. He became quite unable to concentrate on anything or to learn anything, and in addition he became possessed by depression so black that it was perfectly clear to the religious superiors whom he asked to accept him, that he would never be able to live their life of discipline and silence, and remain sane.

He made attempt after attempt to overcome this curious state of mind, going from the Trappists to the Carthusians, from the Carthusians to the Cistercians; but always with the same result —failure. Usually there were reasons coupled with his seeming mindlessness for refusing him—he was too young, or too frail; but when he was given a trial, his depression turned to torment and he had to be sent away.

At length he realized, through an irresistible inner compulsion, that he was to live the life I have described: a life of drastic austerity and penance, not hidden away, but right out in the open, among men, literally in the streets of the cities of the world.

No sooner had Labre understood what it was that he was to do, than his mental condition was cured. He had no idea of the whole meaning of his life, of how many millions he stood proxy for before God, of the enormous burden of mental suffering that was sanctified in his own; but from the moment that he became a wandering beggar his mind was illuminated and filled with peace, which remained with him through all his outward suffering until, like so many of those for whom he had come to be a Christ, he died from exhaustion in the crowded streets.

TERESA MARTIN

I T IS IMPOSSIBLE to write a book about psychological suffering in any form, without referring again and again to Teresa Martin. What Benedict Labre did for the victims of the war, she did for the victims of civilization, the neurotics of our generation—for the neurotics and mentally suffering people that are now in such great majority. She sanctified that worst of all suffering in herself, and, without realizing the vast significance of what she did, entered into it in her acceptance of her father's mental affliction as well as of her own suffering.

At eight years old Teresa fell ill with what was unquestionably a neurotic illness and was baffling to the doctors of her day. The symptoms were those often associated with the "guilt complex"; they were entirely mental or emotional, consisting of fear and distress that was frightening even to watch, and which nothing could relieve. This continued for so long that the child's life even was considered to be in danger.

It is not surprising that she had this illness, for she was an extremely oversensitive child, and the intensity of the piety all round her in her home must have brought on her already precocious spirituality as the heat brings on the hot-house flowers. She was frail in body too, and this, together with her environment, would almost inevitably have resulted in uneven emotional development.

There were certainly natural causes for the curious illness, but there was also the supernatural one—that no one could better offer the burden of psychological suffering than this really good child: no one could sanctify the feeling of guilt better than she. She was preparing for our generation.

Finally the illness was cured by a miracle, and the interesting fact is that after it she never showed symptoms of a neurotic kind again, although she did suffer, with amazing balance, everything that neurotic people suffer in their minds.

She was cured of her illness, and from now on she had unusual spiritual and mental poise, which never forsook her whatever her pain of mind or body. But she was not cured of being herself; she still had the same acute sensitivity to wrestle with, and she was to know all about the suffering that ego-neurotics complain so much of—being misunderstood and exploited. Only Teresa did not complain.

She experienced the terrible sense of emptiness and the numbness of feeling that frightens so many psychasthenics, and passed from the knowledge that she was unappreciated by people to the *feeling*, which is the nearest that there is to despair, that she was forsaken by God.

The well-known story of her torture when another nun rattled her rosary, shows clearly enough that wonderfully though she controlled it, she suffered from acute nervous irritability.

As if it were necessary for her formally to accept the humiliation of mental suffering, the opportunity to do so was given to her in the hardest way imaginable. Her father became mentally ill. His brain was affected by paralysis and he was unable even to recognize his children; Teresa had seen a strange (perhaps telepathic?) vision of him, with a kind of veil over his head and face, which was some sort of warning to her. She suffered intensely when this blow fell—"Words could not express my agony"—but nevertheless she says that the three years of what she describes as her father's martyrdom were the most dear and fruitful years in her life: "Our father must be greatly loved by God since he has so much to suffer. What a delight to share in his humiliation."

Thus the indomitable forerunner of our neurotic age accepted not only that man's suffering, but the mental suffering of all those today who like him must be greatly loved by God, because they have so much to suffer.

HANS CHRISTIAN ANDERSEN

A GENIUS cannot escape from his destiny of Christhood, and he cannot attempt to resist it without disaster. Other men who resist it tend to become mediocre, they tend towards nothingness. They shut the door of their minds against the Holy Spirit, the wind of Heaven, which would have swept through the house of their spirit, bearing with it the seed of life; and they shut themselves into an empty house. But the genius cannot shut the door of his mind, because if he does so the Holy Spirit will sweep down upon him and break open the doors and the walls of his house. It will not come to him in a soft wind, but in a sea of wind in storm breaking down everything that resists it. The genius is a channel through which the universal experience of mankind is poured; all human love and grief and joy, in all their forms, must pass through him. Most men possess their own hearts, but the heart of the genius does not belong to him, it belongs to everyone. His function in life is to give expression to that which is secret in the hearts of all men. He must be the voice of the world, he must laugh with the delight of the whole world, he must shed every man's tears. He must understand in a unique way what it means to bear another's burdens. It is both his glory and his tragedy that he does not belong to himself. He is given to mankind by God, and he is wonderfully close in his sweet and terrible vocation to "The Word of God".

What has been said about guilt and the human destiny of Christhood should have made it clear that the universal experience of mankind *can* only be known and lived in any one man, through the Man who abides in all mankind, Christ.

It *can* only be suffered, without shattering the individual, if he puts up no resistance, but surrenders his soul to the Holy Spirit, through whom he is inlived by Christ, and from whom he receives the fortitude, peace, joy, patience, love, wisdom and understanding that are the soul's stability.

Genius admits no compromise. The human being to whom it

is given must either be a saint, surrendering absolutely to his Christ-destiny, or be broken by his genius.

This may well be the reason for the frequency of tragedy and instability in the lives of great authors. Every one of those listed below was insane, or psychopathic, neurotic, alcoholic, or addicted to drugs.

Blake	Crabbe	De Quincey
Beddoes	Dickens	Rossetti
Boswell	Donne	Ruskin
Bunyan	Dostoievsky	Rousseau
Burns	Ernest Dowson	Rimbaud
Byron	Flaubert	Rilke
Baudelaire	Goethe	Strindberg
Emily Brontë	Gray	Shelley
Elizabeth Barrett	Gogol	Smart
Browning	Hölderlin	Swift
Léon Bloy	Lionel Johnson	De Sade
Carlyle	Charles Lamb	Swinburne
Chatterton	Mary Lamb	Tennyson
Clare	D. H. Lawrence	Francis Thompson
Coleridge	Lermontov	James Thomson
Collins	Nietzsche	Verlaine
Cowper	Edgar Allan Poe	

Many of these wrestled with their own disaster, some overcame it. But their real conflict was with God.

In the soul of the genius the Kingdom of Heaven suffers violence.

> But ah, but O thou terrible, why wouldst thou rude on me
> Thy wring-world right foot rock? lay a lionlimb against me?
> scan
> With darksome devouring eyes my bruisèd bones? and fan,
> O in turns of tempest, me heaped there; me frantic to avoid thee
> and flee?*

The neurosis or frustrating circumstance in the life of a genius is always a conflict between the frailty of human nature and the immensity of his destiny, but it is not always a sign that he has been broken on the rock of his destiny. Sometimes the

* Gerard Manley Hopkins, "Carrion Comfort".

conflict is the means by which he must fulfil his vocation and
enter into the communion with mankind which is its fulfilment.

This was certainly the case with Hans Christian Andersen.
And what conflict he had to wrestle with, both within himself
and in every circumstance of his life. Poverty, ignorance, family
madness and instability, a drunken mother, a selfish and worthless stepfather, his own ugliness and oversensitivity, bullying
and discouragement from his schoolmaster, failure in love—all
this and more is the background of the fairy-stories that hold
the secrets of every human heart.

Hans Christian Andersen was born at Odense in April 1805.
His father was a cobbler; in him a poet was defeated, and he
suffered from almost pathological depression. But he was the
only person in the whole of Hans Christian's life who was close
to him both in understanding and love. Longing to give the
little boy the education that poverty had denied to himself, the
father read aloud to him from the few books he had bought at
the price of real self-denial, made toys and puppets for him, and
a puppet theatre, and encouraged him in his fantasies and his
dreams.

Hans Christian adored him, but before he was ten years old,
the father in a fit of depression enlisted as a soldier, only to
return a few months later broken in health and spirit, and within
two years, when Hans Christian was eleven, he died.

Hans Christian's mother was a washerwoman, a devoted
mother, who now had to work harder than ever for her son,
who gave little promise of ever becoming a breadwinner himself. She loved him dearly and was proud of him, and proud of
the strange, impracticable mind which she could not understand, and of his fastidiousness and extraordinary natural
refinement. She came from circumstances of misery herself. As
a child she had been driven out to beg in the streets by her
parents. Now she kept their one room spotless; everything there
was shining and neat; her little son, though his clothes were of
the poorest, was kept shining and neat too, but this was no easy
task, for he grew at a furious pace. He grew out of everything
the poor woman made for him, as soon as it was made; his
wrists stuck out of his sleeves, his legs grew too long for his
trousers. And he not only grew bigger and bigger, but he grew

more and more grotesque and ugly, and more and more odd: he wrote poems, and stranger still, with those great clumsy feet and long thin legs, he wanted to be a dancer. His hands were huge and looked clumsy too, but he made the loveliest little puppets with them and sewed their clothes himself, and he cut out paper silhouettes that were as decorative and beautiful as the settings for the Russian Ballet. But his mother knew nothing of the ballet.

She did know, however, that his grandfather was mad: he was a harmless lunatic, but sometimes he would wander through the streets of Odense, wreathed in flowers, singing, and then the boys would chase him and he would fly in terror. Hans Christian had seen this and he was to be haunted by it, and by the fear of madness, all his life.

He saw a great deal of insanity, for his grandmother, his father's mother, earned her living by tending the garden of the insane poor, and it was the insane poor who were the first people to whom Hans Andersen told stories.

Soon there were many others, for Hans Christian was driven by a furious urge to give his treasure to the world, and he began in his home town, as a small boy, by almost forcing his way into the homes of the cultured people of the town and reading plays and poems he had written to them. He would even stop people in the street to read his works aloud to them, and when the coming of a troupe of travelling players to Odense started his interest in the theatre, his performance became almost formidable, for now he was fired with the passion to go on the stage, and he not only read his plays and poems but he insisted upon acting, dancing and singing.

He never gave up this habit of forcing himself upon every audience that he could, even strangers, into whose houses he almost pushed his way for the purpose.

This and his oversensitivity leads all his biographers to attribute a naïve vanity to him, but I think there is a very different explanation. The point which I want to illustrate by the story of Hans Andersen is that the strongest passion in his life, the passion which brought fame in the end, was not vanity or ambition, but the absolute need to be in communion with other men, to be one with them, as those who love are one. Hans

Christian did not merely believe in his own genius, he *knew* what he had to give. He *knew* that he had a treasure beyond all price, a gift of sheer beauty, that once it was given would become part of the experience of beauty, of people in all ages, all over the world.

A good-looking, well-dressed youth, educated in a cultured home, might have gone about it in a seemingly more modest way—but only the whirlwind in Hans Christian's soul could drive him out from himself, past all the obstacles that were between that hidden beauty and those he must give it to.

These obstacles increased as he grew older. From the start the gift of beauty had to get past his grotesquely ugly appearance, his ignorance, his own fears and inhibitions caused by his crazy grandfather and his beloved but neurotic father; his ill-fitting shabby clothes. Added to these things, his mother remarried and his stepfather, a worthless, lazy man, content to let his wife help to support him, began the long series of cruel discouragements that afflicted Hans Christian so deeply. He disliked the boy and refused him affection or even interest. The mother, tormented by rheumatism brought on by years of standing in the stream to do her washing, started to drink, and gradually the woman that was so beloved to the strange, lonely son, became blurred and obliterated by the tippler that she had become; long before the poor old woman died, the mother he loved became a memory to her son. Added to all the other barriers between Hans Christian and the world was the shame of his mother's drinking, which everyone in Odense knew about.

When he was fourteen, Hans Christian set out alone with thirty-five shillings, his entire fortune, the savings of his whole life, in his pocket, to seek his fortune in Copenhagen. He had no education and no experience, and incidentally, no talent for his chosen profession, the stage. Many attempts had been made to persuade him to take up a trade, but he refused. "It would be a very great sin," was the final form of his refusal. Nobody understood, but nobody *could* yet understand what this beautiful thing, which it would be "a very great sin" not to give to the world, was. They could not understand because—one more of the obstacles in his way—Hans Christian did not yet know *what* it was himself; he had not yet found his medium, and he had not yet suffered those things through which he was to enter into his glory, he knew only that he had to give the beauty in him somehow. He tried to dance, and his dancing was like that of a frenzied scarecrow; he tried to sing, and his voice, which had been like a bird's before, broke. He wrote pretentious plays and bad poetry. He was refused and rejected everywhere. Before his hour came he was to be sifted like grain. Before he could give a voice to all the inarticulate poetry in man's soul, he was to taste the sordid and ugly realism of life. Before he was to tell the incommunicable secrets of all human hearts, he was to accept the loneliness of unrequited love. For Hans Christian, who before he started on that brave journey to Copenhagen knelt down and put himself into the hands of God, would not be allowed by God to give anything but his own unique gift; he would not be allowed to give instead a passing entertainment to a small audience, or happiness to one woman.

Hans Christian was willing to suffer any hardship rather than commit the sin of forsaking his vocation. To his old mother, who had pleaded with him to give up the stage as his ambition because she believed that he would be beaten and starved in the training, he had answered: "That is nothing ... first one suffers the most awful things and then one becomes famous." And suffer he did. He endured hunger and cold, discouragement and fear; he slept in a dark, airless cupboard, he drew one humiliation after another upon himself. When at last, as the result of his extraordinary persistence, he was given assistance by the State and his education begun, he endured worse torment than ever before. For the schoolmaster Meisling with whom he was sent to board loathed him with the loathing that someone corrupt always feels for someone transparently pure, and someone coarse and insensitive feels for one who is innately fine and sensitive. And Hans Christian *was* pure and sensitive and had a natural nobility of mind. Meisling used every possible means to torment his victim; he ridiculed and reviled him before the others, he denied him all pleasure and recreation, he half starved him at his table, he forbade him to write poetry; and cruellest of all to the boy haunted by the crazy grandfather in Odense, he told him that he would go mad. And as if he was trying to accelerate the fact, he dragged him to witness at close quarters the public execution, by beheading, of a young man and woman.

Meisling's wife was equally bad. She was a wanton, immoral woman, notoriously unfaithful to her husband, and a slut. She made unsuccessful attempts to seduce the boy, now growing to manhood, and violated his sense of decency by a continual flow of obscene talk. The Meislings' home was dirty, an acute misery to Hans Christian, who was homesick for the one room where he spent his childhood in Odense, with its scrubbed wooden floors, its scoured and shining pots and pans, and its snowy white curtains.

The family who had become guardians to Hans Christian were fine and good, and they took him to their heart, but their heart was constricted so rigidly by reserve and convention that it was sometimes difficult to know that it was beating. The Collin family remained loyal, and in their undemonstrative way devoted, to their odd protégé all his life; but they were always faintly shocked by him. To them a display of emotion caused something like physical pain, and Hans Christian was always pouring himself out in unrestrained expressions of affection and gratitude. The one thing that he was reserved about was Meisling's cruelty; a mixture of extraordinary courtesy and extraordinary kindness of judgment made it impossible for him to complain to Collin. Indeed, though he was supersensitive, in continual need of encouragement and hurt most cruelly by the smallest criticism of his work, he never gave way to self-pity. His courtesy prevented him later on from uttering a single word of his grief to the women who rejected his love.

The outbursts, sometimes storms of tears, when his work was criticized, came not from wounded vanity but from the old agonized longing to give the thing he had to give, and then supposing it to be refused, or taken and reviled when he thought he was giving it.

Only at the very end of his life, when in fact he had given all he had to give and he had no more stories to tell, did Hans Andersen ever receive encouragement and stimulus from anyone dear to him. All through the struggling years of his youth, his mind was as famished for sympathy and encouragement as his great gaunt body was for food. Destructive criticism, and he received little else, aggravated the deep inward discouragement that he was always trying to crush.

The fact that Hans Christian was only at ease with those who had some physical disadvantage or with the very poor proves that the other social contacts and friendships which he sought had to be paid for in embarrassment. What seems to many critics to have been the bumptiousness of a conceited young man was in reality the over-compensation that arose from his sense of inferiority.

Whomever he visited, he held in reverence. He never approached *any* human being without making the best of himself, and he could never forget that outwardly, even at his best, he was grotesquely ugly. When he went visiting he brushed his threadbare coat almost into holes, and once, unfortunately for him on a blazing hot day, stuffed it with straw to hide his extreme thinness.

The woman with whom Hans Christian was most at ease, and who came closer to him in sympathy than anyone else, was Henrietta Wulf, the little dwarfed, deformed daughter of Commander Wulf. He never ceased to love and to provide what he could for his poor old mother, and success did not prevent him from going back to Odense and hugging her in the street, even when she was the old drunkard stranger to him that she became. Among his happiest memories was a night in Sweden, when he was already famous, when he sat up until nearly dawn to make new shapes for an old peasant woman who baked gingerbread.

Three times Hans Christian fell in love. He longed for a home and family with the intensity realized only by those whose home has been broken in childhood, as his was. His first serious love was for Ribourg Voight, the sister of a student friend. She seems to have returned his love, but she was already engaged and felt herself to be bound in honour not to break her engagement. So Hans Christian was exiled from her life. Louise Collin and Sophie Orsted slipped away from him, Louise with the evasive tactics of all the Collins, and Sophie with the blithe unconcern of one who was quite unaware that he was trying to summon up courage to propose to her, and who was in love with another man.

Jenny Lind, whom he could have worshipped as well as loved,

refused his offer of marriage with graciousness peculiar to herself that made it possible, indeed inevitable, that he should keep her friendship.

All these deep personal sorrows Hans Christian accepted in silence. Such was the dignity which distinguished him even as the poor shabby child of the washerwoman, and never forsook him even when his nerves broke in old age.

"First one suffers ... then one becomes famous." But becoming famous meant to Hans Andersen giving the pearl of great price, for which he had paid with all that he had, and all that he could not have.

Through the denial of his individual love, the love of all mankind passed through the poet's soul, and his little loves, that might have been passing things and forgotten had they been successful, are left in the world for as long as a child remains in it to enshrine them in his heart.

Henrietta Wulf, the little hunchback, is dear to every child in Thumbelina, who was only an inch high. Jenny Lind's song, which must have died in the singing, lives on in the Nightingale who charmed away death from the king's heart. Hans Andersen himself is immortal, not only in the Ugly Duckling but in the Hardy Tin Soldier, who melted away in the fire of love and was found in the morning in the shape of a heart.

Once when he was in Portugal, Hans Christian compared the soft warm Portuguese wind to a bridal kiss. "But," he broke out, when he had said it, "I do not know what a bridal kiss is like! I imagine so much, I know so little!"

But Hans Andersen fulfilled his humanity. The cost to himself was shown when the effort was over. When it was no longer necessary for him to wrestle with the obstacles between him and other people, with his own inhibitions and fears and torments, they broke in and invaded him.

Odense had been illuminated for him; he had gone back to his beloved people to receive their homage in torchlight processions, bonfires, singing and banqueting, and the old torturing shyness was still upon him—it even brought on his toothache, as it used to do, and stabbed his hour of glory with physical pain. "I know now," he said on his way to his great reception, "what it feels like to be going to your execution."

But he went, as he had gone to everything, not because he wanted his people's homage, but because he wanted their love, he wanted the communion, to be one with them all.

Only when the terrors he had been holding at bay, overcoming daily and hourly all his life, broke over him, was the heroism of his life revealed. Then the thing he had wrestled with secretly and alone was seen. He became the victim of obsessional neurosis, of feelings of persecution, of hypochondria, of anxiety. He went in continual fear of illness, accidents, of assassination, of being robbed. Meisling stepped out of the past into his dreams and the old torments returned. Collin, too, came into his dreams and haunted him by his severity, and brought back his humiliation of long ago when he was forced to ask him for new clothes. Then he would awake weeping with remorse because he had resented imagined humiliations from Collin in his dreams.

He had abnormal fears of crossing open spaces, and of offending people. If he touched someone accidentally with his stick, he wanted to find them again to placate them.

He had obsessional anxiety about missing trains, about blowing out his candle, about putting his letters in the wrong envelopes. He went to the trains an hour at least before the right time, and got up again and again in the night to reassure himself about the candle.

But Hans Christian had won the love he needed now, and in the end he died surrounded and soothed by the love of friends. He was taken to the country home of a cultured Jewish family, the Melchiors, who loved him and shielded him from the popularity which had at last come to him and for which he had not now the strength. And rest brought peace. He died in his sleep at midday on the 4th of August 1875.

Surely, when Hans Christian awoke from that sleep, in which his beautiful soul drifted away from the worn-out, ugly body that had hidden it, he who in the days of his suffering had written in his diary, "Dear God! I could kiss you!" must have echoed the words of his most moving story, "I never dreamed of so much happiness when I was still the Ugly Duckling!"

FRANZ KAFKA

THE WHOLE of Franz Kafka's life was a search for God, frustrated in the very depths of his being by his relationship with his father. This frustration undermined everything else in his life, and unquestionably the continual conflict which it caused in one who was acutely sensitive, acutely aware of good and evil, and possessed by that rare quality among artists, a sense of responsibility to other people as well as to himself, aggravated the illness which caused his death at the age of forty-one.

His story is short and tragic, and it is told with profound insight by his friend Max Brod, who is his only biographer, and his own diaries, published, like most that he wrote, by Max Brod, after his death.

Kafka was born on the 3rd July 1883, in Prague; that lovely old city, built like the setting of a fairy story, destined to be a martyr city, was an apt cradle for him. His father was what is usually called a "self-made" man, and certainly one who was made as he became more by self than God. He was, when Franz was born, a wealthy Jewish merchant, who came from humble beginnings and had worked his way up with much hardship and grit, and who gave the impression that he felt a kind of grudge against his children for the sufferings of his own boyhood. He was a hearty, insensitive type, toughened yet more by his struggle for success in business, and incapable of understanding his scrupulous, oversensitive son. The boy's genius meant nothing to him; he had not the smallest interest in his writing, or in literature at all, a fact which gives extraordinary pathos to an extract from a letter that Franz wrote to him: "My writings were about you, in them I merely poured out the lamentations I could not pour out on your breast."

The letter containing these words was never read by the father; it was written when Kafka was thirty-six years old, in a futile attempt to break down the now insurmountable barrier between father and son. It is not easy to think, in view of both of their characters, that it would have done so, had the older man read it, and evidently the mother thought not, as when it was handed to her to give to her husband, she intercepted it and persuaded Franz not to see it delivered. Part of this letter is still unpublished, part is published in Max Brod's book.* Even a few extracts from it tell the story of Franz Kafka's soul, better than anyone else can do it. But first, a brief outline of the events of his life, to which the extracts refer.

To please his father, and to meet the idea of self-respect formed by his admiration for his father, which seems to have been indestructible, he took up a business career to earn his bread and butter; he was partly motivated, too, by a wish to keep his writing free and "unspotted by this world". His business life was hateful to him, and he had not realized until too late that his body was not strong enough to live two men's lives. To some extent the artist had to be frustrated, which in itself was fatal to his energy.

He graduated as a doctor of Law, and then worked in an insurance company.

He became engaged twice, but broke off the engagement twice, giving reasons which were clearly only a blind for the real one.

In 1914 he became ill with tuberculosis, the result of the conflict in his life, and he was retired on a pension.

Throughout his life he consciously sought for God, God whom he had lost in the darkness of his father's personality, and to whom he had been blinded in the superficiality and materialistic conception and practice of his father's Judaism. He realized that knowledge of God must be knowledge of experience, and assimilated into his being; it could not be outside of his deepest experiences.

For so long as the love of a woman meant marriage to him, it forced him back to his old attempt to identify himself with his father, and resulted in the painful comparison in which his humiliation was grounded. He was humiliated by his own body; and his sense of inferiority, physical weakness, and guilt—guilt before the father—made the physical expression of love seem disgusting to him, and himself in every way unfitted to found a family.

* *Franz Kafka: A Biography.* Secker and Warburg (London, 1947).

He tended more and more to search for God in orthodoxy and
made a profound study of the Hebrew scriptures, and intended
for a time to emigrate to Palestine—a pathetic symbol in the
young Jew of going back to the bosom of the Father.

With these events, which bring us to the last year of his tragic,
short life, in mind, the extracts from his letter may be read,
starting from his childhood:

"I was a nervous child, but I was certainly sulky too, as
children are; it is also true that my mother spoiled me, but I
can't believe that I was a particularly difficult child, I can't
believe that a friendly word, taking me quietly by the hand, a
friendly glance, would not have got me to do anything that was
wanted. Now at bottom you are a kind and gentle man (what
I am about to say doesn't contradict this; I am talking only of
the appearance you presented to the child), but not every child
has the patience and the courage to go on looking until it has
found the good side. You can only handle a child in the way
you were created yourself, with violence, noise and temper, and
in this case moreover you thought this was the most suitable
way, because you wanted to bring me up to be a strong,
brave boy."

And another memory of his childhood:

"You had worked yourself up to such a position by your own
strength, that you had unlimited confidence in your own
opinion. ... From your armchair you ruled the world. Your
opinion was right, everybody else's was mad, eccentric, crazy,
not normal. At the same time your self-confidence was so great
that there was no need for you to be consistent, and yet you
were always right. ... For me you developed the bewildering
effect that all tyrants have whose might is founded not on
reason, but on their own person. ...

"From the standpoint of every little thing you convinced me
both by your example and the way you brought me up. ...
of my incapability. ...

"Courage, decision, confidence, pleasure in this or that, could
not hold out to the end, if you were opposed to it. ...

"In front of you I lost my self-confidence and exchanged it for an infinite sense of guilt. ...

"My opinion of myself depended more on you than on anything else. ..."

Referring to the weakness and indecision in himself which led to Franz's breaking of his engagement, he speaks in his diary of "a will broken by my father," and in the famous letter he says:

"The chief obstacle to my marriage is the conviction which I can no longer eradicate, that to keep a family, particularly to be the head of one, what is necessary is just what I recognize you have —just everything together, good and bad, just as it is organically united in you, viz. strength and contempt for others, health and a certain excess, eloquence and standoffishness, self-confidence and dissatisfaction with everybody else, superiority to the world and tyranny, knowledge of the world and distrust of most people in it, and then advantages with no disadvantage attached, such as industry, endurance, presence of mind, fearlessness. Of all these qualities I had comparatively almost nothing, or only very little, so how should I dare to marry under such conditions when I saw that even you had a hard struggle in your married life, and even failed as far as your children were concerned?"

One might almost imagine, at this point, that Kafka's lifelong preoccupation with his father was not based on love for him, in spite of his obvious wish to be identified with him, through just those things that were impossible. But it was, quite transparently, his father whom he sought to find in his Judaism when he tried to find his faith fully in that; but the father who had shut the door, it seemed, on marriage had also discouraged the boy's religious faith by his own lack of it.

He writes: "I found just as little escape from you in the Jewish faith. Here in itself, was a possible escape, nay more, it would have been possible for us to have found each other in Judaism, or at least for us to have found in it a point from which we could have travelled the same road. But what kind of Judaism did I get from you!" and there follows a description of the visits together to the synagogue, and the shallow and even ludicrous nature of the father's formal religion.

But this little boy who was looking for the father whom he could adore, remembered moments that he cherished, when he felt close to the poor man who all unknowingly set a stumbling-block in his path. He describes two or three of these moments and ends "... during my last illness, you came softly to my room to see me, stopped at the door, just stuck your head in, and out of consideration for me, only waved a hand to me. On occasions like this one lay down and cried for joy, and is crying now as one writes about it."

In the last year of his life, Kafka at last fell in love, and this time more really than before, with the result that what all his own efforts to overcome the humiliation in his soul had failed to do, this love began to do. It is not so amazing as it seems that this happened to him, because Kafka never succumbed to the hesitations and fears that beset him, as nine out of ten people in his circumstances and with his temperament would have done. He violated his own will, and drove himself hard against his own nature, in his pitiful but heroic effort to be that which his father could approve. He shrank inwardly from the double responsibility which he conceived it his duty to face and accept, but he did accept it, and he achieved the miracle of writing books of genius and living the life of a business man at the same time. There are some artists who could do this without a miracle—at least they could write books—but Kafka was one who could do nothing without intensity; it was this fact which wore out the frail body that had caused him so much shame, but proved him so much more manly than his tough father; and this same intensity and self-giving that drove him on in his search for God all through his life.

The deep sense of guilt which his relationship with his father had so aggravated dogged him to the end, and at the end of his life translated itself into a profound consciousness of the sinfulness of all mankind as an almost hopeless obstacle to union with God.

After living for a short time with the Jewish girl whom at last he loved, he was taken to a sanatorium to die. He had intended to marry her, and this time he would have done so, but death prevented it. Her love was as brave and deep as his and gave him a brief independence and capacity for joy. He was able to love and pity objectively, and, as he was dying, to take pleasure in seeing others enjoy the things he could enjoy no longer, food and drink and so on.

For a while he lay in a ward in a bed next to that of another dying man; he noticed without envy and rejoiced in the fact, that when everyone, even the doctors and nurses, had left this poor man, a priest came to him and stayed with him to the end, and that he was able to comfort the man and give him peace.

It is impossible not to believe that when, soon after, Franz Kafka himself died, without any religious consolation, he at last found the adorable Father he had been seeking all his life.

RAINER MARIA RILKE

AMONG THE YOUNGER generation of poets and would-be poets, Rilke is often venerated as the saint of poetry. Yet if ever a man failed to surrender himself to the destiny that genius must accept, it was he.

Just as the soul of a contemplative is laid open to tremendous spiritual forces, the soul of a poet is laid open to the agelong forces of humanity, to the collective love of the whole human race. If, then, he is quite incapable of love himself, inevitably he will be brought to ruin by his destiny.

Rilke left some of the most exquisite poetry that the world has ever known, but it is beautiful as wonderfully set jewellery is beautiful, and has the coldness of precious stones too, flashing off sparks of light, sometimes blushing with eroticism and glowing like rubies, more often radiating pinpoints of pale, flashing colour, like a cut diamond. It is not poetry that has swept through the heart of mankind; it has not even, one cannot help feeling, really passed through Rilke's single heart, or if it has it has passed through it as swiftly as the rush of an angel's wings, picking up nothing from his human nature on the way.

Rilke is a tragic example of the man who is a failure and of the genius that is partly frustrated by incapacity to love.

Certainly everything was against him, even his charm, which made life too easy for him after its beginning.

The beginning was not easy. He was a seven-months' child, and because he was not a girl, a disappointment to his mother; a little later, because he failed to be a boy, a disappointment to his father.

His father, having had to give up a military career for financial reasons, wanted to project his ambitions on to his son. His mother dressed him like a girl, gave him dolls to play with, and alternately spoilt and neglected him. She was an exhibitionist herself, and the worst kind of pietist, over-fervent but incapable of wedding her religion to her life. If it is the mother who lays the foundations of the child's faith, it is not surprising that in

Rilke's case they crumbled away like sand. While he was still a child his mother left him and his father, and his future relationships with her were like those with so many women in his life, a little unreal and carried on almost entirely by correspondence.

At ten years old, already a shivering, neurotic child and one still young enough to need mothering, he was sent to the Military Academy, where—need it be said?—he was bullied unmercifully. He never recovered from the torture of his school life. At one time he believed it his duty to the world and himself to purge his system of it by writing it into a book, but he lacked the courage to re-live his suffering even when it was far behind him in time.

As a young man he exhibited a mass of guilt feelings, which of course he never faced in the open. He became obsessed by sentimentalities for young girls, but wished them to remain virgins and regarded marriage with one of them as a crime, even a murder. This was linked up with a curious fascination with the idea of the deaths of young girls which haunted him all his life— a peculiarity, by the by, which he shared with Dickens. He also associated roses, which were also almost an obsession with him, with young girls; and this is a peculiarity that he shared with another writer, Ruskin, who was also almost unbalanced about young girls and roses, perhaps because the girl who came closest to turning his brain was named Rose.

Rilke was an unsacramental man; he could not realize the oneness of soul and body. Though many women gave him homage that approached a religious cult, and some loved him with genuine love, he could give nothing in response; on his side, "love" and even friendship was seldom anything else but a self-seeking, over-intellectualized, over-analyzed eroticism.

Yet at the beginning of his adult life he was capable of hero-worship, and once came close to sacrificing his own genius for it, a sacrifice which would not have been justified, though it warms one a little to the man to think that he was ever for a moment capable of contemplating it. It was to Rodin that the young poet brought his homage; his admiration for the old sculptor came nearer than anything else in his life to love; he offered him his services as a secretary and for a brief time worked hard in his service. The arrangement ended disastrously, as it clearly had to, and Rodin dismissed his secretary suddenly and rather brutally. But there must have been relief as well as distress for Rilke in the dismissal which set him free to write poetry again.

Now he acted consistently with his one object, of holding fast to his own vocation of poetry, and he was convinced that this was his duty, cost what it might. But this meant, cost what it might to others—his wife and child and his many wealthy women friends; for the first essential, in his own view, for his genius, was that it should cost *him nothing*. His problem was to live fastidiously, as his temperament demanded, in luxury and without the irksome necessity of having to work for his living. But more, he must have solitude, absolute silence and peace in these ideal surroundings. This problem was solved for him by the fanatical devotion of his women friends. On the whole he cultivated only aristocratic and wealthy women friends, and spent nearly the whole of his life living on their hospitality in their country houses and castles.

He had married a young sculptress, Clara, and had one child by her, Ruth. The question of providing for them never troubled him, though when the success of some of his books and the generosity of his publisher brought him some ready money, he was generous to them, from a distance. For of course he was ingenious in avoiding their presence with its distractions and its demands on him. E. M. Butler, Rilke's biographer, writes of his relationship to his only child:

"As for Ruth, Rilke visited her when he was in Germany, which was not very often, wrote to her fairly regularly, spoke of her fondly and even sentimentally; but seemed as totally unaware of his responsibilities as if he were an astral body, tenderly surveying some human child, whose destiny was no concern of his. He was often poetical about her but hardly ever paternal."*

Anything which threatened to force the common lot of men upon Rilke brought his always ready self-pity to a crisis. Naturally, the War in 1914 was a disaster to him, though with typical absence of humour about himself, he first greeted it with heroic

* E. M. Butler, *Rainer Maria Rilke*.

poetry in praise of war! This pose collapsed after ten days of service in the infantry, which brought Rilke near collapse too. He was released to work in the Ministry of War, where he was almost as wretched as he had been in the army, though his occupation was almost formal and his working hours, from nine to three, enviable. After the war he drifted back to the old life of elegant sponging until his death. "Complete solitude, more, invisibility was his only desire."* It became increasingly difficult to please him, for now and then his hostesses made some slight demands on him; they wanted to see and speak to him occasionally in their own homes, and this he found selfish and inconsiderate. Even when the ideal hostess lent him her castle and vacated it herself, he was ever on the look-out for faults.

Naturally, a man seeking to avoid suffering, as Rilke did, suffered more and more through less and less, and his search for solitude and peace ended in the beating of his own heart becoming a torment to him. He became less and less capable of the receptivity on which genius, like religious contemplation, depends, and consequently much of his time was arid and vain waiting for the wind of Heaven, that came less and less often.

Rilke's loss of faith was not, like that of Rimbaud, a revolt against God, for revolt was not in his nature. He did not revolt against God, but he shrank away from the suffering of Christ. That heart of his that he could hear beating in his silence, beating like a clock wearing out in an empty house, shrank smaller and smaller, until it shrivelled up like a dead nut in its shell. His shrinking from Catholicism was his shrinking from Christ, and his shrinking from Christ was his shrinking from the cross.

Once he wrote a letter that contains the thoughts he imagines to be those of a "young worker" about Christ. E. M. Butler warns us that it is not fair to conclude that it contains Rilke's own opinions, as he never published it or any of its contents, but it is certainly very full of Rilke, who certainly never was a "young worker." He writes: "WHO is this Christ who insinuates himself into everything? Who has known nothing of us, nothing of our work, nothing of our affliction, nothing of our joy such as we, today, accomplish, endure, and summon up in ourselves, and who, despite all this, it seems, always demands to

* E. M. Butler, *Ibid.*

be the *first* in our lives. Or do we only put that in his mouth? What does he want of us? He wants to help us, we're told. Yes, but he places himself with singular helplessness in our presence. His circumstances were so completely different."*

The explanation of this astonishing misstatement follows hard on it: "I cannot imagine that the Cross should *remain*, which was never more than a crossroads. Certainly it should not have been stamped on us everywhere like a brandmark."

No, Rilke's heart was too small to meet the love of God, or of his wife or child, or of the friends who lavished all they could upon him—but then, it was not even big enough to risk the degree of suffering involved in the love one gives to a rabbit!

In June 1905, he wrote to Clara: "... yesterday and the day before passed in worry over the little dog, which everybody in the house loved so much; suddenly he grew ill and yesterday evening he died in great torment. It is sad and hard for Lou and her husband. And once again I felt distinctly that one should not draw into one's life those cares and responsibilities which are not necessary, just as I felt it as a boy when my rabbit died."

The last worry of the unhappy poet's life was that he might not die of an illness uniquely his, which no one else could ever share—he refused to hear the illness from which he did die diagnosed, and to discover, even in this, that after all he *was* like some other men. He was afraid of death and hardly allowed the word in his presence. Actually, he died of a rare form of blood poisoning, which most aptly was accelerated in his case by a scratch from a thorn when he was picking roses for a girl.

In the end he was alone, alone more than even he had ever wanted, for he refused the sacraments, and went into eternity an empty shell of a man, excommunicated by his own egoism from all his own kind.

* E. M. Butler, *Selected Letters of Rainer Maria Rilke*, 1902-1926. Macmillan (London, 1947).

RIMBAUD

WHEN A WRITER makes a short résumé of the main events in the life of the French poet, Arthur Rimbaud, one can tell in a flash, from his selection, just what his own values are. In the same way, from the mass of psycho-analytical theories applied to him, one can see at once what theory the writer is determined to prove, for in his tragic life there are symptoms of every possible morbid psychological state, but at the same time there is always some detail which baffles them all.

He was born on the twentieth of October 1854, and by the time he was seventeen he had already written poetry of out-standing genius. Before he was twenty he had abandoned poetry altogether. This much all those who write of him tell us. They usually refer to a scandal with the poet Verlaine, to Rimbaud's subsequent life of restless and unproductive wandering in Abyssinia, and to his return to die in France in 1891.

The extraordinary spiritual crises which occurred with each of these phases of his life are seldom noted, and even his return to the Faith of his childhood on his death-bed, and with it a re-birth of the poet in him, are often left unmentioned. In what is unquestionably the greatest and fullest English biography, *Arthur Rimbaud*, by Enid Starkie, these things are honestly related, but some of them are drained of their significance by the writer's personal interpretation.

I see in Rimbaud an example of a man—or a boy on the edge of manhood—regressing suddenly to the pre-age-of-reason stage of childhood (which I have described in "The Child in Man"), in which the physical strength and capacities of a man are united to the total irresponsibility of a child, who quite innocently has no values but his own egoism, and no restraint but his own littleness. Whether, in his case, this was a patho-logical or a spiritual condition, I could not attempt to say. It could have been the result of mental disease or of sin—there were circumstances capable of producing either or both. I will be content to give just the superficial facts that suggest my theory.

Until his early adolescence Rimbaud was a precocious and pious little boy, of the type likely to rejoice any old lady's heart. He had golden hair and blue eyes, a round face, and the sensual mouth which women find so pretty in a boy, and are so easily misled by. His face was of the type that always keeps a certain look of innocence; the type which arouses the suspicion of an experienced plainclothes policeman, and enchants all others. If poor Arthur delighted his mother's heart, she did not show it. She was a strange, hard woman, and brought her children up with great severity.

During his adolescence the golden-haired, blue-eyed boy suddenly changed to a fiend.

The degeneracy and vice that he now exhibited, indeed flaunted, ran so true to the pattern of revolt and viciousness common to many artists in adolescence, that it is not even interesting, excepting in so far as it points to disturbances on a much deeper level, which may have brought it about. He became dirty, cruel, ridiculously egotistical, drunken and vicious. He took to the wandering so common in unstable adolescents, and among other excursions ran away to Paris, where he had what was probably his first experience of sex, with some common soldiers. Probably this gave him a profound shock, for more than obvious reasons. A genius is one through whom the universal experience of all humanity must pass; his destiny is as sweet and as terrible as that of a saint. The experience of the Christhood of all humanity must pass through both the saint and the genius. In a certain sense, the vocation to be a genius is the vocation to be a saint. Love is the predominant experience of humanity, and if this is vitiated the results can hardly not be disastrous.

Determined to be free of the shackles of his home with its restrictions, its limitations and ugliness, he presented himself, in a filthy and sulky condition, to Verlaine's family—that is to Verlaine's mother-in-law's family, with whom Verlaine lived at the time. He soon wrecked Verlaine's marriage, though it is only just to say that, without him, Verlaine would certainly have wrecked it himself.

After this followed a violent and sordid relationship with Verlaine, during which Rimbaud continued to rage and fulminate against all that was good or beautiful, to revel in every form of obscenity and blasphemy, to pour out hatred and contempt on all human beings—including, at intervals, Verlaine himself. He was eager, and had been ever since this mood had broken out in him, to give an impression of utter depravity, and Enid Starkie tells us "he would invent lewd stories about himself, attributing to himself monstrous and repulsive actions and he used then to be overjoyed when people sitting near him in a café would get up and leave the table." But she tells us, following this and her opinion of the boy's utter inward desolation: "The core of his being was purity and innocence with a yearning for absolute perfection." This is a view which many others share, and I believe that, strange though it may seem, it has far more foundation than his shadowless blue eyes.

When he himself refers, later on, to his "innocence", there is a profound tone of suffering in his voice: "I am no longer in love with boredom. Frenzies, debauches, madness—how well I know its outbursts and disasters—all my burden is laid down. Let us contemplate without dizziness the huge extent of my innocence."*

This is the innocence of the child misshapen by original sin, but without the use of reason to make him responsible for sin.

At some critical moment in his life, Rimbaud failed to surrender to that tremendous destiny of allowing the universal experience of mankind to pass through him, for the rest of humanity—and his resistance broke him.

Partly during and partly after his experience with Verlaine and his final parting from him, he wrote his last literary work, *Une Saison en Enfer*—and after that, silence. Some people think that in the disillusionment and bitterness of his spirit, he renounced poetry deliberately: others that the fierce preciosity of his genius had burnt itself out in a short time, and only dead ashes remained. Personally, I think that when he refused his spiritual destiny as a poet of genius, a terrible spiritual regression threw him back to pre-rational innocence, with all its terror and

* *Une Saison en Enfer*, trans. Norman Cameron. John Lehmann (Cambridge, 1949).

all its impotence. Just as a lunatic in this state often becómes unable to speak as a man, and has to learn to talk (if he can) like a baby, the poet in Rimbaud was unable to speak any more.

From this time, he not only wrote no more poetry, but he became less and less able to accept life, and for a time more and more fantastic in his egoism. He imagined, or pretended to, that he could become equal to God, and that his vicious life, which he was unable to enjoy, was a kind of inverted sanctity, a martyrdom, which would perfect in him the receptivity which he thought essential in a great poet. He believed that, set free from everything that bound and limited other men, he would become the supreme poet-prophet the world awaited, and that he would be then equal to God.

Many people—those who believe that amorality and innocence are the same thing—suppose that during this phase of what seems very like insanity, Rimbaud suffered no remorse. He said that he did not. But he suffered more than remorse, something very like what we believe the damned suffer—the acute awareness of God realized from the despair of hell. This conflict between unimaginable beauty and unimaginable misery is woven all through that last work of his, and with it an ever recurrent sighing for that other childhood of his, the true childhood before this one of regression poisoned by his manhood.

It seems to me that he tells the story of this regression, of his broken self, his failure and his silence, in these words: "Did I not have *once upon a time* a lovable childhood, heroic and fabulous, to be written on leaves of gold, an excess of good fortune? By what crime or mistake have I deserved my present weakness? You who claim that animals sob with grief, that sick men give up hope, that dead men have bad dreams, see if you can tell the story of my collapse and sleep. For my part, I can no more explain myself than the beggar with his continual *Our Father's* and *Hail Mary's. I can no longer speak.*"*

At all events after that the poet was silent in him, and everything that he touched failed and turned to pain. He came back from his restless wandering life in Abyssinia to throw himself upon the compassion of his sister, whom he had neglected throughout their lives, and who devoted herself to him until he

* From "Morning", in *Une Saison en Enfer*, trs. Norman Cameron.

ARTHUR RIMBAUD

died. He came back destitute, mutilated, broken; and with the same streak of childishness that he had displayed all through his life, took it for granted that his own people would care and provide for him. His sister did come to him, and it is from her that the story of his dying has come to us.

He had flouted God, blasphemed and revolted against him, tried to be equal to him, but he had never ceased to be conscious of him, he had never been able to hide his wounds from him, he had lived in conflict with him, the poet in him seemingly defeated and lost, the man in torment, living in the God-consciousness of the damned. He had done all he could to escape, and now at last the regressed child did attain the use of reason, and as he lay dying Rimbaud received the sacraments.

From that moment the poet in him came back, the old visions surrounded him—not the visions of hell, but of angelic beauty—and words were given to him again. He spoke in cadences of sheer beauty, and the words streamed out of him without any effort; the lost poetry that he would now never give to the world was given back to him: "Reason has been born within me. The world is good. I shall give life my blessing. I shall love my brethren. These are no longer the promises of a child. Nor are they made in the hope of escaping from old age and death. God is my strength, and I praise God."

CHARLES DE FOUCAULD

CHARLES DE FOUCAULD and Arthur Rimbaud were born within five years of one another; Rimbaud in 1854, de Foucauld in 1858. Both were Frenchmen, both were born in France. Throughout their lives there was at the same time an extraordinary parallel and an extraordinary contrast between them.

Had they been set side by side as little boys, the contrast in their appearance would have been striking—and also misleading: Rimbaud fair, blue-eyed, and smug, de Foucauld dark, arrogant, with smouldering eyes and a sullen, obstinate mouth.

Both lost their faith in adolescence. This, however, needs qualifying. In her superb biography of de Foucauld, *Desert Calling*,* Anne Fremantle points out that "as there are milk teeth, given the baby mouth to bite infant foods, so there is milk faith, warmed through by the love that cradled it. ... this initial gift of nursery faith must grow with the child, and with him be transformed and be made personal, individual. If this does not happen, and only the ambient faith remains, like skin that sheltered the pupa but is not integrated with it, then either the grown man will slough it, or it will turn flame upon him as upon Nessus and itch and burn until he, of his own free will, either gladly is consumed or miserably tears it and his own flesh from him". And she adds, with equal penetration: "What Charles really lost was his innocence."

The same could be said of Rimbaud and of countless adolescents.

Both de Foucauld and Rimbaud were lonely, unhappy adolescents: Charles, an orphan from babyhood, Rimbaud brought up by a strangely hard mother who almost orphaned him by her severity, and who had been deserted by his father.

Charles was brought up by his grandfather, whom he idolized, but the grandfather died when he was still a very young man, leaving him emotionally alone.

* Hollis and Carter (London, 1950).

Rimbaud had only one friend who understood him in his early youth, a schoolmaster who was removed at the most critical stage of his development.

Both young men abandoned themselves to lives of debauchery, and seemed to want to swamp their loneliness and unhappiness in lust and gluttony and drink.

And both changed suddenly, as if they could no longer tolerate their own purposeless lives, and became travellers. Charles returned to God, and after many years he returned to the desert, the scene of his early travels, to become its apostle. But though he loved the people of the desert and served them, he made not a single convert, and in the end those whom he had come to serve murdered him.

Rimbaud went to Abyssinia, and he too came to love its people, but neither he nor Charles achieved anything that they had set out to do.

When Rimbaud forsook his life of vice, he did not turn to God; on the contrary he turned in on himself, and gradually became isolated from other men; when he died, he died without a friend: "Well, now, I shall ask forgiveness for having fed on lies. And let me be off. But not one friendly hand! And where shall I find succour?"*

When de Foucauld turned from his life of gluttony and lust, he discovered the beauty of God, and when he died he was buried with his life-long friend, whom he had never ceased to love.

Both these men have significance for us, and their intercalation can be worked out further; but now, briefly, the facts about Charles de Foucauld, whom I cite to illustrate the effects upon a man of his objective love for God.

After his grandfather's death, as a young officer, Charles gave himself up to a positive vulgarity of self-indulgence. He became grossly fat and repulsive through gluttony. His idea of having a good time seems to have been sating himself, gorging and stuffing. He made a great display of his extravagance in gluttony and entertained lavishly; at this time, he who was to long for hiding as deeply as Rilke did, but for quite different reasons, appears to have had something of the exhibitionist in him, and

* *Une Saison en Enfer*, trs. Norman Cameron.

in spite of his aristocratic breeding, of which he was perfectly conscious, it is difficult to avoid thinking that he was rather a cad.

He amused himself, as a young officer, by flouting the sensibilities of his more conventional fellow officers and outraging those of his superior officers. In particular he insisted upon flaunting his liaison with his mistress, Mimi, even taking her with him, and the regiment, to Africa. This naturally brought about a good deal of embarrassment for Mimi (nothing at this time could embarrass Charles), but she was treated like royalty, used the name of the Vicomtesse de Foucauld, and for a time lived in what was for her an earthly paradise, more so because she loved Charles. However, this escapade led to his being dismissed from the army. This did not worry him at all. He remained for the time being in Africa, and already it had taken hold of his soul.

When the French army was called to active service in Algeria, Charles wanted to be in the fighting. He volunteered as a private, and was reinstated as sub-lieutenant—this time, however, at the cost of Mimi!

In this campaign Charles met the man who was to remain his life-long friend, Laperrine, a fellow officer then, and he came to love the common soldiers with the real love that is given only when a man shares in the hardships and labours of his men. He never lost his love and respect for the common soldier, and years later when, as a priest, he ministered to them, wounded and dying after fighting in the desert, he realized what the poet Gerard Manley Hopkins was to realize—the Christlikeness of the soldier in his sacrificed life.

Charles de Foucauld never went back to his life of luxury and debauchery after this, but he was not yet converted; first there was his marvellous, and now famous, secret journey through the forbidden territories of Morocco, disguised as a poor Jew. That journey, apart from the obvious wonder and interest, and to him the attraction of danger in it, had deep spiritual significance for Charles. First of all, to maintain his disguise he had to be chaste, and he had to be frugal. Secondly, he saw men about him who, though not Christian, were profoundly aware of the majesty of God.

It is not only a man's body that is purified by voluntary abstinence and by simplicity in eating and drinking, but his mind and soul; and Charles must have realized then, for the first time in his life, the wonder of looking on stars and water and skies of dawn, with clear eyes and a shadowless mind.

At all events, the young explorer had begun to love chastity and poverty, and to long for silence in his soul like the silence of the desert.

In 1888 his conversion came, or more truly it was completed. Outwardly it seemed a lightning conversion, but it had been gathering within him for very long, and was, on the natural level, partly at least the result of his objective attitude to other people; he had always had the power of observing others, of realizing them as themselves, and learning from their lives.

There were the men who adored God in the desert, the soldiers who sometimes were conscious, sometimes unconscious, Christs, and then there was his own family, devoted Catholics, who had something in their lives that Charles was nostalgic for—one in particular, Marie de Bondy, his cousin, whom he had loved deeply from his boyhood; and he attributed his conversion mainly to her. Then there was his sister, named Mimi as his mistress had been, and though she had little outward influence on him, she loved him dearly and there can be no doubt of the fact that her prayers were a great tide of grace drawing him back to God.

It is of interest that Rimbaud, too, was followed through his restless wandering life by the prayers of his devout but rather dull little sister, and in the end it was her tide of grace that drew his soul across the river Styx to God.

From the moment that Charles realized the reality of God, all the objectivity in love of which he was capable went into his love of God. The result was that he was drawn right away from self: not only from his own suffering—for he was to suffer deeply in following his vocation—but also from the misery of his own sins; and, most astonishing of all, from his temptations.

From the hour of his conversion he became naturally chaste. It is amazing that this could be, since he had years of habitual sensuality and indulgence behind him. St Francis of Assisi, a far more fastidious man than ever Charles had been, had to fight his own rebellious human nature literally with fire and snow; St Anthony the Great had to wrestle with the demons of his for years in the desert. But Charles de Foucauld was simply set free. He was given back a state of innocence.

Rimbaud attained the terrible innocence of a child in the pattern of evil, but de Foucauld was given back the primal innocence of the child in God's image. He never wasted himself in remorse, he never looked backwards at all. Having discovered the reality of God, he could not think about anything else, least of all about himself.

The one object of his life from the time of his conversion was to live a life exactly like that of Christ in Nazareth. He did not want to preach or even, at first, to become a priest—but to live as a poor, unknown workman, working with his hands.

He tried to be a Trappist, but he did not find the life poor enough and simple enough—he made himself as poor as any man could, and his clothes were allowed to become as ragged, even as dirty, as those of Labre. From the Trappists he went to Nazareth and became the servant of the Poor Clares, living on bread and water, dressed like a beggar, sleeping in a little hut at the convent door, working most inefficiently as a gardener and odd-job man. He was ideally happy; he rejoiced when the children threw stones at him; and when the nuns, enchanted as they were and edified and amused by their extraordinary servant, gave him dates or sweets on feast days, he saved them and gave them to these children.

But all the time the desert called him, and in the end he went back, as a priest, to be the apostle of the desert. In spite of all his labours there and of the superhuman love he poured out on the tribesmen and the slaves there, he made no converts—not even one—but he said that the only essential thing was that the Blessed Sacrament should be there; and it is a deeply moving and deeply significant fact, that after the priest himself had been sacrilegiously murdered and buried in the sand, the consecrated Host in the monstrance was found thrown down and covered in the sand close to his body. Significant too, that it was found by French soldiers and given, with reverence and awe, by a soldier to another soldier in Communion.

Rimbaud, in his arrogance and his misery, tried to be equal to

God. De Foucauld, in his humility and joy, became one with God in his suffering and death.

His life in the desert was one long act of self-giving to Christ in his brethren, one long act of love. He had longed for silence and solitude, and to be unseen, even more than Rilke did, and one would suppose that he would have found those things in the desert. But he opened his heart—and what is so much more drastic, his door—to all the most needy: the soldiers who came out on military service, the outcasts of the desert, the derelict, the unwanted, the rejected, the negro slaves. It need not be said that his charity was abused; he was exploited, taken in, drained of everything, given no mercy by these people, in whom he continued to look for, and to see, Christ. In the end, some of the tribesmen, those whom he had come to save, murdered him.

He offered no reproach when they came, spoke no word, showed no anger and no fear. One of them shot him at close quarters, through the head, with a revolver; he died instantly.

In the last months of his life, his lifelong friend, Laperrine, had come back as an officer to the desert, and the two men, who understood one another so well, had enjoyed the friendship that their long separation had not broken. When Laperrine died he was buried beside de Foucauld in Tamanrasset. And when it was thought necessary to remove the body of the priest at the time of the opening of his process of beatification, they left his heart in the desert, buried in the soldier's grave with him.

"One part of me," Charles de Foucauld said in his lifetime, "is in the pure sky, that is always above the clouds, but with the other part I love. It is my imperious sweet duty to love mankind passionately and to be interested in whatever is of serious concern to them."

It was said of him by one who knew him personally, that, at the end of his life, this man of sorrows so radiated joy that one had the curious idea that if one listened, one would hear someone singing inside him!

"It is my imperious sweet duty to love mankind passionately."

POSTSCRIPT

Destroy self-love, and there is no more Hell.   St Bernard

T HE VITAL QUESTION for anyone suffering from ego-neurosis is, is there a cure for it?

There is a cure. It is to be found in the first chapter of the children's catechism. It is to know God, and to love and serve him.

The first step towards a cure, with this as with every other disease, is to recognize it for what it is and honestly want to be cured. Only a strong will to be cured will make it possible for anyone to make the repeated efforts necessary.

There are many more ego-neurotics who do not recognize what they are suffering from than who do; and more among Catholics who fail to recognize it than among non-Catholics. There is another reason, too, which makes the cure of ego-neurosis in a Catholic much more difficult than in a person with no religion at all, or with a vague and formless religion—the Catholic ego-neurotic is convinced that he *does* know, love and serve God; in fact, he frequently mistakes his self-love for the love of God, and in all his pious exercises, mortifications and good works he devoutly loves and serves himself. It is almost impossible to make a Catholic ego-neurotic of this type realize that what he believes to be knowledge of God is only a travesty of God. Clearly it is necessary to *know* before we can love or serve, and the ego-neurotic who is deluded about this basic necessity is deluded all through.

The beginning of getting to know God truly is to look away from self to God, to redirect the whole concentration of one's mind. This seems obviously an absurd suggestion to one who is convinced that his long sessions of self-absorption and day-dreaming are prayer, and a certain restful broodiness before the Tabernacle is contemplation.

A person who has no definite beliefs, who is quite uninformed or uncertain about Christ's revelation, or even about the teaching of his own Church, is likely to feel his lack and his need for the knowledge of God. Not only that: if he begins to learn by reading the Gospels, he will be capable of reacting to the wonder of something that is new to him, whilst the Catholic will be so familiar with what he reads that he can hardly feel any shock of amazement, fear or joy in any of it. What is more serious, the Catholic may fail to grasp the truths he reads because he is too familiar with them; he will accept them, but without astonishment, without really laying hold of them or seeing their significance in his own life.

The Catholic ego-neurotic is then the hardest case, and while the treatment, or rather the preparation for the cure, will be the same for Catholic and non-Catholic, the Catholic will have to make a much greater effort to be rid of all his preconceived ideas, and to approach the knowledge of God as something new to him.

How are both Catholics and non-Catholics to find out whether they really are suffering from ego-neurosis or not? I think by the experiment of trying the cure and discovering whether the symptoms become less painful. If anyone suffers from scrupulosity, hypersensitivity, acute shyness, if he believes that he is persecuted, misjudged, frustrated or denied the adulation due to him, let him, instead of presuming that he knows God and himself, assume for a week that he knows nothing at all about God or himself, and begin to learn *about* God as humbly as a newly converted native in the African jungle.

The cure will begin by reading *about* God. For some the reading should begin with the Bible, the New Testament and the Old, but for those who have been reading the New Testament blindly for years, it will be better to read some books which expound the doctrines in it, so that after this they will read the Bible with more realization of the depths of mystery in it. The Bible, the Epistles, and some hard-headed books of dogma and theology will be essential for everyone to start with, followed by some of the great spiritual classics and the books of the saints. Merely pious devotional books should be avoided, though these will have their use later.

Each one will have to find which books, out of a great range to choose from, best suit his mind, and best *exercise* it, for this reading is intended, while giving knowledge about God, to wean the mind gradually from its concentration on self and its wholly subjective fantasies about God. A little wrestling with the angel will help to this end.

The next stage in the cure will be to get to know God experimentally, not now getting to know *about* God, but getting to know him. Objective prayer will be the first step. This must be prayer of adoration and thanksgiving to God for being as he is, lifting the mind out of its habitual wallowing in the "prayer" of self-pity and self-love.

Next the objective attitude to God, which is being learned, must also be practised towards man, and this cannot be done in a better way than through practising the contemplation of Christ in man. It is at this point that the knowledge of God becomes one thing with the love and service of God. We do not see Christ in man, but now we *know* that he is in man, in those of our own household in whom he is most hidden from us. A continual seeking for him in them, an unfailing effort to penetrate his disguise and to discover in which of the infinite variety of ways possible to him Christ is living in each one of those who are part of our own lives, cannot fail to draw off the concentration on self; and the necessity to serve Christ in others cannot fail to break down the barriers of self-protection, self-consciousness and self-love which lead to the frustration of the uncured ego-neurotic.

Although the Catholic ego-neurotic has greater difficulties to overcome in the initial stages of cure, he has the enormous help of the sacraments and the Mass. It is not only in others that he must know Christ if he is to overcome the strangling inhibitions of his self-love and gain the courage to live the creative life of love and compassion towards other men.

Only the knowledge that it is Christ who acts in him, who speaks through his mouth and works with his hands, will enable the ego-neurotic to overcome his shrinking from human contacts, his undefinable fears, his shyness, self-consciousness, and his sense of personal humiliation.

The sacraments and the Mass increase and strengthen the life of Christ in the soul.

The possibilities of the sacrament of Penance as a cure for

ego-neurosis have already been described. All the sacraments increase Christ's life and his power in the soul, and so increase its courage and confidence before life.

Baptism gives Christ's life. We call it Christening, which means simply Christing, making one a Christ. The Holy Communion is receiving Christ whole and entire and through him becoming one with all other men. Confirmation gives the Holy Spirit to the spirit of man, floods him with the glory of Christhood. Matrimony enables men and women to increase Christ in one another through natural love. Holy Orders enables men to increase Christ in the whole world through supernatural love. Extreme Unction brings the strength of Christ's trust to enable man to surrender himself to the eternal love in the hour of death.

Finally in the Mass, the ego-neurotic has a complete cure for ego-neurosis. He can, if he will, find his cure in a perfectly objective, Christocentric participation in daily Mass.

At Low Mass every day, concentrated into a short half-hour of time, is the whole life of man—the pattern of the life which, if it is lived out in the same way, restores man to his real sanity and is a cure not only for ego-neurosis itself, but for guilt which is the cause of ego-neurosis.

Briefly the structure of the Mass is this. First, man comes out of his hiding, and in the power of the Trinity puts himself into the presence of God. (From the Sign of the Cross to the end of the Confiteor.)

In the light of God he knows himself and acknowledges himself to be a sinner, he asks for forgiveness and comes closer to God. Now he breaks into a song of praise and joy; he is looking away from his sins to God's glory. (From the end of the Confiteor to the end of the Gloria.)

He listens to the words that reveal God to him, and learns more about God; he professes his faith in him. (From the end of the Gloria to the end of the Creed.)

And now he surrenders himself wholly to his Christhood, he offers himself to be made inseparable from Christ, to share his destiny. (From the end of the Creed to the Consecration.)

Now he is restored to his Christhood, with Christ he enters into his Passion, in him he is lifted upon the Cross, in him he adores God, with him he redeems man. (From the Consecration to the Communion.)

Finally he receives Christ into his soul again, and in communion with him becomes one with all men, and goes out from Mass to carry Christ into the world in which he lives his daily life.

This is the concentrated plan of man's life, ending as life itself will end when it is lived on this plan, with "Deo gratias—Thanks be to God."